CREATING
BELFAST

CREATING
BELFAST

Technical Education and the Formation of
a Great Industrial City, 1801–1921

Professor Don McCloy

NONSUCH

First published 2009

Nonsuch Publishing
119 Lower Baggot Street
Dublin 2
Ireland
www.nonsuchireland.com

British Library Cataloguing in Publication Data.
A catalogue record for this book is available from the British Library.

ISBN 978 1 84588 937 1

Typesetting and origination by Nonsuch Publishing.
Printed in the UK by Athenaeum Press.

CONTENTS

Acknowledgements

In writing this book, I was guided and inspired by the works of several local authors. Five excellent works deserve particular mention:

Bell, Henry, *Diligence and Skill: 100 Years of Education at Belfast Institute* (Belfast: The Belfast Institute of Further and Higher Education, 2007).

Black, Eileen, *Art in Belfast 1760-1888; Art Lovers or Philistines?* (Dublin: Irish Academic Press, 2006).

Gray, William, *Science and Art in Belfast* (Belfast: *The Northern Whig*, 1904).

McLorie, Alan, *Voluntary Bodies and the Development of Technical Education in Belfast during the Nineteenth Century*, Unpublished MA Thesis (Jordanstown: University of Ulster, 1987).

Neeson, Hugh, *The Origin and Development of Technical Education between 1850 and 1920, with Particular Reference to the Industrial Area of Belfast and its Surroundings*, Unpublished DPhil Thesis (Coleraine: New University of Ulster, 1984).

I should also like to express gratitude to the following organisations for facilitating access to relevant material: the Ulster Museum; Belfast Central Library, especially the Ulster and Irish Studies Department, and its associated Newspaper Library; the Linen Hall Library, and the Public Record Office of Northern Ireland.

Finally, of the many individuals who provided advice and help, I should like to offer particular thanks to Henry Bell, former Senior Lecturer, Belfast Metropolitan College and Trevor Parkhill, Keeper of History, Ulster Museum.

Don McCloy

Captain F.C. Forth, First Principal of the Belfast Municipal Technical Institute.
(Belfast Metropolitan College Archive.)

Prologue

A lifetime's involvement in technical education, as student, lecturer and manager, urged me to put pen to paper – and fingers to keyboard – in an attempt to describe the various trials, tribulations and impediments faced by the pioneers of technical education in my hometown of Belfast. A comprehensive coverage of the subject from its origins to the present day would require more than a single volume, so I've restricted my timescale to the period 1801-1921. These dates are of political as well as technological significance. On the political front, the former date marks the establishment of the United Kingdom of Great Britain and Ireland, and the latter the dissolution of that Union and the foundation of the new Northern Ireland. On the technological front, 1801 was a pivotal year in the transition from manual working to mechanisation; James Watt, for example, patented his steam engine in 1769, and George Stephenson had his first steam locomotive up and running in 1814. At the latter end of the period, the 1920s saw the fledgling Northern Ireland flexing its technological muscles. The *Titanic* had come and gone, and whilst a post-war industrial slump had to be endured, Belfast could boast of the greatest concentration of linen plants in the world, and of the world's largest shipyard, ropeworks, and tobacco factory.

Ireland was relatively slow to reap the benefits of the Industrial Revolution that was occurring on mainland Britain, and it was some time before Belfast really showed that it was capable of picking up the baton of technological advancement. However, when Britain was displaying its technological prowess to the world in the Great Exhibition of 1851, Belfast, with only around 30,000 inhabitants, was already able to boast of some twenty semi-mechanised flax spinning mills, and of embryonic engineering and shipbuilding industries. The town itself was small and pretty at that time. On its south side there was open country beyond the Blackstaff River. In the west, a fashionable residential quarter extended along College Square as far as Albert Street; in the east, the Queen's Bridge led on through pastures to the village of Ballymacarrett; and in the north, Carlisle Circus saw the start of open country, although the area to the west of Clifton Street was under intense development.

In the early 1800s Belfast's trade centred on commerce and shipping, but hordes of labourers, operatives and artisans were attracted to the town as its factories grew in number. As the population expanded, and as the related technologies became more varied and dominant, so emerged a need for technical education – or technical instruction as it was called in those early days. What follows is an attempt to describe, in chronological order, how the townspeople responded to that need.

Creating Belfast shows that Belfast was never backwards in matters educational; for example, the Academical Institution and the Academy, both extant today, were established respectively in 1785 and 1810, and the Queen's College, forerunner of today's Queen's University, opened its doors in 1849. Growing numbers of primary schools, many operating under the National School system, and a much smaller number of secondary (or intermediate) schools, also began to spring up across the town. This book describes how provision at each level of education developed, placing a strong emphasis on their contributions to technical education. All three levels were found, in the main, to be wanting in that particular respect.

Technical education had severe birth pangs. People weren't sure what it was, and even when they did have some idea of its meaning, they weren't convinced that it was worth pursuing. In the most general terms technical education was seen as a way of making people more effective in the workplace. This had been for many years the objective of the apprenticeship system, certainly in the trades. But as science and technology advanced, the amount of knowledge and skill required by practitioners increased in step. It was ultimately agreed that technical education should not be restricted solely to the achievement of manual dexterity and the ability to apply established technique. Technical education would include study of the sciences that underpinned particular trades, and the application of science to industry. *Creating Belfast* follows the evolution of this latter concept of technical education, and how it struggled for recognition by employers, educators and the State.

The need for technical education became steadily more pressing as other countries began to use it to increase the technological proficiency of their industries. But it was some time before the United Kingdom decided to take action on the matter; the longstanding *laissez faire* approach was preferred. In Belfast, the development of technical education in the nineteenth century relied heavily on voluntary effort. A series of pioneering developments ensued, some more successful than others: the Mechanics' Institute (founded in 1825); the School of Design (1849); the Working Men's Institute (1866); the School of Art (1870); the Technical School (1884), and the School of Applied Science and Engineering (1886). Philanthropy, and occasional grants from trade guilds helped these organisations to limp from crisis to crisis.

The Government finally decided to intercede, and to offer some encouragement and support to the providers of technical education. Motivated by a fear of increasing foreign expertise in science and technology, a Department of Science and Art was established in London in 1853. It drew up examinations in science, and schools whose pupils passed those examinations were granted proportionate sums of money. Later, in 1880, the City and Guilds of London Institute began to provide examinations that had a much stronger technical bias than those of the Department of Science and Art, and schools were also able to earn grants for success in those examinations.

Financial inputs from these bodies brought some comfort to Belfast's providers of technical education. However, the sums involved fell far short of the amounts required to ensure the continuing viability of a group of enterprises that relied heavily on fees and donations to keep heads above water. Fortunately, driven once again by increasing competition from other countries, the Government decided to step up its support for technical education. A series of Royal Commissions had brought the matter to a head by demonstrating beyond all doubt that the highly organised and subsidised technical schools on the Continent were extremely effective in improving industrial performance there.

Creating Belfast describes the follow-up to the recommendations of the Royal Commission on Technical Instruction (1884), its effects on Belfast's disparate system of technical education and how, even after the Technical Instruction Act of 1889 had permitted the funding of technical education from the rates, the Belfast Corporation still required much persuasion to make any such contribution. After much cajoling, and complaints from the Town Hall that monies were needed urgently for other public amenities, the Council finally agreed, starting in 1891, to grant small amounts to the schools involved.

Small as it was, the contribution from the City's coffers was welcome. However, even with fees and donations added, it was barely enough to provide Belfast with the up-to-date and well-equipped technical education system that a growing industrial city needed. But a champion was waiting in the wings. Horace Plunkett started wheels turning, and his work, which called for a greater recognition of the particular needs of Ireland, culminated in the Agriculture and Technical Instruction (Ireland) Act, which came into operation in 1900. Shortly afterwards, a new Department of Agriculture and Technical Instruction brought substantial support for technical education. Belfast gained substantial benefit from the new scheme, but only on condition that the Corporation made a meaningful contribution from the rates, and that a Technical Instruction Committee would be formed to oversee the design and operation of a new co-ordinated system of technical education in Belfast. The book's later chapters describe how the Municipal Technical Institute provided the focus for that development, how it subsumed the then-existing providers, how it served the citizens of Belfast, and how its new building in College Square became a familiar and much-loved landmark in the city centre.

A Note on Sources

Archival material played a crucial role in the production of the book. The major sources of such material are listed below.

Belfast Central Library (BCL)

The Ulster and Irish Studies Department, and the associated Newspaper Library were particularly helpful. Early documents about the Belfast Mechanics' Institute are available, as well as bound volumes of annual reports of the Belfast Government School of Art (1871-1902); these latter are under reference GSA,B. There is also a bound volume of the annual reports of the Belfast Working Men's Institute (1879-1889). Some material concerns the formation of the Belfast Municipal Technical Institute, including a prospectus for the year 1914/15. The newspaper archive provides a wealth of information about education in general, and technical education in particular. Press reports cover most meetings of the various management committees.

Belfast Metropolitan College (BMC)

There is surprisingly little archival material available in the very college that sprang from the original Municipal Technical Institute. Some early photographs can be viewed (Hogg was commissioned to photograph the construction of the building), and a disorganised collection of odds and ends includes a few gems. The building itself has changed little over the years and is well worth a visit.

Linen Hall Library (LHL)

Copies of early newspapers are available, but the most productive source of relevant material was the Belfast Printed Book (BPB) catalogue, which extends back as far as 1698. For example, BPB 1831.45 is the first published copy of the Belfast Library of Useful Knowledge, and BPB 1876.3 is a catalogue of the industrial exhibition held in the Ulster Hall in 1876.

Public Record Office Northern Ireland (PRONI)

PRONI was the most abundant source of relevant material. The minutes of the Belfast Town/City Council provide an invaluable and detailed record of the development of technical education in Belfast. Bound volumes of the minutes of Council and its committees can be found under reference LA/7. Reference LA/7/7 provides a particular interesting collection of material; for example, LA/7/7HB contains some prospectuses of the Municipal Technical Institute, and LA/7HD/4 is a copy of the invitation to the formal opening of the Institute. More material on technical education can be found under ED/4, and there is information on Model Schools in ED/8.

The Ulster Museum

The museum's collection of photographs was particularly interesting and relevant. Alexander Hogg took many pictures of Belfast during the years that technical education was increasing in popularity.

I

Belfast Shaped By Science and Technology

Small Town to Industrial City

A considerable quantity of linen had been produced in Ulster long before the 1801 Act of Union came into force. It was a domestic industry, however, mostly carried out in cottages. Belfast itself played only a small part in linen production, with a mere 180 handloom weavers[1] at work in the town in the 1770s. As a thriving seaport however, it handled the shipping of around two thirds of all the linen produced in Ulster at the time. Early Belfast was a centre of commerce, not of industry, and its leading citizens were merchants, not industrialists.

The introduction of cotton manufacture in the 1770s boosted Ulster's textile industry. This great new Belfast industry had humble roots: in 1778 Nicholas Grimshaw persuaded the Belfast Charitable Society that the children of the town's splendid new Poor House in Clifton Street could be usefully employed spinning cotton. With the assistance of Robert Joy and watchmaker Thomas McCabe, Grimshaw installed spinning wheels and a carding machine[2] in the Poor House. That humble introduction to cotton technology was the start of a rapid growth in cotton manufacture. As new mechanised equipment was invented, Grimshaw and Nathaniel Wilson were encouraged to set up Ireland's first cotton mill at Whitehouse[3] in 1784. Horse power and man power were gradually replaced when Belfast got its first taste of steam energy in 1790. However, that experience was not the ideal example of technological planning,[4] for the new steam engine at the Springfield Cotton Mill was used to pump water to drive a water wheel! Fortunately, the new power source was deployed much more effectively elsewhere, and Belfast's cotton industry began to expand, its viability greatly enhanced by the preferential treatment under the Act of Union that placed high duties on cotton imports and paid bounties on foreign sales.

Smithfield was the centre of the Belfast cotton industry; John McCracken's Mill in Francis Street, with some two hundred hands, was typical of the several mills in the area[5]. Between 1800 and 1811 the numbers employed in cotton in Belfast and its environs grew from 13,500 to 50,000. As cotton production increased, that of linen decreased; in 1807, of Belfast's 723 looms, only four were used for flax.[6] However, the cotton industry took a turn for the worse when the Government removed its protection for the industry in 1824. Faced with stiff competition from mills in Lancashire and Yorkshire, the Ulster industry began to crumble. There were only four cotton mills in the whole of Ireland in 1861, and the American Civil War, which started that year, put the last nail in the industry's coffin.

However, the cotton industry's demise was more than offset by an increase in linen manufacture. Technological advances in flax spinning fuelled a resurgence of the linen industry. Up to 1820, the fine linen trade had relied on hand-spinning to produce the yarns required for its specialised products. However, the replacement of hand-spinning by wet-spinning was a great boon to the industry. The wet-spinning process started by drawing the flax through a trough of hot water and this, by loosening the gummy material holding the fibres together, enabled the machinery to spin a finer yarn.[7] Local

Jennymount Mill (Lanyon Building), North Derby Street, completed in 1891.

Ewart's Linen Warehouse, Bedford Street, built in the 1850s.

manufacturers took early advantage of this invention. When Mulholland's Henry Street Cotton Mill burned down in 1828, he replaced it with a flax spinning mill which used the wet-spinning process. By 1840 there were eighteen flax spinning mills in and around Belfast, and their numbers had grown to thirty-two by 1861.[8] The introduction of wet-spinning increased the industry's productivity; so too did the mechanised weaving which was introduced after 1850. Making heavy demands on the Jacquard mechanism, the number of powered looms in Belfast grew from a mere one to some 6,000 between 1852 and 1862.[9]

Linen production flourished, reaching its peak in the 1870s, and, for the next fifty years or so it remained a dynamic industry with a worldwide reputation. In the 1890s the York Street Flax Spinning and Weaving Company reached enormous proportions with some 4,000 workers and steam engines with an aggregate 2,500 horsepower[10] (1,865 kilowatt). The First World War, with its demands for aircraft cloth, brought an abundant new market, and in the early 1920s a boom in demand for dress materials in the USA brought a further period of prosperity.[11] In addition to its many production facilities, Belfast had established itself as a great trade centre for linen. Bedford Street was renowned for the many merchant houses that arranged flax imports from Russia and Belgium, and exported finished goods mainly to Great Britain and the USA.

Shipbuilding also helped to turn Belfast into a great industrial city. Its roots can be traced back to the Ritchie and Maclaine Yard, which opened when Ritchie transferred his business from Saltcoats in Scotland in 1791. The new yard, which made oaken ships, was established near the site of today's Harbour Office. The steamship *Belfast*, launched in 1820, and powered by seventy-horse-power engines manufactured by Victor Coates, was an early success.[12] Two other yards were set up on the Antrim shore of the Lagan in those early days – Charles Connell & Sons, and Thompson & Kirwan – but all three together only managed to turn out fifty ships between 1820 and 1850.[13]

The Lagan of those days was not the ideal environment for shipbuilding, nor, indeed, for marine transport. Twists and turns, mudflats and sandbanks abounded, and water levels were very low when the tide receded. The Belfast Ballast Board (1785) and, later, the Belfast Harbour Commissioners (1847) were anxious to improve matters. Work commenced in the 1840s to dredge the Lagan and cut channels in order to improve maritime access to the town, and to make life easier for the shipbuilding fraternity. Wooden ships gradually gave way to iron ones, and the Harbour Commissioners decided to back the new technology by setting up a shipyard to build iron ships in 1853. This new yard was situated on Dargan's Island (later Queen's Island), which had been con-structed from the mud and rubble gathered during the various improvements to the harbour. It was managed initially by Robert Hickson, who had trans-ferred his engineering works from Eliza Street, but the business was taken over in 1858 by Hickson's general manager – one Edward James Harland. Gustav Wilhelm Wolff, who had been employed by Harland in 1854 as his personal assistant, became the other half of the famous Harland & Wolff duo. The new yard went from strength to strength, and the number of workers increased from 300 to 9,000 between 1861 and 1900.[14] No fewer than 304 ships were produced between 1880 and 1914.[15] Harland & Wolff's formal association with the White Star Line proved particularly successful, with liners ranging from the 3,800-ton *Oceanic* (1871) to the 42,200-ton *Titanic* (1912). In 1880 the firm decided to establish its own engine works, and starting with enormous four-cylinder com-pound engines, Harland & Wolff's engine technology had advanced to double reduction–geared turbines by the 1920s.

A major rival entered the stage in 1880 when Frank Workman and George Clark, both former apprentices in Harland & Wolff, set up their own yard on Queen's Island. The Workman Clark Yard was soon high on the world's league

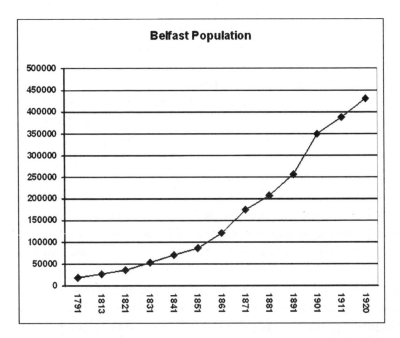

The population of Belfast, 1791-1921.

Some surviving Victorian terrace houses, Hamill Street.

of shipbuilders. Between 1900 and 1923 it produced more ships than Harland & Wolff – 210 against 149 – although the latter had the edge in tonnage terms (1.5 million against 1.3 million tons[16]). Known locally as the 'wee yard', Workman Clark was certainly not 'wee' on the international scale.

The needs of the textiles and shipbuilding industries encouraged the establishment of a third major industry in Belfast – engineering. The town's first large foundry – the Lagan Foundry – was set up in the Short Strand in around 1800.[17] When Stainton, the major shareholder, died two years later, Victor Coates took over the business and carried it through with great success until 1905. The number of Belfast's foundries grew from eight in the 1830s to around twenty in the 1910s.[18] Most had some form of specialisation. Musgrave and Sons, for example, began manufacturing stable and household fittings, such as stoves in 1855. The manufacture of textile machinery offered lucrative business and helped several foundries to grow to enormous proportions. James Combe's Falls Foundry, established in 1845, was by 1852 employing 380 men to produce flax-spinning machinery. And the rapid growth of James Mackie and Sons, set up in 1858, forced a move to the Springfield Road in the 1890s. By the 1850s, several of the larger foundries were manufacturing steam engines; Victor Coates produced particularly large engines, providing the Newcastle-upon-Tyne tramways with a 3,000-horsepower triple expansion engine in 1900.[19] The arrival of electricity brought new firms to Belfast; JH Greenhill began to manufacture dynamos in 1883, and Hugh J Scott started to make motors and dynamos in his Ravenhill Avenue works in 1900. Other notable manufactories included the Belfast Ropeworks (1873) and Samuel Davidson's Sirocco Works (1881), which originally manufactured equipment for drying tea.

These many developments in shipbuilding, textiles and engineering were accompanied by a multitude of other enterprises such as Gallaher's Tobacco (1867). Belfast was a boom town, and its population grew rapidly as the expanding industrial base attracted people from the surrounding countryside and from Great Britain. A vast network of working-class housing extended the boundaries of Belfast. Travel to and from work was facilitated by a growing array of tramways – starting with horse trams in the 1870s, but developing into a modern electrically powered system by 1904.

As these industries and the number of employees grew, the need for technical education for the workforce became increasingly evident.

Science and Technology

The balance of science and technology in the technical education curriculum has long been a contentious issue, so a brief introduction to the merits of each is necessary at this stage.

Technology is the senior partner in the science and technology team. Tools are the trademark of technology, and *Homo Habilis* was making cutting tools from flint flakes some 2.6 million years ago. One of the earliest definitions of technology can be found in Samuel Johnson's 1755 *Dictionary of the English Language*. There it is defined as 'a description or discourse upon arts' – a definition springing directly from the Greek roots *techne* (art, skill or craft) and *logia* (study or knowledge). By art, Johnson meant 'the power of doing something not taught by nature'. So, right up to the nineteenth century, technology was classified as an art. But, in order to distinguish it from the many other arts, it was often referred to as industrial art, and sometimes as mechanical art. Throughout the present book technology will be considered as the application of knowledge and skills to practical tasks.

Whilst the word technology has Greek origins, science finds its roots in the Latin word for knowledge – *scientia*. Science began to develop when humans became curious about their environment; they wanted to understand the seasons, the stars, day and night, etc. The attempts of philosophers like Plato and Aristotle to explain these phenomena provided some of the earliest contributions to the great universal knowledge bank that grows day by day. Later, natural philosophers – as scientists were called in those days – developed the so-called scientific method, which tested hypotheses through experimentation, and great men like Galileo and Newton used this technique to establish famous laws about mechanics and the operation of the universe. In this book science will be considered as knowledge of the world gained through observation and experiment.

Debates about the relative importance and the interactions between science and technology have generated much heat over the years. Basically, science is about knowing, and technology is about doing. The impact of science on technology began to increase from the eighteenth century onwards, when the creators of new technologies found an ever-growing bank of scientific knowledge to draw upon. These new science-based technologies helped engineers meet the ever-increasing needs of Society and the economy. But the role of science in engineering and technology is still often overstated. Science is only one component of the vast bank of knowledge and skills that engineers have to call upon. Whilst science may dictate the limits of the performance of an artefact, it does not prescribe its final form, nor how it can be achieved.

As the years progressed the prospective advantages of a combined scientific–technological approach to industrial problems began to become clearer. As Ireland struggled to increase her manufacturing base in the mid-nineteenth century, Robert Kane, Irish polymath and Professor of Natural Philosophy at the Royal Dublin Society, argued that science and technology should progress hand in hand:

> Science and art, which should distribute by progressing hand in hand, the highest blessings of industry and civilisation, are hence often separated, and the more so, that the persons by whom each is cultivated are kept asunder by the false ideas as to what really constitutes education. The man of science, occupying himself with the interesting paths of abstract discovery, thinks not of community of objects, or of feeling, with the dark, coarse-handed operatives, who, in the furnace or the forge, work up the really practicable solution of his problems; whilst the worker, equally ignorant of the importance of bringing together their respective modes of experiment and inquiry, consider science, like the dead languages, as characterising the position of the upper classes, from whom, intellectually as well as socially, he keeps apart.[20]

Technical education was to become the matchmaker between science and technology.

Popularising Science and Technology in Belfast

If Ireland was to match the economic development of other countries, it was essential that Irish people became informed about science and technology. The Royal Dublin Society (RDS), founded in 1731, was a pioneer in this enlightenment business. Aiming to improve husbandry, manufactures and other useful arts and sciences, it was described in 1780 as having, 'the undisputed merit of being the father of all similar societies now existing in Europe'.[21] The RDS made its mark in Ireland; its work led to the construction of the Botanic Gardens at Glasnevin in 1795, and its collections formed the basis of the National Museum. Also, the transfer of its professors to the Museum of Irish Industry in 1845 greatly enhanced the reputation and capability of that organisation, and influenced considerably the later decision to develop it into a Royal College of Science.

The RDS carried out significant research, but its role in popularising science and technology is of greater relevance here. This was achieved through courses and lectures at the Dublin headquarters and around the country. William Higgins was perhaps the earliest exponent of the public lecture in Ireland. Having set up a chemistry laboratory at the Society's Hawkins Street headquarters in 1795, Higgins advertised a series of courses for the general public. Initial interest was disappointing, but that faltering start did not weaken the Society's resolve to popularise science and technology in Ireland. The Society sent a petition to the Government in 1799 seeking additional grants for teaching:

> The Society, having embraced the important design of communicating to Ireland the benefits of science … feels the necessity of enlarging the lectures, so as to teach the elements and principles of philosophic chemistry in a systematic and experimental course, and also to have a course for them of technical chemistry to demonstrate the application of principles delivered in the former, to various manufacturers and arts.[22]

The application was successful, and new professorships soon followed. James Lynch, for example, was appointed in 1800 and was soon providing three public lecture courses a year, each consisting of twenty-five to thirty lectures covering mechanics, hydrostatics, pneumatics and hydraulics. The RDS's move from Hawkins Street to Leinster House in 1820 provided new opportunities to develop these teaching programmes. Indeed, a continuing growth in interest in such courses required the provision, in 1897, of a 700-seat lecture theatre.

Robert Kane, appointed to a Professorship in Chemistry in the RDS in 1839, made particularly important contributions. During his tenure he demonstrated a remarkable breadth of knowledge through a series of popular lectures on electricity, optics, and mechanics. Kane was appointed President of Queen's College, Cork in 1845 and, in the same year, Director of the Museum of Economic Geology (later the Museum of Irish Industry).

With the transfer of the Society's professorships to the Museum of Irish

Industry in 1854, the focus of the RDS's activities turned towards original research and agriculture. The Society moved from Leinster House to its present site at Ballsbridge in 1922.

Belfast was not solely dependant on these Dublin-based institutions for enlightenment in scientific and technological matters. Local initiative established several organisations aimed at the education of layman and expert, of artisan and dilettante. For example, the Belfast Reading Society, founded in 1788, was originally aimed at the town's artisans.[23] Achieving early popularity, its title was changed in 1792 to the Belfast Society for Promoting Knowledge. In addition to its basic aim of collecting an extensive library, the Society hoped to acquire 'philosophical apparatus and such productions of nature and art as are calculated to enlarge knowledge'. This latter aim led to the establishment of a small museum under the management of one John Templeton, who gathered together a modest collection which included an air pump, thermometers and a barometer. The Society's technological reputation was enhanced by the work of member Job Rider, a clockmaker from Shambles Street, who took out several patents relating to improvements in steam engines.[24]

In 1802 the Society's library secured its first permanent premises in the new

Commercial Buildings, Waring Street, constructed in 1822.

The Old Belfast Museum,
College Square North,
completed 1831.

White Linen Hall, where it adopted the new title – the Linen Hall Library. Further disruption ensued in 1888, when the construction of a new City Hall forced a move across the street to the present day premises in Donegall Square North.

There were other early attempts to provide appropriate educational facilities for the people of Belfast. The Belfast Literary Society, founded in 1801, aimed to provide 'opportunity for intercourse among literary and scientifical, or intelligent and inquisitive men'. It pursued this aim through papers and discussion upon natural history, topography, and the solution of practical questions connected with science, the arts and manufactures.[25]

The Belfast Natural History Society was a more successful venture. Founded in a private house in Chichester Street in 1821, its objective was, 'The cultivation of zoology, botany, and mineralogy in all their branches, more especially the investigation of the natural history and antiquities of Ireland.'[26] Membership grew quickly and it was soon necessary to transfer the Society's meetings to the natural philosophy classroom of the Belfast Academical Institution. However, continuing growth in membership and in the Society's collection of specimens forced yet another move, in 1823, to two rooms in the Commercial Buildings

– rented for £11 per annum, including £1 for setting a fire on winter evenings.[27] Yet further growth persuaded the Society that a purpose-built building was required, and, after considering a site in Queen Street, it was decided to construct the new edifice in College Square North. The foundation stone of the new Belfast Museum was laid by the Marquis of Donegall in May 1830, and the building was formally opened in November 1831. It is interesting to note that the foundation stone houses a time capsule containing memorabilia of the early 1800s. The museum was an instant success. Mechanics and children were charged an entrance fee of threepence, and everyone else sixpence. Easter Mondays were particularly popular; there were some 6,000 visitors on Easter Monday 1853.[28]

The presentation of papers and public lectures was a regular feature of the Society's work. Topics relating to natural history dominated the early proceedings, but other aspects of science, and of technology, gradually came under consideration. This drift led to a name change in 1842, from which time to the present the Society has been known as the Belfast Natural History and Philosophical Society (BNHPS). The change in title, however, did little to increase the emphasis on applied science and technology. In 100 years (1821-1921) only 74 out of a total of 1,155 papers had significant technological content.[29] The 1,081 science-related papers included: uni-valve shells (1822), the eye (1830), polarised light (1844), ocean currents (1859), soap bubbles (1888), and water beetles (1911). The seventy-four technology-related papers included: steam (1834), the electric telegraph (1854), brick-making (1865), glass-making (1869), drinking-water (1874), etching (1883), electrical power transmission (1885), sanitation (1890), horseless carriages (1895), and domestic lighting (1912).

The BNHPS helped to promulgate technical education, with six papers on the theme in the century surveyed. Several short courses of instruction were also introduced. In 1837, for example, Dr J.D. Marshall began a course of twelve lectures on birds, and in 1842 the Revd Dr Bryce of the Belfast Royal Academy started a course of seven lectures on the art and science of education. These lectures were presented in the museum, but others of a more technical nature were delivered at the Queen's College. In 1858 Dr Thomas Andrews delivered a course of six lectures in the chemical lecture theatre at the College. But the single popular lecture remained the most effective way of informing the general public about science and technology. The first such public lecture took place on 30 November 1831, when Professor John Stevelly lectured on 'the wind'.

As the record shows, the BNHPS's interests favoured science, not technology. However, an attempt was made to correct this imbalance in 1891 when an Engineering Section was established under the presidency of W.H. Wilson. Wilson's inaugural address – 'Recent Advances in Mechanical Science' – set the scene for the new development, but it appeared to lose momentum and there is little reference to it in subsequent records of the Society.

The social, as well as the economic advantages of an educated working class were stressed by Belfast's philanthropists. Indeed many newly established (and often ephemeral) organisations emphasised the former over the latter. The Belfast Library of Useful Knowledge, founded in 1831, was one such body. The first issue of *Reality*, a monthly tract costing 1*d*, stated:

> The advantage of knowledge in benefiting the condition of mankind, in dis-
> posing them to be peaceable and well intentioned to each other, and inclined
> to improve their condition without the employment of fierce contention or
> brutal violence, are so great, that it would be trite to insist on them.[30]

The tract was to include items on education, the improvement of the condition of the working classes, political economy, mental and natural philosophy, and natural history. However, lack of support from the intended clientele soon made the venture unviable.

The Belfast Society for the Amelioration of the Condition of the Working Classes was another well-intentioned, but short-lived project. It seems that the workers of the day became disenchanted with a scheme over which they had little control. Another group, the Belfast Working Classes' Association for the Promotion of General Improvement, launched in January 1847, hoped to avoid that mistake by inviting the working classes to join the Association and to partic-ipate in its management. It aimed 'To encourage a taste for reading, and mental cultivation generally, among the working community of Belfast, and otherwise advance their character and condition.' This aim was to be delivered through a monthly *Belfast People's Magazine*, through a reading room in Castle Place, and through a lending library. However, like with preceding organisations, the town's artisans had to endure a great deal of patronising and preaching. A sample reads:

> The intelligent working man will, generally speaking, always be found more
> sober, more honest, more industrious, more skilful, than the ignorant. From
> the first hour of his professional life he has a thousand advantages over his
> neighbour who has known no other school than the work-shop. While the
> one plods mechanically along, trusting to mere imitation for acquiring a
> knowledge of the art which is to be his only capital when he goes out into

the world, his fellow can avail himself of the experience, research, compari-son – genius, in fact – of the wisest and greatest men of his own and other times. The one is the mole who blindly burrows in the earth, hiding himself from the rising sun of enlightenment – the other is the eagle who, soaring into its broad rays, takes in at a glance all that is passing in the busy scene beneath.[31]

In the end, lack of interest from the working classes forced the termination of the Association in 1849. It was clear that other approaches to the education and training of the working classes were needed. These were provided, in the first instance, through voluntary effort. Before introducing the various voluntary initiatives it is necessary to clarify the concept of technical education.

Technical Education Defined

The terms 'technical education', 'technical instruction', and 'industrial educa-tion' were interchangeable in the late nineteenth and early twentieth centuries. However, 'technical education' is used throughout this book except where the context demands otherwise.

Science had long been advocated as an important, if not dominant, compo-nent of technical education. However, the practical and applied components could not be ignored. Robert Kane, Irish administrator and entrepreneur, expressed a view on the matter in 1844:

A person about to be educated for industrial purposes should … be first thor-oughly grounded in the general principles of the natural and physical sciences, and in elementary mathematics … Thus grounded in general education, he should pass to his special branch, according as he is to be a chemist, a maker of machines, a worker in metals, or of other trade. Of all the objects used in his peculiar occupation he should acquire the most minute knowledge; their properties and composition; their adulterations; where they are found; how they are obtained; what can be substituted for them; how they can be made.

To this general education should be added the experience of the workshop. The simplest operation in the arts requires a degree of manipulative skill that no books, no words can give. The most perfect theoretical acquaintance with the construction of machines and the nature of various materials used would not enable a man to do good work. But if the man has obtained the manual skill by working practice, there is no doubt but that the knowledge of the tools he is using and of the materials he worked upon, will enable him to do it better than he otherwise could. The practical education of the artisan in the place of actual working is, therefore, of all the most important, and requires most time. The ultimate object of the previous discipline in science is to enable him fully to avail himself of the opportunities of improvement in his art which the workshop continually affords.[32]

The Devonshire Commission on Scientific Instruction and the Advancement of Science made a crucial point in its 1875 Report, where it defined technical education as, 'general instruction in those sciences, the principles of which are applicable to various specified employments of life … excluding the manual instruction in arts and manufactures which is given in the workshop'.[33] This exclusion of manual instruction from courses of technical education was a crucial factor – one which Kane had foreseen when he proposed that the practical education of the artisan should take place in the actual workplace. Trade societies were adamant that schools and colleges should not be involved in training for trades; they felt that such a move could undermine their own influence on the skills taught to apprentices, and how those skills might be taught. Employers, meanwhile, were concerned that trade secrets might be divulged in any such process.

In the end, it was confirmed that technical education would not offer instruction in the practice of a particular art. To be effective, however, it would need to include some craft instruction, but the major focus of the practical aspects of courses of technical education would be the application, in general, of the relevant sciences to the industries concerned. The Technical Instruction Act of 1889 enshrined the focus on science and the exclusion of trade practice in a long and cumbersome definition of technical education (see Chapter 8). However, when the Department of Agriculture and Technical Instruction was established in Ireland in 1900, it offered a more concise and helpful definition. Technical instruction would include:

…instruction in the principles of science and art applicable to industries, and in the application of special branches of science and art to specific industries or employments, as well as instruction in the use of tools, and modelling in clay, wood, or other material, but it does not include instruction given in elementary schools or teaching the practice of any trade or industry or employment.[34]

Defining technical education was one thing; delivering it was another.

Employers, Voluntary Effort and Technical Education

Apprenticeship is an ancient form of technical education. An apprentice was bound to serve his master for a period of years, during which he would learn the 'mysteries' of his trade. On completion of his 'time', which might stretch to seven years, the apprentice would graduate to journeyman and then, if he were sufficiently competent, to master. Apprenticeship was widespread in Belfast in the nineteenth and twentieth centuries. Harland & Wolff became the largest employer of apprentice, with 1,784 apprentices amongst the 9,791 hands employed in twenty-two trades in 1919.[35]

The terms of the indenture – the written contract between master and apprentice – were rigorous and demanded much more from the apprentice than from the master. This is illustrated in the following extract from an indenture in which John Kerr of Ballymacarrett signed up for a five-year term as an apprentice millwright in Harland & Wolff in 1872:

> ...he shall not waste the goods of his said Masters, or give or lend them unlawfully to any; he shall not commit fornication, or contract matrimony within the said term; hurt, to said masters in their persons or families, he shall not do, cause, or procure to be done by others; he shall not play cards, dice, or any unlawful game with his own or others' goods, whereby his said Masters may have loss, during the said term...[36]

In return for this chastity and respect, Harland & Wolff pledged to teach, instruct, or cause to be instructed the apprentice in the given trade. In this instance John Kerr was paid 6s per week initially, rising to 10s per week in his fifth year.

Apprenticeship focused on the transmission of the craft skills relevant to particular trades: there was little, if any, reference to the underpinning sciences. But that form of training proved to be inadequate as industries grew in size, as the division of labour became widespread, and as science began to influence methods of production. So, whilst apprenticeship continued to be popular throughout the period covered here, later chapters will show that employers and trade societies gradually came to recognise the need for a more effective form of technical education.

As the nineteenth century progressed, the Government became increasingly aware of the economic reasons for providing technical education. But the marketplace, not the Government, was expected to meet the need; this was a matter for industry itself to resolve. However, Belfast's shipbuilding, textiles, and engineering employers were reluctant to support formal off-the-job technical education. In an age of increasing specialisation and mechanisation, they saw few benefits in encouraging workers to familiarise themselves with the sciences related to their particular crafts. They were content, on the whole, with the time-honoured way of doing things – including apprenticeship. There were exceptions, of course, and those few people, along with growing numbers of ambitious young people, provided the momentum for the establishment of formal systems of technical education.

The philanthropists of Belfast took a series of initiatives which boosted the technical education movement. Each is described in detail in later chapters, but a short summary follows:

1825

The Belfast Mechanics' Institute: Springing from a Scottish initiative, the Mechanics' Institute aimed to improve working men's general and scientific knowledge through its library facilities, lectures, museum, and scientific school. It was based in Queen Street.

1849

The Belfast Government School of Design: A branch school of the London-based School of Design, the Belfast School aimed to improve locally produced artefacts, such as damask, through improved design. It ran courses for artisans, but its facilities were also used by the middle classes, many of whom attended on a recreational basis. It was based in College Square North, in the north wing of the Belfast Academical Institution.

1866

The Belfast Working Men's Institute: Learning from the failure of the Mechanics' Institute, the Working Men's Institute provided a social centre as well as a facility where working men could learn the principles of their business. Its Schools of Science and Technology provided a wide range of courses. A successful venture, it was subsumed within the Belfast Municipal Technical Institute in 1902. It occupied a splendid building on the corner of Queen Street and Castle Street.

1870

The Belfast Government School of Art: To some extent a rebirth of the failed School of Design, the School of Art catered for the same sort of clientele, but offered a more wide-ranging and relevant set of courses. Under an astute board of management, it established an influential role in technical education matters, and ultimately became part of the Municipal Technical Institute. Like its predecessor the Belfast School of Design, it was housed in the north wing of the Belfast Academical Institution.

1884

The Belfast Technical School: Designed primarily to meet the needs of a rapidly expanding textile industry, the Technical School aimed to provide practical facilities and practically-orientated courses that were not offered elsewhere. Ever struggling to maintain financial viability, and suffering from severe accommodation problems, the school was subsumed within the Municipal Technical Institute in 1902. It was based in spacious but poorly maintained former industrial accommodation in Hastings Street, off Divis Street.

1886

The School of Applied Science and Engineering: A breakaway from the Working Men's Institute, this school provided courses which had a stronger practical bent than those offered in the Institute. Its work was ultimately subsumed within the Municipal Technical Institute. It was based in the Belfast Model School in Divis Street.

Many artisans who attended these organisations were poorly educated and had to work hard to come to grips with the underpinning sciences of their trades. Many succeeded, but a lot fell by the wayside. The elementary schools and the secondary schools of the day were not giving young people an adequate preparation for technical education.

Technical Education in Schools, Colleges and Universities

What did the early elementary schools do to prepare their pupils for careers in science and technology? Elementary schools played an important role in shaping young people's careers. In the early years of the nineteenth century elementary education was scarce, *ad hoc*, and often delivered in humble hedge schools. The Churches made some attempt to educate their young 'flocks', and various voluntary groups made contributions; for example, a non-denominational Lancasterian School was established in Belfast's Frederick Street in 1810. The establishment of a National School System in 1831 brought focus and much-needed resources to the sector. By 1862 there were seventy National Schools in Belfast, although many were in a dilapidated condition, and many of the children were 'half-timers', sharing their days between the mill and the school.[37] All creeds were catered for: parents of Presbyterian stock, for example, could send their children to schools such as Brown Street and Townsend Street, with 563 and 265 pupils respectively in 1862; and Catholic parents could turn to schools such as Chapel Lane and Donegall Street, with 185 and 196 pupils respectively. The Belfast Model Schools, opened in Divis Street in 1857, attracted both Catholic and Protestant children in their early years; at the time of opening, 389 of the 1,092 pupils were Catholic.[38] The Model Schools attracted the highest-qualified teachers and offered a wide curriculum that included drawing, physical science, and housewifery. However, technical subjects were few and far between in most other primary schools.

There was one exception to this general malaise: Industrial Schools had been springing up across the country since the beginning if the nineteenth century, and one was established in Belfast in 1801. Caring for deserted and orphaned children, the curriculum of these schools included substantial amounts of technical education intended to prepare the children for later life. Industrial schools started to receive State aid in 1868 and this boosted their numbers considerably. For example, St Patrick's Industrial School for boys was opened in Belfast in 1869. In addition to the 'three Rs', its boys were trained by qualified tradesmen in tailoring, cabinet making and boot making. The products of the boys' labours were sold to the general public.[39] A training ship, the *Gibraltar* (renamed the

Grampian), was an interesting Belfast innovation of 1871, but various factors led to its demise in 1899, when it was subsumed within the Balmoral Industrial School for Protestant boys. By 1902 Belfast had a total of six industrial schools catering for nearly 1,000 young girls and boys.[40] Their work was held in high esteem and considered to provide a model technical education. When the Aberdare Commission visited Belfast in 1884, its subsequent report stated, 'no question ... was raised as to the good effects produced by the industrial schools, where the children, never of criminal types, receive an excellent education and training, and are generally, when discharged, placed without difficulty in respectable situations.'[41]

The lack of technical education in the National School system was of such concern that the Government was obliged to set up a Royal Commission in 1897 to determine how much manual and practical instruction should be included in the primary curriculum (see Chapter 2). The review confirmed a sorry state of affairs across the country, with Belfast schools faring particularly badly. It reported that only three handicraft classes and one cookery class were on offer in the city's National Schools at the time. Most schools were dabbling in drawing, but it was poorly taught. The Commission concluded that 'the present system of primary education is so one-sided in its character that it leaves the pupils quite unprepared for technical education.' A Revised Programme ensued, and by 1910 the country's primary curriculum had assumed a more balanced form. At that time all schools were teaching drawing and some 97 per cent were teaching elementary science. At long last, primary-school pupils were receiving some form of preparation in science and technology.

Did Irish secondary (intermediate) schools compensate for the lack of effective technical education in primary schools? For most of the nineteenth century, secondary education was a luxury only to be enjoyed by those who could afford it. Most secondary schools relied on philanthropy of one form or another – some on endowments initiated many years earlier. The schools were frequented, on the whole, by the middle classes, who wished to see their children progress to university or to respected professional careers. Careers in commerce or industry were frowned upon. Today's prejudices in these matters are very similar to those expressed in 1844:

If a boy is to be sent to a profession, great care is taken with his education. Literature and science present themselves to him hand in hand. A reputation, the best passport to professional success, may, it is said, be founded on school and college character, and his ambition is excited by the social and political eminences which professional men may attain. But if he is going to trade, education it is thought would be thrown away on him. If he can read and write and cipher, it is supposed to be enough. Should an ambitious parent desire to give his son a good education, although he is to be in trade, he puts him through college. He devotes the best years of his youth to reading Grecian poetry, and Latin plays; to getting by rote the dialects of the middle ages, and principles of abstract metaphysics, and awakens after the solemnity of getting his degree, to find that he is to obtain his living by principles and pursuits to which his education has had no reference whatsoever.[42]

That set of prejudices helped to produce a distorted secondary curriculum in a large majority of Irish secondary schools – one in which classics, languages and literature predominated. In 1838, the Wyse Commission commented that 'the sciences, even in their most elementary form, are not touched upon'. Fortunately the majority of Belfast's earliest secondary schools were able to avoid that criticism; the curricula of the Belfast Academy (1785) and the Belfast Academical Institution (1810) included scientific content from the outset. Subsequent educational establishments in the town placed varying degrees of emphasis on scientific and technical topics: St Malachy's College (1833); the Belfast Mercantile Academy (1854); the Ladies' Collegiate School (1859); the Christian Brothers' Schools (1866); Methodist College (1868), and St Dominic's High School (1870). Most of them had been providing science classes designed by the Department of Science and Arts in South Kensington, and had benefited from the receipt of results fees.

State support for all aspects of the secondary curriculum finally became available when an Intermediate Education Board was set up in 1878. But the method of support – through payment by results – proved to be unsatisfactory. Amongst its many shortcomings, it discriminated against technical education by allocating more marks and rewards to classical subjects than to modern ones. These factors were highlighted in a review in 1899, and some corrective measures were deployed. However, major improvements in technical educa-tion in Belfast's secondary schools had to await the establishment, in 1901, of the Department of Agriculture and Technical Instruction. Schools were then provided with funds to help them equip science laboratories, classes in science and technology were encouraged, and the Belfast Corporation was cajoled into using the rates to contribute to a system of technical education which embraced all existing components of the city's education system. Those developments led to the establishment of the Belfast Municipal Technical Institute in 1905.

Higher technical education received some early attention in Belfast. The Belfast Academical Institution had planned from the outset to have both School and Collegiate Departments. By 1815, the latter's five professors, including Chairs in Mathematics and Natural Philosophy, were offering an up-to-date programme of advanced studies, including a considerable amount of material of a technical nature. But that development was brought to a halt with the establishment of the Queen's College in Belfast in 1849. A Bachelor of Arts degree and a Diploma in Civil Engineering provided the central plank of the new College's higher technical education provision. Never adequately equipped to deal with the practical components of technical education, Queen's sought collaboration with others who had the necessary resources. When the College achieved university status in 1908, collaboration with the Belfast Municipal Institute began to assume significant proportions, and by 1912 the Institute was providing the practical components of the University's engineering degrees.

2

Technical Education Finds a Place in the Curriculum

Establishing a System of Primary Education

There was surprisingly wide-ranging activity in the field of primary education in the early years of the nineteenth century. However, most of it was unofficial and illegal, and carried out in so-called hedge schools. Popular history places many of these schools in the shadows of hedgerows and in dry ditches, but barns, mud-walled buildings, and respectable buildings were more often than not the venues. Hedge schools were a direct result of the Penal Laws, first introduced in 1695, which included the proscription of any form of Catholic education, 'no person of the popish religion shall publicly or in private houses teach school, or instruct youth in learning within this realm'. Presbyterians also suffered educational restrictions, and many of them turned to hedge schools. The Revd Dr Henry Cooke, for example, a leading Presbyterian of the early nineteenth century, was educated in a hedge school in Ballymacilcurr, near Maghera.

Hedge schools grew in popularity, and by 1824 some 400,000 children were attending around 9,000 such schools.[1] Despite the abolition of the last Penal Laws in 1829, this popularity carried the hedge schools through well into mid-nineteenth century, when they were more commonly known as 'pay schools'. A scattering of official schools offered recognised alternatives to the hedge schools. These came in a variety of forms, but the majority were denominational and felt obliged to proselytise when opportunities presented themselves.

The Society for Promoting the Education of the Poor in Ireland was planned as a non-denominational organisation from the outset. Launched in 1811, and with roots in the Sunday School Movement, the Society planned to support schools where:

> ...the labouring classes may obtain suitable instruction, without any attempt being made to disturb their religious opinions; and that the children of the poor, being thus associated together without distinction, may thereby learn to regard each other without prejudice, and to indulge a charitable feeling for their neighbours, of whatever religious persuasion they may be.[2]

Those liberal principles chimed well with those of the government of the day, so when the Society sought State support in 1814, a positive response quickly followed. Grants grew from £6,000 in 1816 to £30,000 in 1831,[3] and those monies, supplemented by voluntary donations, allowed the Society to support the fitting out of classrooms, to publish booklets on topics like mechanics, needlework and geometry, and to pay gratuities to teachers. The Society also pioneered a successful system of school inspection that was carried through, with minor changes, to the later National School System.

The Society's first school was situated in Dublin's aptly named School Street, but growing income permitted a move to better premises in Kildare Place in 1815. Two Model Schools – one for men and one for women – were established there to exemplify the Society's system of education and also to provide short teacher-training courses. These facilities attracted admiration and support throughout the country. Between 1819 and 1831, the number of schools supported by the Society increased from 133 to 1,621, and the number of pupils from 9,263 to 137,639.[4] By 1825, some 350 teachers had attended short training courses in Kildare Place. There was strong support from all denominations in the early years, but attitudes began to change in around 1820. Catholics were concerned that the Society's committee was dominated by Protestants, that the Society had started to support other educational societies which had overt proselytising tendencies, and that the Society's policy of reading the Scriptures without note or comment was contrary to Catholic dogma. Catholic support dwindled thereafter. In 1831 Lord Stanley, the Chief Secretary for Ireland, asked the House of Commons to withdraw the Society's grant, since, while 'five-sixths of Ireland are Roman Catholic, two-thirds of the whole benefit go to Protestant Ulster.'[5] Indeed, the records for 1831 show that 1,021 of the Society's 1,621 schools were in Ulster.[6] The Government concluded that there was a need for a fresh approach to primary education, but there was a strong consensus that any future system would not use voluntary associations to process public funds.

National Schools

The idea of a national system of education was not a new one; it had already been mooted by a number of government commissions. So the Government moved swiftly to implement such a system – one which would 'unite in one system children of different creeds' and 'banish even the suspicion of proselytism'. To that end, secular and religious education were to be separated, with the latter being taught outside school hours. A multi-denominational system seemed right for Ireland, but it was not long before the various Churches started to voice objections. This is not the place to go into these in detail, although most of the arguments can still be heard today. The National School System never achieved the desired level of non-denominationalism, but it grew nevertheless, and twenty years after its introduction, 4,704 schools were operating under the scheme.[7]

The Model Schools were a particularly noteworthy development – and one in which Belfast played an important part. The Kildare Place Society had established such schools in 1816 and, like several of that Society's other innovations, the National Board decided to develop the concept further. In 1835 the Kildare Place Model School was transferred to new premises in Marlborough Street,

NATIONAL EDUCATION—IRELAND.

OPENING OF THE BELFAST DISTRICT MODEL SCHOOLS, FALLS ROAD.

APPLICATIONS FOR THE ADMITTANCE of Children are received daily, from 9 to 4 o'clock, by the Principal Teachers of the Schools.

Terms, 1s 1d per Quarter.
— 2s 6d   do.
— 5s 0d   do.

Prospectuses and all information in respect to the course of instruction to be had from the Teachers at the Schools. Pupils must be in attendance upon MONDAY, the 4th of May, and the Public Opening will take place on TUESDAY, 19th May, 1857.
Model Schools, 27th April, 1857.   1420

Press notice for the opening of the Belfast Model Schools in 1857. (*Northern Whig* 28/4/1857.)

The Belfast Model Schools in 1921. (*Northern Whig* 28/4/1857.)

where its main function was the training of teachers. It became known as the Central Model School. In addition to this Central Model School, there were to be a further thirty-two District Model Schools – one for each county. Each school would be under direct State control.

This grand plan was modified in 1837, when it was decided to create twenty-five school districts, each with a District Model School from which a Superintendent would supervise all the ordinary National Schools in the district. Each District Model was to have two departments – one for elementary education, and one for science, including workrooms for manual instruction, and each would be attached to a Model farm of some forty acres. The plans materialised slowly. In Ulster, the first District Models opened in Newry and Ballymena in 1849, followed by Coleraine in 1850, Belfast and Ballymoney in 1857, and Londonderry and Newtownards in 1861.

The Belfast Model Schools opened on 19 May 1857. The Falls Road building housed three schools – boys' and girls' schools (for ages seven and up), and an infants' school. There was also an adult department, with classes including drawing, navigation and nautical astronomy, and this at a time when technical education was largely an unknown quantity.

Technical education was high on the agenda. Drawing was growing in popularity at the time, and the Belfast Government School of Design/Art had been preparing National School teachers to teach the subject in College Square North (see Chapter 4). It was a central feature of the curriculum at the Model, where all pupils were required to attend drawing classes. Physical Science also had a high profile in the school; there was a museum, a laboratory and a lecture room fitted out with various models including a steam engine. Girls also had ample opportunity to perfect their practical skills. They had, for example, a bakery, and they were able to practise housewifery skills in the house where the school's student teachers boarded. The Model's practical slant was complemented by a close association with the Model Agricultural School at Musgrave Park in Balmoral.[8] However, that particular venture became a financial embarrassment and had to be sold off in 1875. Its buildings were firstly converted to an Industrial School, but the whole area was later developed as the site for the Musgrave Park Hospital.

The first Headmaster and Headmistress at the Model were G.L. Moore and Miss Collins respectively. Together they ensured that the Belfast Model was indeed a model institution. In addition to providing a wide and relevant curriculum, the school met the National Board's requirement that a wide range of denominational interest should be accommodated. At the time of opening, 1,092 pupils had registered, of these 228 were of the Established Church, 389 were Roman Catholics, 394 were Presbyterians, 57 were Methodists, and 24 other faiths were represented.[9] However, the Catholic hierarchy was not able to accept the separation of religious and secular instruction, and a ban on Catholics attending Model Schools was declared in 1863. By 1872 there were only forty Catholic pupils at the Belfast Model, and numbers had fallen to less than a handful by the end of the century. Sectarian strife affected the school throughout its lifetime. Situated near the Brickfields, riots were a continual source of distraction. The building suffered an ignominious end when it was destroyed by incendiary bombs in May 1922.

The many ordinary National Schools of Belfast should not be forgotten in all of this. In 1862 there were seventy such schools in Belfast (parishes of Belfast and Shankill). The following table provides details concerning six of them.[10]

SCHOOL	DOMINANT RELIGION	AVERAGE ATTENDANCE
Brown Street	Presbyterian	307 day, 256 evening
Campbell's Row	Dissenter	86 day, 38 evening
Chapel Lane	Roman Catholic	185 day
Donegal Street	Roman Catholic	166 day, 30 evening
Springfield	Established Church	82 day, 25 evening
Townsend Street	Presbyterian	226 day, 39 evening

Unfortunately, all National Schools experienced the religious polarisation that had struck the Belfast Model, and many fell far short of expected standards.

Bringing a Practical Component into Elementary Education

The number of its schools had grown from 789 in 1833 to 5,600 in 1860, so, on a purely numerical basis, the National Education system seemed to be thriving. But all was not well. The Churches, especially the Catholic Church, had become disenchanted with the system. However, whilst those concerns needed attention, other factors had assumed greater significance. The National System was evidently far from efficient. By 1860, the annual parliamentary grant to National Schools had risen to £294,000 and questions were being asked about the returns on this expenditure. The answers were not encouraging. It was found that 45 per cent of pupils never got beyond the first book of lessons in 1866, and only 23 per cent reached the third book and beyond.[11] This was far from satisfactory, so a Royal Commission of Inquiry into Primary Education was set up in 1868 under the Chairmanship of Lord Powis.

The Powis Commission submitted the National System to intense scrutiny. It found, in general, that the competence of the teaching force was less than satisfactory, and that school accommodation left a lot to be desired. The Commission's voluminous report, published in 1870, drew many conclusions and made many recommendations (including a rejection of the Model School system). A major recommendation was the introduction of a system of payment by results,

> ...to secure a better return for the outlay and labour of the National System, each teacher, besides a fixed class-salary, should receive an addition according to the number of children whom the Inspector, after individual examinations, can pass as having made satisfactory progress during the year...[12]

This new system of accountability set down strict guidelines for programmes and examinations. The compulsory subjects were reading, writing, spelling and arithmetic for all classes; grammar and geography from third class upwards; needlework for girls from first class, and agriculture for boys from fourth class.

Needlework and agriculture provided a meagre diet of technical subjects, but greater variety could be obtained through so-called Extra Subjects, which could be introduced if the compulsory subjects were being dealt with satisfactorily. The table below shows the relative popularity of some of these subjects in 1899.[13]

Subject	Schools	Pupils	Pupils
Drawing	2,146	98,360	78,025
Algebra	1,357	14,476	9,984
Geometry & Mensuration	827	5,397	3,787
Sewing Machine Work	499	4,917	4,124
Cookery	125	2,887	2,803
Handicraft	10	208	189
Magnetism & Electricity	7	177	122

There were 8,670 schools in the system in 1899, so these figures show that the technically-orientated Extra Subjects were not overwhelmingly popular. And payment by results was having a stifling effect on curricular innovation. Pupils were being crammed so that they would be able to face the inspector's annual inquisition. As a result teachers were tempted to give most attention to the brightest and best-attending pupils. Nevertheless, the National System had brought some benefit to the country. The average daily attendance of pupils on the rolls increased from 37 per cent in 1871 to 65 per cent in 1899, and the country's illiteracy rates dropped from 33 per cent in 1871 to 14 per cent in 1901.[14]

The curriculum's emphasis on bookwork was a matter of concern. So another commission was established in 1897 'to determine how far and in what form, manual and practical instruction' should be included in the primary curriculum. This Belmore Commission, named after its Chairman the Earl of Belmore, presented its final report to the Lord Lieutenant in June 1898. It recommended a considerable expansion in the number of practical subjects: in addition to the three Rs, every pupil should have the opportunity to attend classes in kindergarten and practical handwork, drawing, elementary science, cookery, laundry work, needlework, singing and physical exercise. Significantly, the report recommended that agriculture be removed from the curriculum, but that its salient features be dealt with in the science curriculum. It also proposed that these 'subjects of Manual and Practical Instruction' should not be subject to payment by results. In conclusion, the report asserted that there was a strong desire throughout the country for the introduction of a general system of technical education,

> …the present system of primary education is so one-sided in its character that it leaves the pupils quite unprepared for Technical Education … Now it seems to us that the changes we recommend would go far to remedy this defect. The system of National education, modified as we propose, would give an all-round training to the faculties of the children, and would thus lay a solid foundation for any system of higher education – literary, scientific, or technical…[15]

The Belmore Report was well received by the National Board, so implementation was able to follow fairly swiftly. A new programme – the Revised Programme – was up and running in National Schools in September 1900. Payment by results was abolished for all subjects. Of the new subjects, two are of particular relevance to the theme of this book; (a) Kindergarten and Manufacturing Instruction, and (b) Object Lessons and Elementary Science. The former commenced with simple exercises with coloured balls, progressed through paper-folding, knots, wire-bending to building cardboard models, and, in fifth and higher standards in urban schools with workshops, culminated in woodworking. Object Lessons and Experimental Science provided a different kind of hands-on experience. It included four alternative science courses: experimental science; agriculture and horticulture; light and sound, and electricity and magnetism. The teaching of all four strands was assisted by object lessons, where pupils could make their individual observations about an object, e.g. an apple or a wheelbarrow, before entering into a dialogue with the teacher.

The following table shows how the practical subjects were received in schools over the first ten years of operation of the Revised Programme.[16]

Year	1900	1905	1910
Total Schools	8,684	8,659	8,314
Drawing	5,942	8,587	8,314
Object Lessons & Elementary Science	3,096	8,423	8,031
Kindergarten & Manufacturing Instruction	1,293	4,447	6,366

| Needlework | 1,700 | 6,279 | 6,369 |
| Cookery | 263 | 360 | 2,437 |

Thus, on the whole, the Revised Programme appeared to be meeting its objective of giving manual and practical instruction a more significant role in Irish elementary education.

Irish Intermediate Education

Secondary education – or intermediate education as it was originally called in Ireland – did not enjoy the relatively substantial State support that primary education attracted in its early years. There were a few private schools and academies scattered across the country, and Protestants could turn to the diocesan schools and the royal schools. Whilst the Penal Laws were in force, better-off Catholics (and Dissenters) tended to send their children overseas for their higher education, but by the mid-nineteenth century religious orders like the Christian Brothers and the Ursulines had started to set up their own intermediate schools. The Government was generally content with these piecemeal developments, recognising that intermediate education was a commodity that well-to-do parents should be able to purchase if they so wished.

Belfast took an early lead in the field of intermediate education. Voluntary effort had seen the opening of the Belfast Academy in May 1786. Originally situated in Long Lane (now Academy Street), off Donegall Street, and in close proximity to St Anne's church, the Academy had strong Presbyterian connections. The Revd Dr James Crombie, the first Principal, was Minister at the First Presbyterian church. The academic work, which was divided amongst four schools, included languages, rhetoric, moral philosophy, jurisprudence, civil government and history.[17] But there was a clear intention from the outset to encompass scientific and practical topics as well as the academic. The original prospectus included arithmetic, algebra, astronomy, navigation, bookkeeping, and experimental philosophy. Crombie referred to these latter subjects in his annual report for 1792:

I have likewise used my utmost diligence in forming scientifical and literary classes, and have engaged the ablest men, upon whom I could prevail, to undertake courses of lectures on the most useful subjects. In this, too, my labours have been attended with some success. Dr Stephenson teaches two courses on Chemistry, little, I believe, if at all inferior to those read in the best universities. Mr Porter is now giving an extensive course on Natural Philosophy; and, considering the short time allowed for preparation, and the great inconvenience with which he had to struggle, his lectures and experiments are greatly superior to what could be reasonably expected.[18]

By opening these lectures on 'useful subjects' to the general public, the Belfast Academy established itself as a pioneer of popular education.

The Academy had originally hoped to establish a collegiate side where university-level work would be conducted. However, the associated costs, and the arrival of a prestigious competitor in the centre of town, put paid to those ambitions. The Academy moved to new premises on the Cliftonville Road in 1880, and the 'Royal' epithet was added to the title in 1888.

The Academy's great rival, the Belfast Academical Institution, was the town's next major educational innovation. Again driven by Presbyterian interests, its founders aimed to establish a non-denominational and liberal organisation. The original objects made it clear that science would be a major part of the curriculum.

The project moved ahead quickly, and the Academical Institution was formally incorporated in 1810, and opened officially to boys and young men in

The Belfast Academical Institution in 1820. (Benn, *History of the Town of Belfast*, 1823.)

Early science logo of the Belfast Academical Institution. (Robb, *The Book of the Royal Belfast Academical Institution*, 1913.)

February 1814. It was based – thanks to the largesse of Lord Donegall – on a large central site at the west end of Wellington Place. The royal descriptor was added to the title in 1831.

The Institution comprised two departments – a school department and a collegiate department, the former embracing schools of English, mathematics, classics, French, writing, and drawing, and the latter, which was essentially a training college for the Presbyterian ministry, centring on a Faculty of Arts with Chairs in mathematics, classics, logic and *belles-lettres*, moral philosophy, Irish, Hebrew and oriental languages, divinity, and anatomy.[19]

The increasing reputation of these two Belfast schools seemed to justify the Government's *laissez-faire* approach to intermediate education. But there was evidence that the system, in total, was not meeting the country's needs, and a view that the Government should be more proactive in the matter. A select committee (the Wyse Committee) was set up in 1835 (shortly after the introduction of the National School System) to inquire into ' the existing condition of the endowed schools and to suggest plans for their improvement and the advancement of education'. The Committee's report proposed an expansion of the system, operating on a non-denominational basis, and funded by the State. It described a growing need for people skilled in the sciences,[20] and noted that, of the middle and upper classes, 'the great majority … is necessarily destined to agricultural, commercial, and, in some instances, to manufacturing pursuits.'

In arguing for State-supported schools to meet these needs, the Committee praised the two Belfast schools:

> These defects have been in some degree supplied by private Commercial Schools, and by Mechanics and other Institutions, but in none with the effect observable in the Belfast Institution and Academy. The introduction of the mechanical, physical, and moral sciences in these establishments, to an extent unknown in other parts of the country, has been effected without difficulty, and been productive of satisfactory results.[21]

Despite its many sensible recommendations, the Wyse Report was shelved. The Government continued to be wary about funding secondary education, and it was only too aware that any attempt to introduce non-denominationalism would be doomed to failure.

Meanwhile, the number of intermediate schools grew slowly in Belfast, with only three other major establishments joining the Academy and the Royal Belfast Institution (RBAI) by 1859:

1833 – St Malachy's College
1854 – Belfast Mercantile Academy (Belfast High School from 1942)
1859 – Ladies' Collegiate School (Victoria College from 1887)

This slow rate of progress prompted the Government to set up a Royal Commission on Endowed Schools. Its report, published in 1858, criticised many of the existing schools, and, like the earlier Wyse Report, proposed State support for intermediate schools. It urged modernisation of the curriculum, which should 'embrace instruction not only in the Classics and Mathematics, but in the English language and literature, foreign languages and the experimental and natural sciences'. And schools should also offer bookkeeping, mensuration, drawing and singing.[22]

The people of Ulster were generally content with these proposals, and a deputation of clergymen and businessmen travelled from Belfast to Dublin in 1859 to present the Lord Lieutenant with a supportive petition. They asked for non-denominational schools, for competent teachers, and for efficient instruction.[23] The Presbyterian General Assembly also supported the proposals, largely because of the lack of classical schools where candidates for the ministry could be trained. It seems that the Government was on the verge of responding positively to the recommendations, but Catholic opposition to the extension of mixed education beyond primary-school level blocked the way ahead.

The expansion of Catholic intermediate schools under direct Church control continued, with twenty-seven new schools founded between 1850 and 1867.[24] The next three major schools to be established in Belfast were:

1866 – Christian Brothers' Schools
1868 – Methodist College
1870 – St Dominic's High School

The Government's determination not to fund denominational education, and the Catholic Church's determination not to participate in mixed denominational education, together constituted what seemed to be an intractable problem. However, by the 1870s, demands for intermediate schools that would prepare young people for the professions and for university life had reached such a level that the Government was forced to act.

State Support for Intermediate Education

For most of the nineteenth century the only State contribution to science and art instruction emanated from the Department of Science and Art (DSA), based in South Kensington in London. The DSA was set up in 1853 following the Great Exhibition of 1851, which had made it abundantly clear that other countries were catching up with, if not overtaking, Britain in the race for global technological supremacy. It was assumed that an improved technical education system would correct this situation, so schools were encouraged to offer scientific and applied art courses drawn up by the Department, and were rewarded through a system of payment-on-results. Irish schools fared reasonably well in the scheme's early years, earning some £5,000 in results fees compared to around £30,000 in England and Wales.[25] In Belfast, RBAI, the Belfast Model, and the Christian Brothers' Schools were the most active providers of DSA courses. In 1870, twenty-eight Belfast schools participated, including a few elementary schools and some evening schools. Of the latter, the students of the Working Men's Institute performed consistently well. Of the other schools, RBAI started to run DSA classes in 1863, the Model in 1861, and Methodist College in 1876: the CBS schools were able to boast of 600 passes in Drawing in 1899.[26]

A broader system of payment by results than that offered by the DSA offered a solution to the intermediate school problem in Ireland. Already employed in National Schools, an extended system of payment by results would allow the Government to fund intermediate schools of all creeds without appearing to support denominational education. The Intermediate Education (Ireland) Act of 1878 put such a system into practice. A Board of Commissioners was appointed to manage the scheme. There was a major flaw in the new system, however; it neglected to mention the education of girls. But that omission was corrected promptly after the Lord Chancellor was visited in his London offices by two Belfast ladies,[27] Mrs Margaret Byers, Principal of the Ladies' Collegiate School, and Mrs Isabella Tod, Secretary of the Ladies' Institute. Both were formidable supporters of women's education and women's emancipation.

The Intermediate System involved three grades of examination in its early years – Junior, Middle, and Senior. Examinations were organised in seven divisions: Greek, Latin, English, Mathematics, Modern Languages, Natural Sciences, and Music and Drawing. This diet, unfortunately, ignored the advice of the 1858 Commission to include a range of utilitarian subjects, so the intermediate school curriculum continued to be dominated by language and literary studies. The position was exacerbated by the fact that, in terms of results fees, classical subjects were worth more than modern ones, and schools increasingly opted for the financial attractions of the Intermediate Board's offerings than the often more demanding DSA subjects. Nevertheless, the Belfast schools did their best, within the limits of resources, to make inroads into the growing domain of technical education. At RBAI, for example, the appointment in 1883 of Robert Barklie, former superintendent of the Working Men's Institute, brought a fresh approach to the teaching of science. Chemistry and Physics were taught using an experimental approach.[28] It was reported at the annual prize-giving in 1886 that 'pupils are instructed in the practical use of the various tools used in mechanical processes, and are also taught to make the apparatus used in the illustration of the various branches of physical science'.[29]

Nevertheless, the academically-biased curriculum, and the stultifying tendencies of payment by results were taking their toll. This was compounded by a lack of funds; of the Intermediate Board's annual income of £32,000, £8,000 went towards prizes and £12,000 towards administration, leaving a mere £12,000 to be distributed across schools.[30] Some additional income became available after 1890, when part of the monies gathered from the

CAMPBELL COLLEGE,
BELMONT, NEAR BELFAST.

THE GROUNDS (70 Acres) AND BUILD-
INGS ARE NOT EXCELLED BY
THOSE OF ANY SCHOOL IN THE
UNITED KINGDOM.

Boys are prepared for Universities, Wool-
wich, Sandhurst, Indian Police, &c., as well as
for Professional and Business Life.

There are CLASSICAL and MODERN
SIDES, a SCIENCE DEPARTMENT, with
fully-equipped Physical and Chemical Laboratories, and a COMMERCIAL DEPARTMENT,
in which Boys are thoroughly prepared for a
Commercial career.

Advertisement drawing attention to Campbell College's Science Department. (*Northern Whig*, 2 September 1915.)

METHODIST COLLEGE,
BELFAST.

PREPARATION for the PROFESSIONS,
COMMERCE, ENGINEERING, and
TECHNICAL INDUSTRIES by Staff of
Honour Graduates.

Special provision in College Workshops for a
FULL TRAINING in Hand and Machine
Tools for Boys preparing for ENGINEER-
ING.

Special Laboratories and Equipment for
Advanced Courses in Experimental Science in
TECHNICAL INDUSTRIES.

Advertisement demonstrating Methodist College's interest in matters technical. (*Northern Whig*, 13 September 1915.)

Local Taxation Act (see Chapter 9) was directed towards technical education. However, this windfall only provided temporary relief. All of these factors persuaded the Government to review the Intermediate System in 1899 when, under the chairmanship of Chief Justice Palles, a parliamentary commission produced a report which recommended peripheral adjustments to the system rather than root-and-branch overhaul. Payment by results was replaced by a system of capitation fees, and the Board was permitted to appoint inspectors. Of most significance to the cause of technical education, all subjects, classical and modern, were given equal weighting.

The establishment, in 1899, of a Department of Agriculture and Technical Instruction (DATI) brought further benefits to technical education in schools. Science and drawing in intermediate schools were funded by DATI from 1899 onwards, and local schemes of technical instruction had to support such developments in intermediate schools (see Chapter 10). The press advertisements (previous page) show that technical instruction had achieved a firm foothold in Belfast's intermediate schools by the 1910s. Methodist College, for example, appointed its first engineering lecturer in 1918, and there were two such teachers in post in 1926.[31] Campbell College was a relative latecomer to the secondary-school scene in Belfast. Founded as a boarding school in 1894, thanks to the largesse of H.J. Campbell, linen baron, it could boast a 100-acre site in east Belfast.

The DATI's Experimental Science programme proved popular in Belfast schools. In 1910, Belfast boys won sixteen exhibitions in the subject, seven going to pupils of RBAI, and four to pupils of the Christian Brothers Schools.[32] Overall the Belfast schools performed more than satisfactorily in the annual intermediate examinations. The following league table shows the number of exhibitions and medals won by Belfast pupils over a nine-year period, 1907-1915.

Boys		
School	Exhibits	Medals
Belfast Royal Academy	15	5
Campbell College	17	8
Christian Brothers' Schools	25	3
Mercantile College	6	2
Methodist College Belfast	27	9
Royal Belfast Academical Institution	98	24
St Malachy's College	22	4

GIRLS		
SCHOOL	EXHIBITS	MEDALS
Belfast Royal Academy	3	7
Methodist College Belfast	32	13
Mercantile College	4	1
St Dominic's High School	4	–
Victoria College	56	25

Judged on results, RBAI was by far the outstanding boys' school, and the boys and girls of Methodist College, Belfast's pioneer of mixed-gender education, together performed extremely well. The girls of Victoria College recorded exceptional results. In 1890, for example, they won seventeen prizes and exhibitions out of a total of twenty-three for Ulster and a grand total of fifty-three for all-Ireland.[33] But their consistent success attracted criticism as well as praise. In 1892, an article in a Dublin paper asked, 'did you ever read anything more scandalous than the avarice of this female Orange and Freemason nursery in Belfast?'[34]

Early Steps Towards Higher Technical Education

At the time of the Act of Union there was only one university in Ireland – the University of Dublin, with Trinity its sole college. The Relief Act of 1793 had opened Trinity to non-Anglicans, but the Presbyterians of the north of Ireland preferred their prospective ministers to be trained elsewhere. The large majority of these young men headed for Glasgow and Edinburgh, mostly the former, but the northerners were unhappy with this state of affairs; they wanted a seminary on their own doorstep.

When the Belfast Academy was founded in 1785, there was hope that it would provide the required higher education in literary and philosophical studies. As far back as 1786, Dr Alexander Haliday, Belfast's leading physician of the day, had appealed to the Government for support for higher work at the Academy.[35] Whilst his appeal fell on deaf ears, the Academy continued to press its case. The second Principal, Revd Dr W. Bruce, recorded that, in his early years, he had striven energetically 'to extend the limits of Academical Tuition to the Outline of a Collegiate Course.'[36] But despite those efforts, the Academy was never able to attract the financial support necessary to achieve collegiate standing.

The Academical Institution made greater progress on the collegiate front. It had planned, from the outset, to have both School and Collegiate Departments. By 1815, the latter was able to boast five professors, including Chairs in Mathematics and Natural Philosophy, and, unlike the Academy, the Institution was successful in attracting a parliamentary grant of some £2,000 towards their salaries. Many distinguished persons occupied these chairs. James Thomson, for example, Professor of Mathematics from 1815 to 1832, was a renowned mathematician whose reputation was enhanced through two very distinguished sons – James, who later became Professor of Engineering at Queen's, and William, later Lord Kelvin. Two others outstanding in the field of science and technology at the time were Thomas Andrews, Professor of Chemistry and Fellow of the Royal Society, and Andrew Ure, the Institution's first Professor of Natural Philosophy and Chemistry, and populariser of science.

The Institution's Collegiate Department was soon offering an up-to-date programme of studies, including a considerable amount of material of a technical nature. In 1825, for example, a prize in natural philosophy was awarded for the best 'Essay on the comparative advantages of Steam, Wind, and Water, as prime movers for Machinery, illustrated by references to the best experiments that have yet been made on these powers.'[37]

The Academical Institution attracted considerable numbers of pupils and students. In 1825 there were 302 pupils in the School Department and 160 students in the Collegiate Department. Of the latter, 116 were preparing for the Presbyterian Ministry.[38] Collegiate examinations were conducted orally by the professors, and were often attended by members of the governing body. Success was rewarded with a General Certificate signed by all the professors and by the Moderator of the Synod of Ulster. Graduates came from all corners of Ulster; of the 485 certificates awarded between 1817 and 1839, eighteen went to Belfast students, fifteen to Donegal students, and ten to Monaghan students. The United States provided three students.[39]

That run of success was brought to a halt, however, when the large majority of the Institution's higher work was transferred to the new Queen's College in 1845.

Higher Technical Education at Queen's

As explained previously, Trinity College, with its close affiliation to the

Established Church, was not able to meet the needs of prospective Presbyterian clergy. The Catholic Church had similar concerns, and after vigorous protestation, its needs were acknowledged in 1795 by the establishment of a Catholic College at Maynooth. Initially enrolling both lay and clerical students, Maynooth College had by 1817 established itself as the national seminary for the education and training of Catholic priests. Recognising that that turn of events left lay Catholics with a very restricted range of higher education opportunities, Robert Peel's Conservative Government introduced a Colleges Bill in 1845. Three non-denominational Queen's Colleges – Belfast, Cork, and Galway – were created. They opened their doors to students in 1849, and were united the following year under the Queen's University of Ireland, which examined and awarded degrees. However, the non-denominational nature of the new colleges once again brought censure from the Catholic hierarchy.[40] At the synod of Thurles (1850) the faithful were warned of the 'grave and intrinsic dangers to which … the faith and morals of studious Catholic youth are exposed'. The new colleges progressed, nevertheless, and the Catholic Church responded by establishing its own university in St Stephen's Green in 1854 – despite the fact that, without a charter, it would not be able to award degrees.

Each Queen's College had three faculties – Arts, Law, and Physic (Medicine). The Faculty of Arts was to provide a sound general education which the professions could build upon in the other two faculties. In each college, the Arts were to include 'those branches of modern Literature and Science, now essential to be known by every well educated man.'[41] Special attention had to be paid 'to those branches of practical and applied Science, upon which the subsistence of the people and the well-being of the State is so materially grounded'. Trinity College had already taken a major step in that direction in 1841 when it opened a School of Engineering. A two-year course leading to an Engineering Diploma gradually evolved into a degree. But students were hard to come by; only 130 graduated in the twenty years to 1861, and 400 in the thirty years, 1852-1882.[42]

The choice of a site for the northern college created some acrimony. Armagh, Londonderry, and the Royal Belfast Academical Institution led the contenders, but the Government decided on (what was at the time) a large rural site on the southern boundaries of Belfast. The Queen's College, Belfast, designed by Charles Lanyon, was opened formally on 20 December 1849. Its new professors included three former staff of the RBAI: Thomas Andrews, Professor of Chemistry; John Hodges, Professor of Agriculture, and John Stevely, Professor of Natural Philosophy. In addition to their subject expertise, each had an intense interest in the popularisation of science and in the education of working men. The School of Engineering was led by Professor John Godwin, who managed to hold down a senior post at Ulster Railways whilst running his school. Godwin was succeeded in 1857 by James Thomson, brother of Lord Kelvin, and an inventive genius in his own right, and when Thomson moved to Glasgow in 1873, he was succeeded by George Fuller, a former Professor at University College London.

So there was a well-qualified body of professors in place to carry the Queen's College forward. There were degrees in law and medicine, but the three-year Bachelor of Arts (BA) and the two-year Diploma in Civil Engineering (DipCE) were the central planks of the new college's higher technical education provision. The BA course included classes in Physics, Chemistry and Mathematical Science. The first year of the DipCE covered Mathematics, Chemistry, Mineralogy, Geology, Drawing, Surveying, and Mapping, and the second year included Natural Philosophy, Theory of Machines, and Civil Engineering. As originally designed, the DipCE programme required students to complete a further three years of practical work under a recognised engineer before they were permitted to sit examinations. In 1851 the required period of practical experience was reduced to two years.[43]

All was not well, however: the new Queen's Colleges were not flourishing. Between 1849 and 1859, the average annual attendance at Queen's Belfast was only 189 – out of a disappointing average of 421 for all three colleges. At Belfast the DipCE was only attracting a handful of students. This lack of growth persuaded the Government to set up a Commission of Inquiry (Kildare) in 1857. But the ensuing Report,[44] published the following year, was 'not dissatisfied' with the small enrolments, and went on to identify a list of mitigating factors – the great famine; the hostility of the Catholic Church; the pre-eminence of Trinity College; the lack of an effective system of intermediate education. So there was little significant change.

The review, however, brought some changes in course content and length. In the DipCE, for example, the requirement for a period of practical experience was abolished altogether in 1857. But the course's emphasis on practical matters was maintained by extending the two years of study to three, and including new subjects like experimental physics, office work, field work and engineering excursions. The Diploma was superseded in 1868 by the degree of Bachelor in Engineering (BE).

The following table lists the numbers of students attending a selection of classes over the period 1856 to 1863.[45] It shows that Physics and Chemistry were the most popular of the scientific/technical subjects. The positive effect of the extension of the DipCE course to a third year is evident in its later years.

	1856/7	1857/8	1858/9	1859/60	1860/1	1861/2	1862/3	1863/4
Engineering	17	14	10	16	13	16	25	30
Chemistry	70	60	74	81	64	89	89	81
Practical Chemistry	10	11	14	21	21	20	24	28
Laboratory	15	10	11	10	12	15	15	8
Mathematical Physics	19	26	25	24	64	67	72	69
Experimental Physics	37	41	28	42	87	86	94	95
Practical Mechanics	2	7	3	4	4	-	2	5

Numbers attending the Queen's University of Ireland crept steadily upwards in the wake of the Kildare Commission. In the decade 1869-1879, average annual attendance had reached 400 at Belfast, out of a total of 806 for the three colleges. But the University's science and engineering courses never really took off; in the thirty-year period 1851-1881, only 67 DipCEs and BEs, and 683 BAs were awarded at Belfast.[46] Arguments based on mitigating factors were no longer sufficient, and Government turned to root and branch measures.

The Queen's University of Ireland was replaced by a Royal University of Ireland in 1879. Purely an examining body, the new university allowed students access to examinations without having to attend classes. It catered for students of the three Queen's Colleges, for students of other institutions, including those with a Catholic culture, and for the man in the street. It also catered for women and indeed it granted the first degree to a woman in 1882. However, like the Queen's University, the Royal University failed to live up to expectations. The colleges atrophied, and in 1901-02 there were only 349 students at Belfast, and only 632 in all three colleges together.[47] So, in 1908, much the wiser after years of bitter experience, the Government pushed through its Irish Universities

Act, which established what turned out to be a remarkably durable system of higher education. Trinity College was left untouched; the Royal University was abolished; the Queen's University of Belfast was inaugurated; and a National University of Ireland was set up with colleges at Cork, Dublin and Galway, and with Maynooth a recognised college. By 1909, numbers at the new Queen's University had risen to 580.[48] The progress of higher technical education at Queen's in the early 1900s will be considered further in Chapter 11.

3

Adult Education and the Belfast Mechanics' Institute

Earlier chapters showed that neither children nor adults had easy access to effective technical education in Ireland throughout the first half of the nineteenth century. The situation was marginally better in Great Britain, where the Industrial Revolution was demonstrating the value of technical skills. However, in the context of today's 'hi-tech' industries and their interactions with the education system, it seems a curious fact that Britain's industrial heyday placed few demands on the education system. Technical advancement had come to depend upon amateurs and self-made men like Arkwright, Bramah, Crompton and Maudslay, none of whom had been formally educated in science or technology. The entrepreneurs of the day were, in the main, 'practical men' who had derived their knowledge and skills from practice, and whose expertise had been developed 'on the job'. Self-sufficiency was the slogan of the day, and the concept, influenced by John Wesley's preaching, was championed by many. Samuel Smiles's book *Self Help*, which sold 20,000 copies when it first appeared in 1859, extolled intellectual self-improvement, even 'at the cost of some effort or sacrifice'. Smiles perhaps overstated the case when he wrote, 'The great Inventor is one who has walked forth upon the industrial world, not from universities, but from hovels; not as clad in silks and decked with honours, but as clad in fustian and grimed in soot and oil.'

The working men of Belfast attempted to put Smiles's self-help philosophy into practice.

Birth of the Mechanics' Institutes

The first attempts to provide organised technical education were aimed directly at the working classes. The major impetus for such development had Scottish roots, and was based largely on Professor John Anderson's pioneering work in Glasgow on the popularisation of Natural Philosophy. Anderson (1726-1796), a major figure in the history of technical education, had started courses at the University of Glasgow in the 1780s for 'town's people of almost every rank, age and employment'. Covering the whole gamut of Natural Philosophy, his courses were supported by a fifteen-chapter, 400-page book *The Institutes of Physics*, first published in 1786. Anderson was proud of this particular development, indeed he mentioned it in his will,

> It is well known that by a course of experiments, which I have given annually
> for many years according to the plan in my Institutes of Physics, upon the
> Tuesdays and Thursdays, the Manufacturers and Artificers in Glasgow have
> become distinguished in a high degree, for their General Knowledge, as well
> as for their Abilities and Progress in their several Arts.[1]

That will bequeathed the bulk of Anderson's assets to the establishment of an Anderson's Institute, which was to develop his work with the artisans of Glasgow. Dr Thomas Garnett, Professor of Natural Philosophy, organised these popular courses until he left to take up a chair at the Royal Institution in London in 1799. But his replacement, Dr George Birkbeck, carried the work to even greater heights: indeed Birkbeck may safely be regarded as the originator of the Mechanics' Institute movement. He made a practice of visiting workshops and factories where, 'he soon observed the mechanics to be, – not what they have been represented, doltish and stupid as they were ignorant; but what they really are, – acute observers and curious inquirers'.[2] His lectures on the Mechanical Arts were entertaining and well received; no fewer than 500 attended the fourth in the series.[3] The Prospectus for these lectures illustrates Birkbeck's enthusiasm for the subject:

I have become convinced that much pleasure would be communicated to the mechanic in the exercise of his art, and that the mental vacancy which follows a cessation from bodily toil would often be agreeably occupied, by a few systematic philosophical ideas upon which at his leisure he might meditate. It must be acknowledged, too, that greater satisfaction in the execution of machinery must be experienced when the uses to which it may be applied and the principles upon which it operates are well understood than where the manual part alone is known, the artist remaining entirely ignorant of everything besides; indeed I have lately had frequent opportunities of observing with how much additional alacrity a piece of work has been undertaken when the circumstances were such as I have now stated.[4]

Birkbeck, originally trained in medicine, resigned his Glasgow post and moved south to England in 1804. He was succeeded by Dr Andrew Ure, who later joined the staff of the Belfast Academical Institution. By 1806 Birkbeck had settled into a medical practice in London, but the duties of this post did not distract him from his abiding passion for education. He became a founder member of the London Institution for the Diffusion of Science, Medicine and the Arts, which was set up in 1809 to popularise science amongst the educated middle classes. But his work with the poorer classes of Society had left an indelible mark and was an inspiration to others. Timothy Claxton, one of his many admirers, opened a Mechanical Institution in London in 1817, but it was short-lived, closing in 1820 when Claxton moved to Russia. In Scotland, Edinburgh – Glasgow's eternal rival – followed the Anderson's Institute model in its Edinburgh School of Arts, established in 1821. Two years later, that particular development, compounded by disagreements between the Mechanics' Class and the management of the Anderson's Institute, persuaded the Mechanics' Class to initiate the establishment of an independent Glasgow Mechanics' Institution. Birkbeck was asked to advise, and the new institution opened its doors in 1823.

Pressures were brought to bear to open a similar type of institution in London. Thomas Hodgskin and Joseph Robertson of the Mechanics' Magazine started correspondence on the subject with Birkbeck, and this culminated in a meeting in the Crown and Anchor Tavern in the Strand in November 1823. It was agreed to form a London Mechanics' Institution. The first classes were held in a disused chapel in Monkwell Street, and the new institution soon had nearly 2,000 students on its books.[5]

Mechanics' Institutes became popular across Britain. For example, the

Manchester Mechanics' Institution commenced business in 1824 under the chairmanship of Benjamin Heywood. Its promoters included the engineer William Fairbairn and Eaton Hodgkinson, who had contributed much to the development of the theory of strength of materials. The preamble to the Institution's rules made it clear that theory, not practice, would be the focus:

> It is not intended to teach the trade of the Machine-maker, the Dyer, the Carpenter, the Mason, or any other particular business, but there is no Art which does not depend, more or less, on scientific principles, and to teach what these are, and to point out their practical application, will form the chief objects of this Institution.[6]

The Mechanics' Institute movement grew remarkably quickly. By 1826 every large town and most of the smaller ones had institutes; by 1850 there were some 610 institutes in England and a further twelve in Wales, with around 600,000 members in total.[7] *The Mechanics' Magazine* supported the cause. Founded in 1823 by Thomas Hodgskin, it aimed to provide working men with 'Accounts of all new Discoveries, Inventions and Improvements' together with 'Plans and Suggestions for the Abridgement of Labour'.

Mechanics' Institutes in Ireland

The aims and objectives of the Mechanics' Institute movement proved attractive to Irish philanthropists. There was already much concern about the poor education of the working classes in Ireland, and this had led to the establishment of adult schools by the London Hibernian Society and the Benevolent Evening Schools' Society. The former catered for some 1,000 adults and 28,000 children in 347 schools in 1816, and the latter enrolled around 700 poor men and boys in 1812.[8] Instruction in those schools was, however, restricted to basic literacy.

Whilst industrial developments in Ireland could not match the great boom in Britain at the time, there was, nevertheless, an initial burst of enthusiasm for the philosophies behind the Mechanics' Institutes. A Dublin Mechanics' Institute was established in 1824, and many other towns followed suit. Institutes sprang up across the country, but many were short-lived; between 1825 and

The old Exchange Building where the Belfast Mechanics' Institute was conceived in 1825. (Benn.)

The old Exchange Building is still recognisable at the corner of North Street and Donegall Street.

1870, no fewer than twenty-seven achieved varying degrees of success.[9] The north-east of Ulster, with its growing industrial base, seemed the area most likely to benefit from such a development. The local press commented in 1825, 'The manufacturing interest of the North of Ireland, render it peculiarly well adapted to the furtherance of the objects which such Institutions have in contemplation, and if the thing be entered into here with proper exertion we have no question of its success.'[10]

There was, indeed, an initial vigorous response from the north-east, with Armagh, Newry, Dungannon, Portaferry, Downpatrick, Dundalk, Lurgan, and Glenarm vying to outdo each other. But Belfast, with a population of 40,000 and a growing industrial base, was expected to set the pace. The citizens of Belfast responded favourably when the matter was opened for debate at a public meeting in the Exchange Rooms on 21 March 1825. The meeting room was crowded with hundreds of artisans, mechanics and local dignitaries. Local educators played a dominant role. The meeting was presided over by Revd Thomas Dix Hincks, Professor of Hebrew and Oriental languages and President of the Faculty of Arts at the Belfast Academical Institution. Speakers included John Young and James Thomson, Professors of Moral Philosophy and Mathematics respectively at the same institution, and the Revd R.J. Bryce, Mathematical Master at the Belfast Academy. All speakers presented strong and stirring advocacy for the establishment of a Belfast Mechanics' Institute (BMI). For example, the Revd Bryce stated that it would:

…bring forward men of genius who would enrich the arts by useful inventions, and although it cannot be expected that every one will turn out a Watt, yet, in this large and flourishing town, there may be many Watts in embryo, and should the Mechanics' Institute only produce one Watt in the course of a century they will be amply rewarded.[11]

Six resolutions were passed at the meeting:

That as the establishment of Institutions for the instruction of Mechanics in the scientific principles of the arts which they practice, as also in other branches of useful knowledge, has been productive of incalculable benefit in other parts of the empire, a Society for this purpose be established in this town, to be designated the Belfast Mechanics' Institute.

That such Institutions are likely to be most useful when chiefly supported and managed by Mechanics themselves.

That the objects of the Institution shall be the establishment, first, of a library, to consist chiefly of Works on the different Arts and Sciences. Secondly, of Lectures on the various subjects connected with the Institute. Thirdly, of a Museum of Models and a general collection of Philosophical and Chemical apparatus.

That the Subscription shall not exceed one British shilling, per month, payable in advance.

That the friends of knowledge and improvement, be invited to contribute towards the accomplishment of all the aforesaid purposes, by donations of Money, Books, Specimens, and Apparatus.

That a committee of twenty one, two thirds of whom shall be Mechanics with power to add to their number, and seven to be a quorum, be now appointed, to draw up a set of laws for the constitution and government of the Institute; and that those laws be submitted to a meeting, to be called on the first Monday in May, which meeting shall consist of all those whose names shall have been previously received, and who, upon the adoption of the proposed laws, or of such other laws as they may approve of, shall, in themselves constitute the Belfast Mechanics' Institute.

Committee members were elected as follows:

Samuel Pierce, Founder
John Thomson, Engraver
Henry Searson, Bookbinder
William Bell, Machine-maker
George Samson, Printer
Washington Owen, Smith
John Petrie, Confectioner
R. Martin, Cotton Spinner
Michael Gaffiagin, Architect
W. Green, Machine-maker

Mr Boyd, Iron Founder
A.H. Thornton, Manufacturer
John Davis, Carder
James Hope, Weaver
Revd T.D. Hincks, Professional
Professor Thomson, do
Dr Young, do
Revd R.J. Bryce, do
Professor Stevelly, do
Mr Robert Bradshaw, do
Mr Alexander Coleman, do

Resolution Two, moved by Robert Bradshaw of Milecross Lodge, Newtownards, followed the model already adopted at the Dublin Institute. Bradshaw quoted Lord Byron, who was a strong advocate of practical men having control of their own affairs, 'lest they should be deceived by and ultimately ousted by others more cunning than themselves'.[12]

The interest displayed by Belfast's leading educationalists is noteworthy. The aims of the proposed Institute complemented those of the Belfast Academical Institution whose founders had planned to bring scientific training to the working classes. One newspaper went so far as to assert that 'the learned Professor of Natural Philosophy in the Academical Institution will cheerfully extend … the benefit of his patronage, and valuable assistance'.[13] The newspaper was right, as it turned out, and Professor Stevelly ended up on the Board of the Institute. Professor Young, Secretary to the Faculty of Arts at the Academical Institution at the time, was at pains to confirm the support of his institution. He explained that he and his colleagues had hailed, with ardour, the idea of a Belfast Mechanics' Institute and, 'they will contribute all the aid in their power to forward its designs, and promote its interests; and the consequences will be, that it will reflect as much honour on the Academical Institution as the Academical Institution can confer upon it.'

As directed by Resolution Six, the committee commenced the work of drafting the definitive rules and regulations for the Institute. Members were grateful for the assistance and advice freely given by the Cork Mechanics' Institute which had been set up a year earlier.[14] The new rules were presented at a meeting on 17 May 1825. The Belfast Mechanics' Institute was to promote 'the Knowledge of the Arts and Sciences' and the Institute's objectives, originally described in Resolution Three were modified to:

The objects of the Institute shall be – First, to found a LIBRARY; secondly, to establish and support LECTURES on such Scientific Subjects as are practically useful to the working classes of the community; thirdly, to form a collection of MODELS and of PHILOSOPHICAL APPARATUS; fourthly, to establish a SCIENTIFIC SCHOOL.[15]

The last of these – the formation of a scientific school – was a significant addition to the original set of objectives.

Purchases for the library were to be confined initially to the different arts and sciences, and courses in mechanics and chemistry would always take precedence over other subjects. The membership of the board was increased to twenty-four, but two thirds were to be 'operative tradesmen' – defined as persons, whether masters or journeymen, who actually worked at their respective callings.

The meeting was informed that, up to 6 May, the list of members had grown to an impressive 401, covering no fewer than seventy trades and occupations.[16] Of these, the leading seven were; Machine-makers (forty-three), Carpenters (thirty-three), Smiths (twenty-seven), Engineers (sixteen), Textile Artisans (sixteen), Founders (thirteen), and Cabinet-makers (eleven). The small representation from the textile industries is noteworthy, bearing in mind its then-dominant position in the North's manufacturing industry. This has been attributed to the structure of the industry at the time, and the apathy of both workers and employers.[17] In addition to these operative tradesmen, there was a sizeable representation of middle-class professionals including professors, teachers, attorneys, accountants and architects. The good news about membership was tempered somewhat by an announcement that, to date, the list of donors was comparatively small.

The Programme of Work

With a management structure in place, the work was now able to get underway. For the first few months, weekly meetings of the Institute were held in the Lancasterian Schools in Frederick Street. There the 'operative tradesmen' turned out to be a formidable team: the records show – in the typically patronising manner of the day – that:

...the rules were considered seriatim and were debated with such an admirable display of shrewdness, strength, judgement, and courtesy of demeanour on the part of the mechanics as to frequently elicit the marked approval of the Chairman and the learned gentlemen by whom he was surrounded.[18]

Members paid particular attention to the development of an earlier proposal to establish a Scientific School for teaching Arithmetic, Algebra, Geometry and Trigonometry, and the application of same to the arts.

The purchase of property in Queen Street brought a degree of permanence to the new Institute. However, whilst there was a substantial piece of ground attached, the building itself was a modest acquisition – a small low, two-storey house, the schoolroom occupying the top floor, and the schoolmaster's living quarters the lower.[19] It seemed ill-fitted for its intended purpose – certainly for chemical investigations. The footnote to McCormac's inaugural lecture in 1829 describes the upper floor of the Institute:

The room of the Mechanics' Institute was formerly a stable-loft, and is capable of containing not more than fifty or sixty persons. It is low in the ceiling, and possesses no large chimney by which the noxious fumes arising from chemical processes might be carried off.[20]

The Belfast Academical Institution honoured its promise to assist the Institute. For some time, it had been providing popular lectures on science, initiated in 1814-1816 by Professor Andrew Ure who had earlier played a similar role in Anderson's College, Glasgow. Professor Stevelly continued this work. A course of public lectures was held in the evenings in the Academical Institution. As the advertisement for the course indicates, arrangements were made to permit members of the Mechanics' Institute to attend free of charge.

The large majority of Institute members attended the earliest in this series of lectures, but interest tailed off after only a few weeks. Unfortunately, the Revd Bryce's course on geography which followed in 1826 did not inspire a resurgence of interest in Institute lectures. Its content and style would not have appealed to the average artisan. For example, having implied that some artisans were poorly motivated, and others were intellectually deficient, Bryce asked, 'Because they will not, or cannot ascend with us to the highest regions of human contemplation, shall we not allow them to taste the sweets of an humbler department of knowledge?'[21]

The Science School was also having problems. In 1826, the Institute had found temporary accommodation in 7 Fountain Street, where the Revd J. Phillips, teacher at the Scientific School of the Mechanics' Institute, provided classes from eight to ten o'clock on Mondays, Wednesdays and Fridays. Arithmetic, Algebra and Geometry were taught with particular reference to their applications to Mensuration, Gauging, Surveying and Dialling. However, that interesting diet was not sufficient to attract a viable group of students, and that fact, combined with several complaints about Phillips's teaching methods, persuaded the Directors of the Institute that Phillips had to go. But Phillips, also Master of the Classical and Commercial Academy in King Street, took the matter extremely badly, and vented his spleen in the local press where he described the Directors as:

> Poor miserable wretches? Their parsimony has rendered them ridiculous throughout the three kingdoms; and, were strangers to draw the general character of Belfast from them, considered as the Patrons and Managers of the Mechanics' Institute, it would be held up to everlasting scorn and contempt.[22]

Nor were the planned monthly scientific meetings a raging success. The inaugural address in the series was delivered in December 1829 by Professor Henry McCormac, a local physician and member of the Belfast Academical Institute's Faculty of Medicine.[23] But its subject matter, 'The Best Means of Improving the Moral and Physical Condition of the Working Classes', was hardly designed to excite and enthuse the average artisan. More sermon than lecture, the printed version of McCormac's address was prefaced by a lengthy quotation, in Latin, from Bacon's *Instauratio Magna*. However, the esoteric content was tempered to some extent by a practical footnote that advocated the better use of Church facilities and resources for the furtherance of working-class education. McCormac proposed that:

> ...the construction of upper stories in the places of worship of the different sects, for the purposes of libraries, lecture rooms, and public instruction generally ... [and] the clergy, who have frequently much spare time on their hands, might usefully devote a portion of it each day in the week to the instruction of their flocks both rich and poor, male and female, in the different sciences of the mind, and in the illustration and explanation of all the varied objects and processes of art and nature.

> **Belfast Academical Institution.**
>
> POPULAR LECTURES ON MECHANICS AND
> ON CHEMISTRY.
>
> A COURSE of LECTURES on MECHANICS
> will be delivered in the INSTITUTION by Professor
> STEVELLY.—To commence on Monday, the 23d of May,
> at Half-past SEVEN o'Clock in the evening, and continue
> on every Monday, Wednesday and Friday evenings, until
> the course be completed. Before the close of the summer a
> Course of LECTURES ON CHEMISTRY will be de-
> livered, of which further notice will be given.   399

Professor Stevelly's lectures, as advertised in the *Belfast Newsletter* on 20 May 1825.

Sententious pieces like the above did little to arouse the interest of artisans. However, there is at least one surviving record of a satisfied customer.[24] When the small and ephemeral Belfast Franklin Forum celebrated its anniversary on 8 January 1827, one of the assembled company – a mechanic by trade – rose to toast the memory of Dr Anderson and prosperity to all Mechanics' Institutes:

> I cannot let this favourable opportunity pass, without humbly, and grate-fully acknowledging that I have been much befitted, in my line of trade, by the Belfast Mechanics' Institute. I have been shown why I execute my work in a particular manner, and the results that arise from such an application; whereas, before I became a member … I was unable to give any reason for so doing…
>
> I cannot help referring again to the Belfast Institute; which may be truly called a Mechanics' Institute, as it derived very little assistance from the great and wealthy … Withal, it is not, thank God, on the decline; but rather advancing rapidly. It possesses a valuable collection of books, principally relating to what is of the greatest utility to the operative. There is also attached to the Institution an evening school, in which is taught the senior and junior branches of the mathematics…
>
> Men who, before the establishment of such societies, went to the ale-house for want of a better way of spending their time, are now better employed either at the Scientific School, or in reading at their fireside the books of their own Library.

BELFAST
MECHANICS' INSTITUTE.

ARRANGEMENTS have been made, in consequence of which all Members of the Institute ARE ENTITLED to attend Mr. STEVELLY'S LECTURES on MECHANICS and CHEMISTRY, upon shewing their Tickets.—The first Lecture will be given at the ACADEMICAL INSTITUTION on MONDAY, the 23d inst. at Half-past SEVEN, P.M.

THE ADJOURNED GENERAL MEETING OF THE INSTITUTE will be held on TUESDAY, the 24th inst. in the *Lancasterian School-House, Frederick-street,* to consider the remainder of the proposed Laws, and transact such other Business as may come before them.

(337

A notice from the *Belfast Newsletter,* 20 May 1825, inviting members of the Mechanics' Institute to attend Professor Stevelly's lectures.

Incipient Decay

The Institute's Board seemed unable to address the growing lack of interest in its various activities. Members were informed of a sorry state of affairs at their sixth annual meeting in 1831, 'It appeared from the annual report, which was read by Mr John Grey, the Secretary, that the affairs of the Institute are not in a flourishing condition, which is to be attributed chiefly to the depressed state of trade and the small remuneration of labour.'[25]

The Science School collapsed. The resignation of its teacher Mr McKee, and the very small numbers in attendance, forced the Directors to conclude that they could no longer expect the Institute to carry such a heavy burden. Their alternative proposal, however, seemed unlikely to reinvigorate the Institute: it was noted that 'The Revd Dr Bryce proposes to give a course of lectures this season, *gratis,* on the causes of the present distressed condition of the working classes, and the means of rectifying it.' Subsequent lectures did little to move the emphasis from the esoteric to the practical. Another lecture by McCormac in 1832, this time on the more promising topic of chemistry, stirred up a theological storm concerning the geological age of the Earth.

The Belfast Mechanics' Institute seemed bound for an early demise. Secretary Samuel Archer had drawn attention to early warning signs when his first annual report in 1826 reported a fall off in members. Elsewhere it was noted that 'within five years the Institute was moribund and neither the lecture courses nor the Scientific School had taken root'.[26] Fatigue after a long week's work, lack of financial support, economic depression, lack of interest in knowledge not immediately related to their everyday domestic and working experiences, and, perhaps the most significant reason of all – lack of basic literacy – were contributory factors in the dwindling interest amongst artisans. Another major factor was an apparent lack of active participation by the leading industrialists of the town. The Manchester Mechanics' Institute, for example, had benefited greatly from the active support and encouragement of the great engineer William Fairbairn.

The deteriorating state of the Queen Street building had not inspired confidence in the project and matters had not improved some eighteen years later, when the *Belfast People's Magazine* reported:

> The school-room is a perfect disgrace to Belfast. Its low ceiling and imperfect ventilation render it so injurious for occupancy for any length of time, that Mr Millar, the persevering master, has, on more than one occasion, suffered in health from this cause. Will not the trustees of this useful institution look to this?[27]

With so many factors working against the Institute, further decline towards the moribund state seemed inevitable. The Belfast Directories ceased to refer to the Institute between 1832 and 1838. Activities had almost ground to a halt by 1838, when books, apparatus and the property in Queen Street had to be sold to meet debts of £507.

Reincarnation and Final Demise

A revival in the fortunes of local trade rekindled an interest in the Institute's work,[28] and in November 1838 the local press reported that a meeting had been planned to 'appoint a provisional committee of management and make such other arrangements as may be necessary to complete the reorganisation of the Institute'. The few remaining members of the Institute met on 3 December in a building formerly occupied by the York Street Methodist Chapel. The attraction of subscriptions was top of the agenda. *The Northern Whig* threw its weight behind the campaign to bring new life to the Institute. It urged the wealthy citizens of Belfast to support the cause, 'they have a substantial apology for not coming forward more energetically. We hope that the prospect now opened up for the permanent re-establishment of the Belfast Mechanics' Institute, will not be blasted by indifference, the effects of which have already proved so fatal to its progress.'[29]

Sufficient monies materialised to allow the re-purchase of the Queen Street premises. As a marketing ploy, annual subscriptions were reduced from 12s to 10s per annum. The future looked a little brighter. New experiments were tried; a course in French for ladies was offered in 1839, but such a venture was a long way from the original aims of the Institute. The support and interest of the Belfast Academical Institution appeared to dwindle, and those few lectures that did materialise in 1841 were delivered by leading members of the Belfast Natural History and Philosophical Society – a body which was itself becoming increasingly involved in public lectures on scientific matters. However, yet again, the topics delivered at Institute lectures – galvanism, entomology, and the pulverisation of light – were clearly better suited to middle-class than working-class audiences.

Most of this was to no avail, and the Belfast Mechanics' Institute began its final descent into oblivion. But there was, at least, one cheering aspect of the work in Queen Street: despite the unsatisfactory state of the accommodation,

MECHANICS' INSTITUTE.

THE SCHOOLS at the MECHANICS' INSTITUTE, QUEEN STREET, have RE-OPENED, after the Christmas Recess, in which upwards of One Hundred Pupils, mostly Children of the Working Classes, are receiving a liberal education. There are, also, EVENING CLASSES at the above Institution, for the instruction of Operatives and others in the following branches, namely:—

Writing,	Geography,	Classics,
Arithmetic,	Mensuration,	Mathematics,
Grammar,	Bookkeeping,	and Drawing.

The principal Teacher, Mr. MILLAR, will be most happy to give every information as to Terms, Hours of Attendance, &c., to those who may desire to avail themselves of the advantages thus held out to the Public.
Institute, 17, Queen Street.

The Mechanics' Institute is advertised in the *Belfast People's Magazine*, 1847. (Number 2, Volume 1, February 1847.)

the premises had became predominately a primary school, and a successful one at that.

With 200 pupils on the rolls, the school was flourishing in the mid-nineteenth century, but the chief connection between the school and the Institute seemed to be the fact that members of the latter could enrol their children at the former for half the usual fee.

Mid-century saw the Belfast Mechanics' Institute in a sorry state: its name had disappeared from the street directories, and a prominent publication of 1851 had noted its suspension.[30] The Queen Street School continued to attract young people, but classes for working men had practically ceased. The library was also providing an increasingly unsatisfactory service. In 1865, the Institute was finally laid to rest when its few remaining assets were merged with the Belfast People's Reading Room to form a new Belfast People's Library Institute. The new Institute had the laudable objective of promoting increased literary and scientific knowledge among the working classes of Belfast. This objective was to be achieved through:

> ...the maintenance of cheap reading and news rooms, circulating libraries and lectures and other means of promulgating literary and scientific knowledge amongst the working classes. Amongst these other means the formation of a collection of models and philosophical apparatus and the establishment of a scientific school shall be kept in view if the funds of the Institute should hereafter be sufficient for such objects being efficiently carried out.[31]

The careful phrasing of the second sentence displayed a lack of confidence in the future of the new Institute. It struggled to survive, and was ultimately amalgamated with the Belfast Working Men's Institute and Temperance Hall in 1872.

Following the model developed in Great Britain, the establishment of a Mechanics' Institute in Belfast in 1825 seemed a good idea at the time. However, the Institute's protracted decline and fall was the culmination of many adverse pressures and circumstances. The Board of Directors carry much of the blame for the Institute's failure. The evidence indicates that the Institute was allowed to drift from its original laudable aims and objectives. Lectures seemed to be more suited to middle-class audiences, than to tired and anxious artisans, and they were often more concerned with the workers' morals than with their technical efficiency. A pronounced lack of input from employers and practising professional engineers allowed conservative voices from higher education institutions to dominate proceedings. The Institute's establishment did, however, help to identify the need for an improved system of technical education in Belfast; and it helped to inspire a sense of inquiry and self-development in the artisans of the day. Whilst the Mechanics' Institute failed, other organisations sprang from its ashes. For example, the Belfast Working Classes Association, established in 1847, had many similar aims.

4

Teaching Art and Design in Belfast

Knowledge of the underpinning sciences, and skills in the use of tools to make and assemble artefacts, are important components of technical education. But many artefacts, no matter how well constructed or shaped according to the underlying sciences, will not meet the approval of the public if they don't look right or don't feel right. Such ergonomic and aesthetic considerations require the expertise of persons educated and trained in such matters. Schools of Art and Design produce such people.

The need for people with such skills became increasingly evident in the second quarter of the nineteenth century. But the gulf between the fine and applied arts was widening at the time, and the portrait painter and sculptor were becoming more and more divorced from the designers of cambric and the manufacturers of ornamental ironwork. The academies of art had distanced themselves from the applied arts, and had set themselves up as self-styled guardians of a liberal profession. Those trends had an adverse effect upon the quality of British products. James MacAdam, Secretary of the Royal Belfast Flax Improvement Society, summarised those effects in 1848:

Of the great staple productions of Belfast, in common with other manufactures of the place, many articles which were formerly estimated merely according to the intrinsic value of the material composing them, are now, to a considerable extent, dependent for the success of their sale upon the ornamental style in which they are brought into the market ... the prosperity of a manufacturing population is intimately connected with their skill and proficiency in combining the ornamental with the useful arts. When articles of equal utility and durability are produced, in different localities, the preference will always be given to those which excel in elegance and beauty…'[1]

The situation reached crisis level in the United Kingdom in 1824 when a reduction in tariffs attracted a flood of foreign products. Of these, the French ones, with their particularly high quality of design, proved especially attractive to the more affluent of British consumers. This French invasion was tolerated for a considerable time before the Government decided that something had to be done. Chivvied by William Ewart, the Liverpool MP, the Government finally decided, in 1835, to set up a Select Committee on the State of the Arts and Manufactures in England 'to inquire into the best means of extending a knowledge of the arts and of the principles of design among the people (especially the manufacturing population) of the country'.[2] Reporting in 1836, the committee criticised the art academies, 'they degenerate into mannerism and fetter genius', and the Royal Academy was accused of being cliquish. The committee concluded that the arts were not receiving sufficient support in Britain, and there was an urgent need for more attention to design. But the major concern derived from the growing gulf between art and manufacture, '…to us, a peculiarly manufacturing nation, the connexion [sic] between art and manufactures is very important'.

The Government responded swiftly by establishing, under its Board of Trade, a Government School of Design for the Improvement of Ornamental Art. The school, funded to the tune of £15,000, and housed on the top floor of Somerset House on London's Strand, was opened in 1837. Its object was to 'afford the manufacturers an opportunity of acquiring a component knowledge of the fine arts as far as the same are connected with manufactures'.[3]

'Plans Gang Aft Agley'

The pioneering Government School of Design soon ran into trouble. There was an ongoing tension – should it focus on drawing, or should crafts and technical processes be its major business? At one extreme, some thought that the country would be best served by academies where high art was the major interest, and the needs of industry were of secondary importance. At the other extreme, there were those who argued for institutions with a strong practical bias – designing, manufacturing and selling artefacts. The first Principal of the School of Design, William Dyce, struggled valiantly to resolve this issue of identity, but he gave up and resigned in 1843. The Government, however, had already concluded that the school was showing sufficient promise, and was persuaded, in 1841, to provide £10,000 to extend its work to branch schools around the United Kingdom. Manchester and York were amongst the first (1842), Glasgow was opened in 1844, and Paisley followed in 1848.

Unfortunately, jealous, bickering professionals, uninformed politicians, and unenthusiastic industrialists combined to impede the development of the schools. An anonymous critic complained to *The Times* in 1845:

> In England we have had a School of Design for nine years, it has cost the country nearly £20,000, what has been the result. When decorators will be wanted for the House of Lords are there now pupils adequate, or do any give promise of being so. Or will the architect be obliged (as was done not two years since in another place) to send to Munich for half a dozen.[4]

The state of affairs had reached crisis point in 1848 when the Government, in some desperation, decided to call in a troubleshooter. They turned to Henry Cole, a man of many interests and great ability. Cole had already added reforms of the Record Office and of the Post Office to an impressive and growing list of achievements. The Board of Trade approached him for advice on the Schools in September 1848, and, renowned for his less than respectful view of high art, few were surprised when Cole plumped for a practical approach to design education. He proposed that the schools should be self-supporting, and should earn money by designing furnishings for government establishments and for the Royal Palaces. This notion was politely rejected, however, on the grounds that it would offer unfair competition to other designers. Angered by the rejection, Cole used his final report to the Board to berate the management of the Schools:

> ...[looking] to the want and sympathy and cordial co-operation everywhere; to the neglect of the provincial schools, and their gradual decline; to instances of improvident expenditure; to the daily growing dissatisfaction of manufacturers, and, in short, to the absence of any palpable satisfactory results, about which there could be no dispute, I find my opinion of the unsatisfactory working of the school, so confirmed, that I am impelled to express my belief, that by no means short of a complete change of system, can the school fulfil its object, and its duty to the public.[5]

That obloquy produced no tangible change in the system, but Cole was on the warpath. An unstoppable force[6] – epitomised by his motto (from Ecclesiastes) 'Whatsoever thy hand findeth to do, do it with all thy might' – he used his Journal of Design and Manufactures to help shape opinion on the question of the Schools of Design. The resultant debate, spurred on by Cole's tireless determination, forced the establishment of a Select Committee in 1849. However, chaired by Milner Gibson MP, with Cole attempting to pull strings in the background, the outcome of the committee's conclusions was considered by many to be bland and disappointing. Cole's demands for wholesale change had been rejected. The work of the schools was praised, 'the Schools, though far from having attained that degree of perfection of which they appear capable, are decidedly producing very beneficial results'. And complaints that the work of the Schools was not sufficiently practical were passed over on the grounds that their objective was to produce designers, not designs. The last straw, as far as Cole was concerned, was the general acceptance of the system of management.

Later sections of this chapter will show that Cole had the last word in this matter. The stage is set, however, for the entry of the Belfast Government School of Design.

The Belfast Government School of Design

A school of design for Belfast was not an entirely new concept. The Academical Institution had opened a small academy on its premises in 1814, and operating outside normal school hours, it had twenty male pupils on its books by 1815.[7] A succession of three drawing masters saw the academy through to 1870 when it was disbanded. The first principal, the Florentine Gaetano Fabrinni, left in high dudgeon in 1820 to set up his own private academy in a central room in the White Linen Hall. He moved to Little May Street in 1836 – just as the London School was being established. In 1847 Fabrinni, an entrepreneur, decided to take advantage of the Government's growing interest in applied art and design, so he organised evening classes for 'industrious Mechanics, anxious to improve their taste in the Arts, Decorative and Ornamental'. But failing health, and his death in 1849, put an end to those plans.[8]

Public, rather than private interests, began to speak out. A drawing school

The Government School of Design, London, in 1843. (*London Illustrated News*, 1843.)

had already been set up in the Royal Dublin Society, but Belfast's needs required local provision. In 1836, the catalogue of the first exhibition of the Belfast Association of Artists referred to the need for a local institution.[9] The preface to that catalogue – the 'Address to the Public' – proposed that part of the proceeds of the exhibition should go towards 'a normal school of artistic education, at which lectures on the principles of designing and colouring will be an essential part'. The idea lay unexplored, however, until it was revived in 1845 by the Belfast Society for the Amelioration of the Working Classes, which body, of transient existence, proposed a wide-ranging scheme of education for the working classes, including a School of Design. The matter received further consideration in 1847 when the Belfast Working Classes Association declared, 'In order to have a direct elevating effect upon the arts and manufactures on which we depend for subsistence, a School of Design will shortly be initiated by the committee of our association.'[10]

How would the Government react to such a proposal? Ambrose Poynter, Inspector of Branch Schools of Design, had already made an exploratory visit to Belfast in 1846, but the ravages of the potato famine had forced a postponement of any new development on the educational front. Momentum did not flag, however, and promotion of the scheme was assisted by local members of parliament who pressed the Board of Trade for funds to establish schools of design in Ireland. Two years later, after some negotiation with the Lord Lieutenant for Ireland, parliament voted £1,500 for the establishment of three schools in Ireland – in Belfast, Cork and Dublin. Each city was to receive £500, but on condition that a matching amount would be raised from local sources.

The Belfast development was given a thorough airing at a public meeting in the Town Hall on 27 November 1848. A paper, read by James MacAdam (see above) highlighted the lack of skilled designers, especially in the sewed muslin trade, which employed upwards of 150,000 people at the time. Stating that some £80,000 was spent annually on the purchase of foreign designs, he argued that a Belfast School of Design would help to generate local designs and provide work for local people. In a later paper to the Dublin Statistical Society[11] MacAdam re-emphasised the needs of the sewed muslin trade, and added the needs of the linen trade. He also identified a wide range of other trades which could benefit form the establishment of a Belfast School:

> In ornamental ironwork, much might be done with facilities for procuring designs. In Belfast, machinery of the most finished kind is turned out, including steam engines, iron steamboats, flax-spinning machines, etc ... As yet, little ornamental work has been executed ... Among the minor branches of employment in Ireland on which the action of Schools of Design could have a salutary effect, may be mentioned – paper-staining, glass-staining, book-binding, engraving, and lithography, stone-cutting, and stucco work, building, cabinet work, and carving on wood and metal, house-painting, and uphol-stery, working in the precious metals, etc.

A good deal of support was raised for the new project. By the spring of 1849, £376 had been promised by various benefactors. But lack of financial support from the town council was a major disappointment: Cork Council had provided an annual grant of £200 towards that town's School of Design, but in Belfast the Town Council argued that it was prevented by legal reasons from so doing.

A meeting of subscribers, held in the Commercial Buildings on 30 May 1849, confirmed a general enthusiasm for the project. A thirty-three-member local Committee of Management was elected, thirteen of them representing the textile trades, and eight representing other trades dependent on design skills. Lord Dufferin was elected President; Charles Lanyon and William Thompson,

Vice-Presidents; W.J.C. Allen, Treasurer; and James MacAdam Jr, Honorary Secretary.[12]

With finances available, and a Management Committee in place, it only required staff and suitable premises to get the project underway. Of the former, the Board of Trade appointed Claude Lorraine Nursey as Headmaster. Nursey had played a leading role in the formation of a School of Design at Bradford, and was a former Headmaster of the School of Design in Leeds. He was supported by a second master – David Wilkie Raimbach. The question of accommodation was resolved relatively easily. With the impending establishment of the Queen's College, Belfast, the Royal Belfast Academical Institution would no longer be offering university-level education in its Collegiate Department. The resulting redundancy of a block of rooms at the northern extremity of the RBAI grounds provided an ideal opening for the new School of Design. The annual rental of £150 was welcomed by RBAI, but only on condition that the art students would use the College Square North entrance. The RBAI proprietors wanted no intermingling of their pupils with the art students who would be predominantly working class. The north wing 'could be isolated, giving the persons attending the new establishment a distinct entrance, and keeping them apart from the other departments'.[13]

Work Gets Underway

With everything in place, the Belfast Government School of Design (BGSD) opened its doors for business on 6 December 1849. Some 130 pupils had already enrolled on the public classes, and by Christmas a further twenty-seven had entered the private classes. Private classes ran in the evenings and were largely aimed at artisans; public classes, on the other hand, were intended for the better off, and usually ran during the day. Those attending public classes were charged a small fee – men 1s 6d, and women 9d per month. For the better-off families who wished to send more than one of their members to private classes, the charge was one guinea per quarter for the first pupil, and half a guinea per quarter for every additional member of the family.[14] The Committee of Management saw advantage in offering such diversity of provision,[15]

The primary object, in the establishment by Government of Schools of Design, is to afford, to the lower classes, through the assistance of the State, an easily accessible education in decorative art. But, at the same time, full sanction and encouragement have been given to making these resources available for the instruction of other ranks of Society; private classes have, therefore, been organised, at a higher rate of charge.

The Government Schools operated a national curriculum drawn up by the Board of Trade. In its original form, this curriculum was divided into twenty-two stages; ten concerned with drawing ornament, the figure, and flowers from the flat and the round; seven with painting the same types of examples; three with modelling them; and the last two stages devoted to composition in design. All students followed the ten drawing stages, but thereafter individual students could choose between painting and modelling. The various stages were modified somewhat during the first few years of operation, but a major change was the introduction of a twenty-third stage entitled 'technical studies' which included workshop practice and applied design.[16]

The School's first annual general meeting of subscribers was held on 25 January 1850. By that time 137 pupils had enrolled on the public classes – with 119 of them under thirty years of age. It was noted with concern that only eighteen women had joined the classes.[17] The annual report praised the encouragement provided by the several prizes and scholarships offered by local benefactors. Particularly noteworthy was Lord Dufferin's prize of £50 for the best design of a damask tablecloth. This tablecloth was to be displayed at the Great Exhibition in London's Crystal Palace the following year, but, nearer the event, it was decided to divide the prize amongst damasks, embroidered muslins, cambric, linen ornaments, and embroidered vests.[18]

The BGSD was formally inaugurated on 10 April 1850. A splendid affair, the 500 people who were there gathered were enlightened by uplifting speeches, and entertained by an exhibition of examples of the skills of local and foreign artists and designers. Lord Dufferin, the President, explained the origins and objectives of the Schools of Design:

... a lamentable ignorance of art was manifested among our workmen, especially among those engaged in what are called fancy trades – the silk trade, the ribbon trades, the china trade, and others – though an earnest desire for instruction appeared to prevail among them ... though it was immediately to the designers and manufacturers that this artistic education was to be offered, there was another pupil no less ignorant, no less in need of the schoolmaster, and infinitely more refractory than either the manufacturer or designer – and that was the public itself.[19]

Whilst on his feet, Dufferin took the opportunity to express concern at the lack of women ('lovely disciples') attending the school. With many hundreds of women employed in the sewed muslin trade, and in fancy needlework of various kinds, this was both a surprise and a disappointment. But His Lordship's patronising manner did not go down well with the Belfast women. A later speech, in 1855, referring to 'sweet girl graduates in their golden hair', did little to improve the situation.[20]

It became an established tradition to award the School's prizes at an annual social event (a conversazione), which included a display of works of art by students and established professionals. The conversaziones were attractive and

The old buildings of the Belfast Government School of Design survive today as part of the Royal Belfast Academical Institution.

well-organised affairs; for example, the 1851 event was described as follows:

> The number of visitors was very great – probably not less than five hundred ladies and gentlemen – and the tout ensemble was exceedingly graceful to the eye. The large suite of apartments above and below, in the wing of the Institution devoted to the school, was thrown open, and brilliantly lighted, and decorated with fine specimens of native art and industry; and the continued change of feature, produced by the constant entry and departure of groups of well-dressed men and beautiful women, in their graceful evening costume, contrasted here and there with the bright uniforms of the officers of the garrison who mingled in the promenades, produced a series of pictures most temptingly inviting to the eye of the artist.[21]

Measuring Success

After the first few years, the BGSD seemed to be progressing satisfactorily on all fronts. The financial position appeared sound, and the President was able to report at the 1852 conversazione that the Belfast public was continuing to contribute generously to the school. In the year ending June 1851, public subscriptions amounted to some £400 – a sum well in excess of the £78 subscribed in Dublin, the £100 in Cork, and even the £300 in Manchester.[22] The annual grant from London was £500, but was increased to £600 the following year.

Considerable numbers of students attended the classes, but much greater interest might have been expected from a thriving town like Belfast, with its population of around 100,000. The 1852/53 annual report[23] recorded 152 students in public classes and 60 in private, and the following year's report[24] listed a total of 245 pupils (public classes, 109; governess's class, 12; ladies' class, 29; gentlemen's class, 14; schools, 81). The appendix to the report for 1853/54 also referred to an additional 117 pupils attending 'especial' classes, but the nature of these classes, perhaps extramural, was not explained. It also listed the occupations of pupils, although the stated total of 231 does not tally with the above-mentioned 245.

Architect, 1

Bookseller, 1

Cabinet-makers, 4

Carpenters, 4

Chemists, 2

Clerks, 16

Constabulary, 1

Dentist, 1

Designers/Apprentices, 6

Drapers, 3

Draughtsman/Mechanical, 1

Engineers, 2

Engravers, 7

Fitter, 1

Flax Trade, 2

Grocers, 2

Hackle-maker, 1

Hardware, 1

Japanner, 1

Linen Lapper, 1

Linen Trade, 4

Litho Writer, 1

Marble Carvers, 2

Mechanics, 3

Messenger, 1

Metal Turner, 1

Moulder, 1

Painters, 6

Pawnbroker, 1

Penners, 2

Plasterer, 1

Provision Trade, 2

Sewed Muslin Trade, 23

Schoolboys, 100

Ship Carpenter, 1

Spinners, 3

Stone Carver, 1

Stone Cutters/Masons, 5

Storemen; flax/yarn, 2

Student of Divinity, 1

Surveyors, 3

Teachers, 2

Undetermined, 4

Weaver, 1

Whitesmith, 1

Woodcarver, 1

TOTAL 231

The Belfast School introduced several operational innovations. It collaborated with other educational institutions; for example, in 1853 the school's staff contributed to the teaching of forty boy pupils in Fountain Street National School, twenty boys and twenty girls in May Street National School, and fourteen boys and three girls in Mr Hutton's private school.[25] The development of art in such schools was encouraged in 1850, when the committee agreed to admit teachers without fee so that they could qualify to give elementary instruction in art to their charges. By 1852, the School's own advanced pupils were helping to design and deliver drawing classes at Newtownards and Carrickfergus.[26]

Prizes and scholarships added to the students' motivation. £20 was awarded in prizes to the various classes in 1851, and this sum was increased to £50 the following year.[27] Ten of the students' designs – those which had won school prizes offered by Lord Dufferin and others, as well as a few of the better unsuc-

The bill for decoration of the School of Design's conversazione in 1851. (Public Record Office Northern Ireland.)

cessful designs – were manufactured and sent forward to London for the Great Exhibition of 1851. There they received considerable praise from the jurors, and were valued, in total, at £100. Thanks to Lord Dufferin's largesse, fifteen of the school's pupils were able to spend nine days at the Exhibition.[28]

Those prizes and medals drove the students on to greater things. A further spur was provided by cash scholarships that allowed the winners to devote more time to their chosen specialisms. The report of the 1851 conversazione records the award of scholarships of £20, £15 and £10. The Belfast School was the first to offer such scholarships.

Belfast students performed well in examinations and were able to hold their heads high in the national arena. In 1852, for example, nine won medals awarded by the Department of Practical Art in the annual exhibition of drawings submitted by students from the various Schools of Design across the Kingdom. These medals recognised exceptional work at all twenty-three stages of the curriculum; for example, Samuel McCloy, engraver and later Master of the Waterford School of Art, had covered stages five to twenty-three, and Patrick McGivney, sergeant of constabulary, was working at stages two to six.[29]

Whilst enrolments might have been higher, there is clear evidence that the school was making a useful contribution to local industry. Inspector's reports

The School of Design pays the rent: 'The Treasurer will please pay to the Treasurer of the RA Institution the sum of seventy five pounds for one half year's rent of the School payable in advance on 1st Novr last. Charles Lanyon, Chairman. J.W. MacAdam, Hon. Secretary. Belfast 3rd Dec 1849.' (Public Records Office Northern Ireland.)

made the point. The 1851 report, for example, states:

> The progress of the Belfast School continues to be satisfactory, and it has identified itself with the manufacturers of the town to a degree which no other school has ever attained within the short period that has elapsed since its establishment. The manufacture of linen bands and headings has very greatly increased – probably threefold – since the establishment of the school, and the improvement of the quality of these articles in a still greater proportion is directly due to the pupils of this school. The embroidered waistcoat trade is also increasing, and the school has undoubtedly contributed to its advance.[30]

Unfortunately, the sense of satisfaction deriving from these successes was marred somewhat by the ever-present concerns about resource-related matters. The lack of a suitable facility for the display of sculptures was one such issue. Poynter, the Government Inspector, commented on this shortcoming during his visit to the School in October 1850, 'the room containing the collection of casts was totally unsuitable for the purpose, whether as regards space or light.'[31] The Board of RBAI was not prepared to erect a new building for this purpose, but it agreed to reduce the annual rent of the existing building by £50, and to donate an adjacent plot of ground for a purpose-built sculpture gallery. Charles Lanyon, the renowned local architect (and vice-president of the BGSD), drew up the necessary plans and estimated the total cost of build and fitting to be £650. Appeals to the public brought some response (Dufferin himself promised £50), but other competing claims on the public purse restricted progress. The 1853 annual report identified the major cause of delay as 'the movement originated by the lamented young Nobleman ... having for its object the foundation of an Athenaeum'.[32] The young Nobleman – the Earl of Belfast – had generated considerable interest in his proposal for an Athenaeum that would draw together the various cultural and intellectual strands of life in Belfast, and could well include the BGSD. The proposal, however, never came to fruition, and the construction of a sculpture gallery for the BGSD had to wait another half century.

Decline and Fall

Worries about the lack of a sculpture gallery were nothing compared to those about to be generated by the new management regime in London. The Great Exhibition of 1851 was a major turning point in the British approach to design. Held in the Crystal Palace in South Kensington, the object was to display the fruits of British manufacture to a world audience. However, it also exposed a great deal of bad taste in design. Many British designs were over elaborate, and many were blatant copies of Continental designs. Indeed, *The Times* was extremely critical of the pretentiousness of the excessively elaborate manufactured goods, and was only able to admire the building itself and the machinery on display therein.[33]

Henry Cole, a close confidante of Prince Albert, had played a leading role in the creation and operation of the Great Exhibition, so he was ideally placed to use the lessons learned to further his case for a reorganisation of design education. The Board of Trade was persuaded of the seriousness of the situation and decided in 1852 to establish a new department – the Department of Practical Art. It was to take responsibility for design education, and was to be run by Cole, with part-time assistance from the artist Richard Redgrave.

Cole moved quickly to redesign, re-launch, and rename the Schools of Design: the Belfast Government School of Design became the Belfast

Government School of Art in 1852. In London, the Central School was moved from Somerset House to Marlborough House on the Mall, and a new head-master was installed. Cole then turned his attention to policy: he wanted a greater practical dimension to the work of the new Schools of Art; he wanted art education to permeate down to the National School system, and encouraged the appropriate training of schoolteachers; and, in order to improve public awareness of good taste, he wanted the pupils of the Schools of Art to include greater numbers from the middle and upper classes. But, above all, he insisted that the schools should be self-supporting.

The speed of change was further accelerated by the establishment of a Department of Science and Art (DSA) in 1853. By definition, the Department of Practical Art had been limited to art-related matters, but the 1851 Exhibition had clearly demonstrated that science had as much, if not more, to offer the enterprising manufacturer. The DSA embraced the work of the former Department of Practical Art, and took responsibility, in Great Britain, for the School of Mines, the Geological Survey and the Industrial Museum of Scotland, and, in Ireland, for the Committee of Lectures in Dublin, the Royal Dublin Society and the Museum of Irish Industry. This wide remit was shared between two Joint Secretaries; Henry Cole heading the Arts Division, and Lyon Playfair, the Science Division.

There was little subtlety in Cole's approach to change. In March 1853, the provincial schools received a bombshell in the form of a Board of Trade Minute. It started ominously:

> It was understood, on the establishment of the Schools, that a Government Grant was promised for a limited period of three years, upon the condition that a sum equivalent to it was raised in the locality; and, on the expectation that, after three years, the Schools would be so established and supported as not to require any further assistance from Government.[34]

That sentence prefaced a depressing message: any future Government grant would be restricted to items concerned with 'the direct costs of instruction' – defined as masters' salaries, teaching, scholarships and training. The grant could not be used to cover items such as the maintenance of the school, its rent, the salaries of officers, or prizes.

Cole's many dicta were set down in circulars and documents, and it was only a matter of time before the provincial Schools of Art began to groan under the burden of the new bureaucracy. Belfast did not escape the deluge of paperwork.

The annual report for 1853/54 included the following *cri de coeur*:

> Instead of devoting all their time to the details of local management, and to
> the development of the usefulness of the classes, in accordance with the wants
> of the locality, their attention has been most disagreeably occupied with a
> voluminous and contradictory tissue of letters and printed circulars from
> the Department, the tenor of which completely put it out of those projects
> which, they believe, their local experience best fitted them to conceive.

A series of acrimonious exchanges between Cole and the Committee of
the Belfast School of Art was soon underway. Cole was reminded that the
Government had initially granted Belfast £500 per annum, and had indicated
that this sum could well be increased, depending on performance. Indeed, the
grant had been raised to £600 in 1851.[35] But Cole was unmoved, blaming the
School's unsatisfactory financial position on its high costs per student, and criti-
cising the fact that only around 200 citizens of such a large town were attending
the School's classes.

The financial outlook was now far from promising; estimates in Belfast predicted that £315 would be required to cover the various costs not directly
related to instruction, and Secretary MacAdam predicted that fees and donations would fall short of that figure by some £70. In response to this increasingly
unsatisfactory situation, and influenced, perhaps, by MacAdam's threat that the
committee would resign, Cole agreed to make up any deficit that might arise
in the year 1853/54. Thereafter, however, the Belfast Government School of Art
would be on its own.

To make matters worse, Cole decided in June 1854 that the DSA's contribution to Masters' salaries would in future be limited to £50 per annum, leaving
the provincial schools to make up the rest from fees and donations. At this
point in time, Master Nursey and his assistant Raimbach departed to Norwich
in somewhat mysterious circumstances. In 1855 Lord Dufferin was forced to
admit, 'Mr Nursey, a most excellent instructor, was conjured away from us (in
a manner I could never clearly understand) and located at Norwich.'[36] Without
teachers, and in considerable financial difficulty, the Belfast Government School
of Art was forced to close in the autumn of 1854.

The School's doors remained closed for a full year before Lyon Playfair, Cole's
colleague Joint Secretary at the DSA, agreed to visit Belfast in the autumn
of 1855 to see if anything could be salvaged from the sorry mess. The local
press did its best to support the School's side of the debate, asserting that the

closure had been the result of 'the autocracy of Mr Cole, and the unwilling-ness of the committee to submit to his dictation'.[37] Much more amenable than Cole, Playfair agreed to a compromise whereby the DSA would pay a Master at £150 per annum, and would support an assistant on a smaller scale. Public donations helped to clear outstanding debts of £300, and a new, more business-aware Finance Committee was formed. And RBAI extended its generosity by reducing the annual rent to £75.[38] All of this reassured Dufferin, who was able to report in December that 'the misunderstanding with the Government … caused by Mr Cole's interference, has been overcome'.[39] So the Belfast Government School of Art was able to re-open in its original building on 4 February 1856. A new Master, JD Croome was appointed, and was later joined by an assistant, R. Hale.

Business seemed to be back on track, with pupil numbers rising to 607 (including 257 schoolchildren) by June 1857. But, whilst these were greatly in excess of the numbers of earlier years, and must have encouraged the commit-tee, financial insecurity once again raised its ugly head. An indifferent response from the public to exhibitions in the School, and the continuing inability of the Town Council to contribute to the School through the rates, combined to convince the committee that financial stability was unachievable. With debts of £177, the decision to close was taken on 8 June 1858, and the doors of the Belfast Government School of Art were closed and barred on the 15 July. They were not to open for another twelve years.

5

The Belfast Working Men's Institute and Temperance Hall

The idea of a Working Men's Institute for Belfast was first mooted in August 1866, when a group of interested gentlemen met to discuss how the welfare of the town's working classes might be improved. The rapidly growing number of factories and mills in Belfast had created the need for a better-educated workforce, but it was agreed at the outset that the moral welfare, as well as the intellectual welfare of the workers should be addressed. The dangers of alcohol were a particular concern at the time, and the Irish Temperance League, formed around 1858, had provided a platform for the great Irish Temperance Mission. Belfast was anxious to join the battle against the demon drink, so a committee was formed to start the planning of an Institute which would uplift, as well as instruct, the working men of Belfast.

The committee's work led to the establishment of the Belfast Working Men's Institute and Temperance Hall which was formally opened in 1871. Edward Allworthy, Secretary, described the Institute's intentions in the original prospectus in 1866,

Hitherto Belfast, the capital of the North of Ireland, with its teeming population of the Working-classes, has had no Working Men's Institute; no public place where the Artisan and Mechanic may meet with his friends; and secure from the counter-attractions of the 700 public houses that stud our streets, can have a cup of coffee, spend an hour or two in social intercourse, read the papers of the day, or periodicals bearing on his own trade, and where he might hear lectures, scientific and useful, at a moderate charge; while towns much smaller in England and Scotland – even in Ireland – can boast of one or more.[1]

The lack of any reference to the Belfast Mechanics' Institute, which had striven to meet some of the same objectives, is surprising; more so when the new Institute building was to be sited only a few hundred metres along the very same street! With £2,000 donated within the first few months, £1,800 was directed towards the purchase of ground where the east end of Queen Street met Castle Street.

Construction of a suitable building, estimated to cost £4,000, commenced in the autumn of 1866. In the meantime the founding members arranged meetings in the premises of the Working Classes' Refreshment Reading Rooms in numbers 3 and 5 John Street. (John Street, between North Street and Donegall Street, was demolished in the 1880s and replaced by Royal Avenue.) The foundation stone of the new building was laid on 14 May 1870 on an extremely wet Saturday afternoon, but Thomas Gaffikin, Chairman of the General Committee, read the weather as a good omen, 'a baptism of cold rain water was poured upon the incipient institution, in seeming token of the temperance principles in which it should be reared'.[2] Another contemporary described it as 'nature's apparent effort to test the temperance advocates' appreciation of cold water'.[3] The same commentator described how nature continued to resist the scheme; the separate names Temperance Hall, and Working Men's Institute, had been engraved on the Queen Street front of the building, but the former seemed to receive the rougher treatment from the elements, 'for it has since been almost completely removed by atmospheric denudation'. It is a moot point whether the workers themselves had assisted this process of denudation. Temperance was not high on their list of priorities; they were more concerned with their own education and training. At a public conference in the new building on 11 November 1871, Mr Hunter, a representative of the working men of Belfast stated:

What was wanted in this building, and which he hoped would be carried out, was that it may bring working men – bona fide working men – into contact with the principles of their business, bring the hand of the practical operative into contact with the clear head of the theorist, so that working men might know the principles on which they were every day carrying on their several avocations.[4]

The Formal Opening Ceremony

It took five years to complete 'an edifice that would do credit to the largest city in the Empire'. Even by today's standards, its facilities were comprehensive and impressive:

> The building contains on the ground floor a large and capacious News Room, where a selection of the various periodicals will be provided for the subscribers. A culinary department will be fitted up with all the accommodation necessary to enable the manager to provide various kinds of refreshments at a cheap rate. On the first floor there is a Manager's Office and a Committee Room, a spacious Library, which, it is hoped, will ere long be stocked with a choice selection of popular literature; and a splendid room for the purpose of free lectures on general topics connected with the arts and sciences – not neglecting those other subjects that affect our social interests. Over the entire building there is a large public hall, capable of containing twelve hundred persons, with orchestra and band gallery available for occasions requiring that accommodation; there are also comfortable apartments for the manager, who will reside on the premises; and smaller rooms for games and amusements, and a smoking room.[5]

The Belfast Working Men's Institute and Temperance Hall was formally opened with much pomp and ceremony on 15 November 1871. It was a great occasion, made all the more colourful by the display of flowers, and the gowns of office of the various dignitaries. The colour spectrum was further enriched by the many flags and banners of organisations such as the Oddfellows, the Linen Finishers' Society, the Ironfounders, the Stonecutters' Society, the Independent Order of Rechabites, and the Good Templars.[6] Supporting the temperance theme of the Institute, the banner of the last-mentioned was emblazoned with the stirring words, 'Brethren, Water, Strength; Peace and Plenty; Wine a Mockery.'

The proceedings commenced at noon with a stirring rendition of the national anthem, the conclusion of which signalled the start of a dignified procession to the platform. Lord Dufferin (Lord Lieutenant of County Down), the Mayor, members of the Town Council, Councillors, the President and professors of the

Queen's College were among the distinguished band of worthies.

The Mayor, Philip Johnston JP, delivered a speech which, following the usual pattern of the day, contained the full quota of self-righteous, condescending and patronising remarks:

The Belfast Working Men's Institute, decorated for Queen Victoria's visit in 1885. (Welsh Collection, Ulster Museum.)

I rely more on what men do for themselves than on what is done for them; and, therefore any exertion on the part of the industrial classes to show that they intelligently appreciate their position, and desire themselves to take a share in improving it, is to me far more encouraging than any amount of subscriptions and donations from wealthier men ... Intemperance is at the bottom of many disasters, and is generally the parent of pauperism and crime. I earnestly hope and trust that this Institution may be the means of winning many a worthy man from acquiring habits of inebriety, which must in the end lead him down the path to ruin and to misery...[7]

And, after informing his audience that he had 'been for many years brought by my business into frequent contiguity with the working classes', the Mayor took advantage of the occasion to share his views on industrial relations:

It is not my prerogative to enter upon what may be the cause of this conflict between capital and labour ...I do not say who is right or who is wrong, but evidently uneducated and unthinking men are not capable of taking the proper stand in the great conflict between capital and labour; and it's difficult to argue with them, believing, as I do, that most of their difficulties would vanish, were there a better comprehension of the real facts and principles at stake...

The artisans and mechanics among the audience must have been greatly relieved when the speeches came to an end. However, yet another uplifting experience was awaiting; a choir and orchestra delivered an ode written by Francis Davis. One verse is sufficient to demonstrate its general tenor – the new Institute would be:

A beam of love and loveliness,
Revealing to remotest lands,
In works of holiest form and hue,
What Irish minds, and hearts, and hands,
For God, for man, and art can do.[8]

Fortunately, for them, Belfast's working men and women were then released to enjoy some real entertainment in the accompanying exhibition. The exhibition had been arranged, not only to entertain and educate, but to raise badly needed funds.

Attracting Funds

The Institute was in financial difficulty from the beginning. The cost of the building and its contents had been assessed at £4,000 in 1866, but, as ever, this turned out to be a gross underestimate, with costs rising to some £7,000 by the time of completion in 1871. Donations from public benefactors were not sufficient to meet this growing commitment, so the Institute had to look for other sources of income. The Belfast and North of Ireland Workmen's Exhibition of 1870, held in the Ulster Hall and launched on the 17 May (only three days after the laying of the Institute's foundation stone) was one such potential source. Arranged as a prologue to a grander international event in London later that year, the Belfast Exhibition included machinery, tools, textiles, furniture, ceramics, and stationery. There were also fine art, archaeology and natural history sections, but these attracted a great deal of criticism from the artisans who felt that they, and their work, had been under-represented. In defence, the Secretary, W. Kirkpatrick, explained that he had felt 'obliged to supplement our Exhibition from other departments than the workshop, and that the beauties and instruction of antiquity, science and art, might not inappropriately be blended with the produce of our more humble labours'.[9]

It seemed the mechanical arts, and their practitioners, had once again been relegated to the back seat. However, despite the bickering, some 70,000 people visited the Exhibition before it closed on 4 June. The proceeds amounted to about £700, of which Kirkpatrick received £200, and £150 was donated to the General Hospital. The distribution of the remaining £350 turned into an undignified row, the outcome of which remains a mystery. A donation of £50 to the Belfast School of Art is on record,[10] but it remains unclear whether any workmen were rewarded with visits to the London exhibition, or if the Working Men's Institute (WMI) received any monetary benefit from the event.

So, on its opening day, the embryonic organisation still found itself in debt to the tune of £2,000. Further donations were sought from the gentlemen and merchants of Belfast. In addition, having learned a lot from participation in the Belfast Exhibition of the previous year, it was decided to organise an exhibition to run concurrently with the formal opening of the WMI; as well as promoting the new organisation, this held promise of raising funds. The people of Belfast were generous in providing material for the exhibition, 'The inhabitants of the town have been most liberal and generous in forwarding to the Exhibition Committee all those objects of interest, value, and curiosity, which render Exhibitions so agreeable and attractive.'[11]

The exhibition used practically every room in the new Queen Street building, including the large theatre on the top floor, where working models connected with the engineering and carpentry trades were displayed. Indeed, these splendid models (dominated by model ships) bore particular testimony to the skills of local artisans. With the need to attract large numbers of visitors, the organisers decided to widen the range of exhibits to include fossils, flint tools, bronze and iron-age implements, specimens of local products, photographs and paintings. There is no clear record of the number of visitors to the exhibition, nor of the monies collected, but, whilst the event helped to publicise the WMI, the proceedings from the exhibition seemed to have done little to stem the continuing deterioration of its financial position.

The WMI admitted its first members in July 1872, and the first Committee of Management, composed of working men, was elected at a public meeting the following August. At that meeting the new members were shocked to learn that the Institute's debts had grown to more than £4,000, and there were no funds for furnishing rooms, purchasing books or newspapers. The organisation was teetering on the edge of extinction, and matters reached breaking point in 1874 when the Trustees proposed to resolve the financial crisis by selling the Queen Street building.[12] After some heated exchanges, the Trustees agreed that the Committee of Management would assume full control of the WMI, and would take full responsibility for wiping out the debt. The town's artisans were now in control!

The Industrial Exhibition and Bazaar of 1876

Growing numbers of courses helped to meet recurrent expenditure, but more cash was needed to clear the residual building debts. A major step in that direction was an Industrial Exhibition and Bazaar, opened in the Ulster Hall on 23 May 1876. This was a large and wide-ranging affair, requiring the construction of temporary buildings on the vacant ground adjacent to the Ulster Hall.

The Exhibition embraced five departments: fine arts; scientific and mechanical appliances; textile fabrics; economic products, and antiquities and curiosities. There was a supporting display of fancy work and a ladies' bazaar.

The associated pageantry outshone that of the WMI's opening ceremony five years earlier.[13] Opening the Exhibition, the Duke of Abercorn felt obliged to remind his audience that the arts had a well-established hierarchy. He remarked that, 'We give a moderate share of attention to the Polite or Fine Arts; but our chief study is of the Coarse Arts, through which our town has risen from comparative obscurity to comparative wealth and power.' The assembly was then treated to a choral rendition of an 'Ode to Industry', whose cloying sentiments matched those of the ode delivered at the WMI's opening ceremony:

> Man, arise and speed thy mission –
> Labour of the Brain and Brow;
> Heaven assigns a high ambition –
> Glorify thy Maker now.[14]

The more secular objectives of the Exhibition were described by the President James Henderson:

> ...stimulating and developing local industry and the mechanical skill and talent of our numerous artisan population, by giving encouragement to emulation in improvement and progress, by affording an opportunity for inspecting the results of ingenuity, skill and taste in various departments, and by granting facilities to our operatives to remedy the defects in their own products by comparing them with the results of the ingenuity of others.[15]

Sacred and secular objectives aside, the Exhibition was well received by the public. Excursion trains were organised, 'to give our country cousins facilities for visiting town and inspecting one of the largest collections of articles of utility and vertu ever displayed in the North of Ireland.' Section B, scientific and mechanical appliances, turned out to be extremely popular. The press reported:

> Although there are other sections in the exhibition in which the eye of the visitor will be more attracted, and where, possibly, more pleasure can be had, in none will his interest be so thoroughly aroused, or his observation and judgement more earnestly appealed to than in Section B...[16]

Section B included an impressive array of the high technology of the day, including:

> Flax Hackling machines, Preparing and Spinning Machinery and Looms … In addition … Steam and Gas Engines, Pumps, Gas Meters, Weighing machines, Nail-Cutting Machines, Slide lathes, Fluting machines, Patent Bottling Apparatus, Confectionery Boiler, Lithographic printing Machine … There are also working and other models of Engines, Ships, &c., including a perfect model of Marine Engines of SS Britannic; and a complete model of the SS Germanic, which made the quickest passage on record across the Atlantic.[17]

The fact that this equipment was on loan from local companies was evidence of the growing stature of the WMI within the industrial community. The above figures show some typical catalogue advertisements.[18]

More than 100,000 people visited the Exhibition by the time of the formal closing ceremony on 14 August 1876. Entrance fees amounted to more than £2,000, and the proceeds from the ladies' bazaar added a further £7,746.

Science Classes

The WMI's day-to-day recreational diversions attracted much custom. The library, the newsroom, the amusement room (with its bagatelle and billiards table), and the refreshments room, offered welcome respite from the cares of daily toil. Membership increased steadily in the first few years; from 413 in 1873 to 473 in 1875. And the number of visitors – each paying 1*d* entrance fee – rocketed from 8,818 to 29,104 over the same period.[19] However, the Institute's educational provision soon became its forte.

The session 1872-73 saw the establishment of the WMI's Science School. Under the aegis of the Department of Science and Arts in South Kensington, such schools were intended to instruct artisans in the sciences underpinning their particular trades. A payment by results system had been introduced by the DSA in its campaign to raise the quality of teaching in its Science Schools, and the professionalism of the Institute's few staff, and the interest and motivation of its mature students, soon brought a steady stream of income from this source.

The Ulster Hall at the time of the 1876 Exhibition; the vacant ground to the left (now Bryson House) was used for a display of mechanical appliances. (Lawrence Collection, National Library of Ireland.)

Much of the success of the science classes was attributable to Robert Barklie, Secretary to the WMI, Science Master, and Superintendent of the WMI's Education Department. Barklie had served an apprenticeship in the spinning trade, and after some years in the bleaching, dyeing and printing industries, he qualified at Queen's College, Belfast. He was later admitted as a Fellow of the Chemical Society. Before joining the WMI he had taught for sixteen years at both primary and intermediate levels. A remarkable man by any standards, Barklie was an excellent manager, as well as master of a wide range of scientific and technological subjects. In later years he was also able to offer the public his services as an analytic chemist; the 1886 annual report included a piece advertising Barklie's ability to undertake all kinds of commercial, agricultural, and medical analyses – especially water analysis, and analyses connected with linen manufacture. This work, and his outstanding contributions to the WMI, ultimately earned him Membership of the Royal Irish Academy. He was later appointed public analyst in the city.

The inaugural set of science classes – seven in total – established standards of performance which were maintained throughout the WMI's lifetime. The Institute's students performed exceptionally well. Pass rates exceeded those in the rest of the United Kingdom, and prestigious prizes and studentships were won (a national silver medal in organic chemistry, and two studentships to the Government School of Mines in London). The first annual meeting of the WMI acknowledged these achievements, and wished to build upon them. Thomas Gaffikin moved,

> That this meeting, deeply impressed with the necessity and importance of having a systematic teaching of the elements of science placed within the reach of the artisans, and believing that the classes taught in this Institute are calculated in an eminent degree to further the cause of technical education, heartily expresses the hope that these will be largely taken advantage of by the industrial class, and cordially recommends the Institute to the sympathy and support of the merchants, manufacturers, and other employers of labour.[20]

Barklie welcomed this encouragement. In the Institute's annual report for

Musgrave's stoves were on display at the 1876 Industrial Exhibition and Bazaar. (Anon, *Official Catalogue; Industrial Exhibition and Bazaar,* location LHL.)

105

PRIZE·MEDAL,
LONDON, 1862.

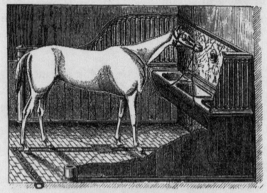

MUSGRAVE'S PATENT
STABLE FITTINGS

Musgrave's stable fittings were also presented at the 1876 Exhibition. (Anon, *Official Catalogue; Industrial Exhibition and Bazaar*, location LHL.)

1875 he stated that the numbers enrolled in the various classes had increased from 101 to 166 between 1874 and 1875. This growth, and the performance of the students, did much for the WMI's reputation. Speaking at the 1876 Exhibition and Bazaar, D. Fortune, a member of the WMI's Board, reported that he had:

> ...the honour a few weeks ago to take part in the annual meeting of the various Working Men's Institutes in the United Kingdom ... and it was his particular pride and gratification to be able to report that they had accomplished in Belfast in connection with the Working Men's Institute a success that had no parallel in the history of any institution in the United Kingdom.[21]

Whilst that report might have lacked objectivity, the views of the British Association for the Advancement of Science could not be so criticised.[22] When the Association met in Belfast in 1876, it agreed to grant the sum of £100 to the WMI for the purchase of scientific apparatus. Speaking for the association, Professor Redfern commented, 'When they looked at the number of persons in the classes, and the success of those classes, the Working Men's Institute has very strong claims upon the people of the town.'

Classes, taught in the evenings and on Saturdays, covered an increasingly broad range of subject material. In 1879, for example, 353 candidates sat DSA examinations in fourteen subjects. Of particular note was the ongoing superior performance of the WMI's students compared to those in the rest of the United Kingdom[23] (see table). The Belfast students still maintained that edge in 1888 when their success rate was 72.2 per cent compared to the UK's 67 per cent.

Subject	Candidates	% Pass	% Pass
Mathematics	49	69.4	59.3
Theoretical Mechanics	14	78.6	68.1
Acoustics, Light and Heat	52	71.2	47.5
Magnetism and Electricity	53	81.1	74.3
Inorganic Chemistry	65	67.7	61.5
Organic Chemistry	14	78.6	84.1
Geology	9	77.8	50.0
Analytical Physics	14	64.7	58.1
Botany	32	62.5	54.3
Biology	2	50.0	n/a
Physiography	11	100.0	48.9
Agriculture	14	100.0	76.1
Inorganic Analysis Laboratory	14	57.2	73.9
Organic Analysis Laboratory	10	88.9	75.0
Overall	353	73.4	60.3

Working Men's Institute Examination Results 1879.

An important development took place in 1879 when the Pharmaceutical Society of Ireland formally recognised the WMI as a school where students could study for the Apothecary's Diploma. Only four other institutions had received such recognition – Trinity College, Dublin; the Royal College of Science in Ireland; the Carmichael School of Medicine, and the Queen's Colleges. The thirty up-to-date workbenches in the Institute's chemistry laboratory allowed up to 120 students to perform practical analyses. Queen's College, Belfast, on the other hand, could only cope with fifteen students.[24] The WMI facility allowed men who were at work during the day to qualify for an Apothecary's Diploma through evening attendance.

EDUCATIONAL CLASSES—Classes in connection with the SCIENCE AND ART DEPARTMENT in Mathematics, Mechanics, Acoustics, Light and Heat, Magnetism and Electricity, Chemistry (Inorganic, Organic, and Practical), Geology, Botany, Biology, Animal Physiology, Physical Geography, &c., conducted by

ROBERT BARKLIE, F C.S., Q.C.B.
E. P. DEWAR, M.A , Ex-Sen. Sch , Q.C.B., and
WILLIAM TAYLOR, Lab. Asst., Q C.B.

TERMS—Payable in advance—2s. 6d. for One Subject, and 1s. for each additional Subject ; or 5s for Five Subjects for the Session of Seven Months for those who attend the May Examinations. All others 5s. per Quarter per Subject.

The Working Men's Institute advertises its wares in the official catalogue of the 1876 Industrial Exhibition and Bazaar. (Anon, *Official Catalogue; Industrial Exhibition and Bazaar*, location LHL.)

Strengthening the Technical Dimension

The DSA's classes were chiefly concerned with the theoretical aspects of the various subjects. There were some illustrations of the application of those theories to practice, but, on the whole, the related technologies received little attention. That shortcoming was addressed with the establishment, in 1880, of the City and Guilds of London, and its associated technologically biased classes. The WMI grasped the opportunity to widen its portfolio, and a Technical School was set up in parallel to the existing Science School. By 1882, the Science School was running twenty-two classes, and the Technical School eighteen classes.[25] The range of subjects listed in the 1882–83 Prospectus were:

Science School
1. Practical, Plane and Solid Geometry
2. Machine Construction and Drawing
3. Building Construction
4. Naval Architecture and Drawing
5. Pure Mathematics
6. Theoretical Mechanics

7. Applied Mechanics
8. Sound, Light and Heat
9. Magnetism and Electricity
10. Inorganic Chemistry (Theoretical)
11. Inorganic Chemistry (Practical)
12. Organic Chemistry (Theoretical)
13. Organic Chemistry (Practical)
14. Geology
15. Mineralogy
16. Animal Physiology
17. Elementary Botany
18. Biology
19. Metallurgy
20. Steam
21. Physical Geography
22. Principles of Agriculture Engineering

Technical School
1. Alkali Manufacture
2. Bread Making
3. Coal-Tar Distilling
4. Spirit Manufacture
5. Photography
6. Textile Fabrics; Manufacture of Linen
7. Telegraphy
8. Electrical Instrument Making
9. Metalworking Tools
10. Woodworking Tools
11. Fuel
12. Manufacture of Oils, Colours and Varnishes
13. Bleaching, Dyeing and Printing of Linen
14. Gas Manufacture
15. Electro-metallurgy
16. Weaving and Pattern Designing
17. Electric Lighting and Power Transmission
18. Mechanical Engineering

An expanding portfolio attracted increasing numbers of students – approaching 600 by the mid-1880s. Examination successes were reflected in the substantial sums of money accrued from the DSA's payment by results scheme. In 1882, for example, the WMI's classes earned £689 of a total for Belfast of £1,242.[26] The annual report for that year stated that only eight of the DSA's 1,421 science schools across the Kingdom had earned more results fees![27] That situation still pertained in 1884. The report also included a list of the top nine earners of results fees, and, whist the WMI maintained ninth position in terms of fees earned, the list showed that in terms of prizes gained per student, the WMI's students topped the field. The following table extends that list to cover the four top performers in Ireland:

School	Entries	Prizes	Results
Manchester Board School	750	–	£1,048
Newcastle-on-Tyne	350	35	£917
Bradford School of Science and Art	322	6	£888
Anderson's University, Glasgow	1,376	47	£839
College of Science, Glasgow	900	52	£773
Allen Glen Institute, Glasgow	320	44	£759
Manchester Mechanics' Institute	700	42	£740
St Thomas's Charterhouse, London	500	9	£668
Belfast WMI	300	49	£557
Dublin Central Model School	100	0	£391
Sullivan Schools, Holywood	80	7	£173
St Malachy's College, Belfast	85	1	£122

In 1884 the total number of science schools in Ireland was 163, of which 91 were in Ulster. Irish science schools had a total of 4,619 students, and together earned £4,775 on results.[28]

In addition to DSA prizes, many of the Institute's students won scholarships, including those to Queen's College, which allowed them to achieve even greater distinction. In 1878, for example, R.H. Matthews won a Local Exhibition, worth £50, and proceeded to Queen's where he won a Science Scholarship and performed exceptionally well in his first year of studies – third place in Chemistry, third place in Experimental Physics, third place in Practical Chemistry, and fourth place in Anatomy.

There were many other examples of exceptional performance. In 1886 James Young, a working shoemaker from Ballymacarett, was placed third out of seven in the national competition for Royal Exhibitions, and in 1887, John Smith, a practising carpenter, gained third place out of twenty-five in the Whitworth Scholarship competition, and ninth place out of twelve in the National Scholarship competition. Smith, described as the only bona fide artisan in the latter competition, was the only candidate to succeed in both competitions: he won a total of £450 in scholarships.

The WMI's alumni had passed the 5,000 mark by 1890; many of them proceeded to distinguished careers.

The School of Applied Science and Engineering

With student numbers nearing 600 by 1885, the WMI's accommodation in Queen Street was stretched to the limit. This seemed to have been a particular problem for the mechanical engineering classes, which were organised and taught by William J. Fforde, an excellent teacher who, associated with Harland & Wolff, had joined the Institute in 1881. The 1884/5 prospectus described him as a Senior Mechanical Engineer and First-Class Honorman of the DSA. Clearly an enterprising gentleman, Fforde decided to resolve the accommodation issue by moving the relevant classes lock, stock and barrel to the Belfast Model School in Divis Street. There he was treated generously by the Commissioners of National Education who only charged for the heating and lighting of classrooms (£25 per annum). It is not clear whether Fforde's initiative received the whole-hearted blessing of Robert Barklie, but it is interesting to note that the WMI's annual reports for the period make no reference to such a move.

Fforde was promptly replaced at Queen Street by T.P. Rennoldson who was also associated with Harland & Wolff. But the gradual decline in Queen Street successes in City and Guild engineering examinations – only six in Mechanical Engineering in 1887 – suggests that competition from the Model School classes was beginning to have an effect. Factual evidence is elusive, but a contemporary observer reported that 'Mr Fforde's complete success followed.'[29] Some of that success can be inferred from the press report of the first prize-giving of 'Mr Fforde's Science and Technology Classes'. Held in St George's Hall on 30 January 1887, the ceremony attracted a considerable audience, including James Musgrave (Chairman), James Barbour, F.W. Smith, and Professor Fitzgerald.

Unfortunately the press report[30] of proceedings contained no statistical information. The annual report, read by the secretary George Wood, was considered
to be of 'a most satisfactory character'. Professor Fitzgerald noted the success
of the classes, and remarked that 'he knew of no classes of a similar character in
any country which approached in size those of Mr Fforde'.

The Model School evening classes in engineering became known as the
School of Applied Science and Engineering. Fforde was still active thirty years
later in Belfast's new Municipal Technical Institute.

Working with Industry

The industrialists of Belfast and its environs did not always adopt a benevolent attitude to technical education. Dr Porter, President of the Queen's
College, confronted them in his speech at the WMI's 1880 prize-giving ceremony:

> I have been glancing at the list of the Executive to see who the members
> of the Executive are. I find they consist of the leading merchants of Belfast.
> Well, I say, no thanks to the leading merchants of Belfast for taking an inter-
> est in this Institution, and the subjects which are taught in this Institution.
> If it were not for the advantage which they receive from this Institution and
> kindred centres of education they would be unable to carry out the work
> that they now carry on with such success ... Belfast has been successful,
> but to what does it owe its success? ... I say mainly – to the talent, to the
> learning, to the skill, to the industry, and to the perseverance of the working
> men.[31]

Dr Porter went on to implore employers to offer some form of recognition to
those employees who had pursued classes in technical education:

> But what I should like to see ... whenever any young man is studying here,
> and is able to obtain from this institution a certificate of merit – of having
> obtained honours – then I believe that in the merchants' offices in town, and
> in our great manufacturing establishments in town, such as the spinning mills
> and the great shipbuilding yards of Messrs Harland & Wolff, and other places;

and in such a great establishment as Dr Richie's, would it not be well if these young men would be received there on better terms than those who had not the same advantage on their side. Let some years be struck off their apprenticeship – let them have to serve only half time, or let them obtain higher salaries, because they are worthy of it.

There was a clear need for such recognition. Over the years many of the WMI's best students had been awarded exhibitions to allow them to continue advanced technical education in London – and many went on to achieve excellent results. However, this local talent was not being put to effective use at home:

> Not one of the total number of exhibitioners has obtained as the result of his collegiate or technical training employment in Belfast. One of the most distinguished ... was most anxious to devote his entire attention to the linen trade, could not get employment even at apprentice's wages ... is about to leave for a lucrative appointment in Spain. This shows how local talent and scientific and technical education is appreciated in Belfast.[32]

Investigations in 1883 by the Royal Commission on Technical Instruction (RCTI)[33] confirmed that many Belfast employers had little interest in technical instruction. A majority, indeed, were openly antagonistic to the concept: they saw no advantage in educating workers in the sciences underpinning their trades, and, in a *laissez faire* Society, they considered such an education as of greater benefit to the individual concerned than to the employer. In their view, all the knowledge workers needed could be gathered on the shop floor. In an age when science was making inroads to the production process, this was a dangerously short-sighted view.

That narrow view was compounded by management's attempt to maintain traditional hierarchies. For example, bleachers and dyers – in an industry where the new sciences were bringing about a revolution – were discouraged from attending classes in technical instruction because 'they are getting to know a great deal too much'.[34] Linen manufacturers were equally unreceptive. H. McCance, a local industrialist and examiner for the CGLI informed the RCTI that 'in 1882 out of sixty candidates for the examinations in linen manufacture there were none from Belfast'.[35] But W.Q. Ewart, a giant on the local industrial stage, appeared to be more concerned that 'all who were trained in the classes wish to be foremen or managers at once'.[36]

Foremen and managers guarded their positions and status jealously. Few, if any, attended classes at the WMI. Those who did seek enlightenment preferred to travel to Glasgow and other centres in Britain. Robert Barklie informed the RCTI that 'with one or two exceptions the managers have received no scientific training ... and have no scientific attainments ... and the foremen do not like to attend the same classes as apprentices in case they fail in the examinations'.

The Closing Years

The last two decades of the ninteenth century saw a steady decline in the fortunes of the WMI. Its effectiveness suffered a major blow when Robert Barklie resigned in 1883. Having established a reputation as an innovator and entrepreneur, it was no great surprise when Barklie succumbed to an offer to lead the Natural Science School of the Royal Belfast Academical Institution. He remained at RBAI until his retirement in 1894.[37]

Other factors impacted adversely on the viability of the WMI. The debt on the Queen Street building was an ongoing burden. Reduced to £2,000 by the proceeds of the 1876 exhibition, the Institute's management had been able to effect further reductions by setting aside small sums annually. By this means, the shortfall was reduced to £1,000 by the early 1890s, but a gradual falling off in public support at that time forced the Institute to devote practically all of its revenue to recurrent expenditure. The financial position improved marginally in 1891 when the City Council agreed to make a modest maintenance contribution to the various providers of technical education (see Chapter 8). The WMI's share of these monies amounted to a mere £75 in 1891, but the grant rose to £225 in 1894, and the Institute received a total of £2,000 in the decade 1891-1901. The School of Applied Science and Engineering received £725 over the same period.

The management committee decided, once again, to seek salvation through an exhibition. The Belfast Art and Industrial Exhibition opened on 11 April 1895. It was preceded by a great row about whether the visiting public should have access to alcoholic beverages. Held in the White Linen Hall, the Exhibition had twin objectives, 'the liquidation of a debt upon a building intended for the social improvement of the industrial class, and an effort for the development of the commerce and manufactures of that com-

In the courtyard of the White Linen Hall in the 1870s. (Lawrence Collection, National Library of Ireland.)

munity of which they form so important a part'.[38] The idea of using the White Linen Hall for the exhibition venue was attributed to W.J. Alderdice, the then President of the WMI. To be demolished three years later, the Linen Hall's buildings and grounds provided the ideal venue for such an event. With the engineer R.I. Calwell in charge, work on transforming the site began in December 1894.

The organisation of the Exhibition was the responsibility of an Executive Committee, chaired by the Lord Mayor, W. McCammond, and served in a secretarial capacity by the multi-talented Robert Barklie. Eight sub-committees shared the burden of planning the event: finance, art, mechanical, economic products, home industries, textile fabrics, natural history and antiquities, and entertainment. Together they arranged for 360 exhibits – a display dominated by Irish manufacturers, but including examples of products from Britain, the USA, the Continent, India and the colonies.

The Belfast Art and Industrial Exhibition turned out to be an impressive affair. It fulfilled the twin objectives of inspiring local manufacturers and alleviating the WMI's debts. However, the WMI was now facing pressures from other quarters. Social and industrial changes were rampant in Belfast, and other organisations were springing up in response to the associated needs. Many of them were in direct competition with the WMI,

> The fact is, the growth of the city is gnawing at the vitals of the institution. Kindred establishments are springing up on every hand, and the more successfully do they appeal for public support the more do they affect the membership of that institution, which in its early years had few such rivals to contend with. In recent years this has been particularly the case, and that it has been able to hold its own so well is creditable to its management and the manner in which its affairs are directed.[39]

The establishment of the Belfast Free Public Library in 1888 reduced substantially the number of visitors to the WMI's reading rooms. The classes run by the Belfast Technical School in Hastings Street, the Belfast Government School of Art, and the School of Applied Science and Engineering were offering alternative educational opportunities to the artisans of Belfast. The whole system of technical education was ripe for rationalisation.

6

A New Belfast
School of Art

Planning and Organising

The closure of the original School of Art in 1858 decimated the provision of art and design education in Belfast. Whilst the bare essentials of art education continued to be taught in the Drawing School of the Academical Institution, the lack of advanced provision was a matter of concern to some of the town's more enlightened and public-spirited individuals. William Gray, whose overall contribution to the education of Belfast's artisans was outstanding, voiced this concern in a letter to the press in 1868.[1] Under the heading of 'Science and Art in Belfast', he berated the town's existing intellectual associations for their ineffectiveness; the Belfast Natural History and Philosophical Society was severely criticised, and its museum was considered to be of little use as an educational facility. Gray, who had been associated with the original School of Art, went on to deplore the fact that Cork, Dublin, Waterford, and the relatively small town of Clonmel could all boast successful schools of art, whilst Belfast, Ireland's most successful industrial town, could not.

Gray's proposal for a new School of Art attracted a good deal of support. The whole-hearted backing of Francis Davis Ward, of Marcus Ward's, brought an early seal of approval from local industry, but the organisation and administration of the plans for the school were driven forward by two academics – John Carlisle, Principal of the Royal Belfast Academical Institution (RBAI), and Professor Wyville Thomson of Queen's College. Thomson sent a circular to all those considered to be interested in the topic, inviting them to a meeting in RBAI on 15 March 1870. There, with an audience which included Gray and the Mayor, Dr Sam Browne, it was agreed to establish a Provisional Committee to give further consideration to the proposal.

The Provisional Committee met in the RBAI on the 22 March when, with the Mayor in the Chair, the proposal to establish a School of Art was unanimously adopted. A sub-committee was delegated the tasks of clarifying the relevant regulations of the Department of Science and Art (DSA), and providing assurance that there would be no recurrence of the acrimonies gen-erated under the old Cole regime of fifteen years earlier. Members were also asked to visit existing schools of art in order to learn from their experiences. The sub-committee reported on 6 June that its investigations had satisfied members that the project was a viable one. The new DSA regulations reduced the amount of interference from London, and, whilst self support was still a requirement, the achievement of that happy status was considered to be well within the reach of the proposed school. The Provisional Committee's deci-sion to establish a School of Art was justified and confirmed. The objects of the new school were,

> ...to afford instruction to the artisan classes of Belfast and its neighbourhood
> in art, elementary and advanced, in all its branches, freehand and figure draw-
> ing and designing, architectural and mechanical drawing, painting in oil and
> water colours, and modelling ... and also to provide instruction in all such
> departments of art to the middle and higher classes, both male and female,
> under competent masters, at such hours and with such scale of fees as the
> Board of managers shall decide.[2]

Carlisle was the major author of the Constitution and Rules of the new organisation. A thirty-strong Board of Managers was elected, chaired in the first instance by J. Combe. Membership included three qualified engineers (CE) – Sir Charles Lanyon, W.H. Lynn and R. Young; industrialists such as E.J. Harland, V. Coates, and Sir James Musgrave; educators like Vere Foster, Professor Thomson and J. Carlisle; and public entrepreneurs such as William Gray.

The old School of Art had found it hard to make ends meet, so the Board of the new Belfast Government School of Art (BGSA) was particularly anxious that those days of worry and penury would not be revisited. Public responses to pleas for support were extremely encouraging. The Board decided to accom-modate the new school in the original buildings at RBAI, where the old school's collection of casts and sculptures, and its art and design library still remained. A lease of seven years at £80 per annum was agreed with RBAI, but this was later changed to thirty years at £100 per annum.[3] William Dunville, the distiller, generously agreed to cover this expenditure in its entirety from the Sorella Trust, a charitable trust founded in memory of his sister Sarah. Another example of public largesse was Vere Foster's guarantee of the headmaster's salary for the first two years. Contributions of a similar size and nature might well have saved the original school.

A building grant of £300 from the DSA contributed to the alteration and fitting out of eight rooms in the RBAI's north wing. In addition, the DSA was able to provide relevant equipment at one quarter of cost. Those sums were complemented by donations and annual subscriptions which, including the Dunville contribution, amounted to more than £700. Of the donations, the two largest – £100 each - came from J. Charters and J. Ward (a director of Marcus Ward). The Board was particularly encouraged by generous responses from industry; for example, the Northern Spinning Company, John S. Brown, Richardson Brothers, and Combe and Company each donated £25. These one-off donations, which totalled £587, were supported by ongoing annual subscriptions of some £208.

Teachers were an essential resource. The headmaster, Thomas Mitchener Lindsay, was appointed in the autumn of 1870. Highly recommended by the DSA, Mitchener provided an excellent service to the BGSA before resigning in 1880 to take up a post as art master at Rugby School.

Getting Down to Work

When the BGSA opened on 17 October 1870, the Headmaster's inaugural address indicated that, whilst all classes of Society would be served, the school would devote particular attention to the needs of artisans:

> We especially invite the cunning artificer in brass and iron; we shall be disappointed if we do not meet the young mason, cabinetmaker, upholsterer, joiner, carver, and gilder, housepainter, and decorator in our classes; we have no hesitation in saying that we can impart instruction of practical value to the operative, no matter what the craft by which he earns his daily bread.[4]

Artwork from the front page of the 1881–82 Annual Report of the Belfast Government School of Art.

That emphasis was not evident, however, in the first published timetable of classes, where artisan classes found themselves at the bottom of the list.[5]

Morning Classes for Ladies
Tuesday, Friday: 1p.m. to 3p.m.
Terms: £1 5s per quarter

Morning Classes for Gentlemen
Tuesday, Thursday, Friday: 9a.m. to 11a.m.
Terms: £1 5s per quarter

Special Classes for Schoolgirls
Tuesday, Thursday, Friday: 8.45 to 9.45a.m, or 3.15 to 4.15p.m.
Terms: 12s 6d per quarter

Special Classes for Schoolboys
Tuesday, Thursday, Friday: 8.45 to 9.45a.m. or 3 to 4p.m.
Terms: 12s 6d per quarter

Artisan/Public Evening Classes
Tuesday, Wednesday, Thursday, Friday: 7.30 to 9.30p.m.
Terms: 6s 6d per quarter, or 2s 6d per month for Elementary Classes; 10s 6d per quarter for Advanced and Special Classes.

(The teaching year was divided into four terms, or quarters.)

The school's curriculum was largely dictated by the examination requirements of the DSA in South Kensington. It initially fell into three categories:
Elementary, Advanced, and Special.[6]

ELEMENTARY: Freehand and model drawing; shading from copies; practical
geometry, and linear perspective.

ADVANCED: Drawing and painting the figure, flowers, landscapes, ornament,
etc., from copies and from nature; drawing and shading from the antique;
systematic instruction in the principles of ornamental design, and illuminat-
ing.

SPECIAL: Orthographic projection; engineering and machine drawing; building and construction; architectural drawing; the projection of shadows, and
modelling.

The breadth of instruction is evident in the list of examinations for 1900:[7]

Geometry
Geometrical Drawing
Principles of Ornament
Perspective
Painting Still Life
Freehand Drawing (Adv)
Light and Shade
Advanced Model Drawing
Machine Construction
Drawing from Life
Drawing Antique from Memory
Architecture

Design
Historic Ornament
Painting Ornament
Anatomy
Building Construction
Architectural Design
Modelling Design
Casting Models
Modelling from Life
Modelling Antique
Drawing Antique

Polytechnic Aspirations

From the outset, the curriculum of the new school demonstrated the Board's determination to extend its influence beyond the confines of fine and decorative arts. In fact, the Board attempted to establish a polytechnic institution where the teaching of both applied science and arts would be of great benefit to local industry, and would at the same time help to shape and raise the profile of technical education in Belfast.

To that end DSA classes in Practical, Plane and Solid Geometry, Machine Drawing, and Building Construction were included as ongoing components of the School's portfolio. In 1876 reference was made to the 'decided increase in the awards given for scientific drawing and machine and building construction, subjects so essential for the technical education of artisans'.[8] Headmaster George Trobridge, who replaced Lindsay in 1880, took every opportunity to promote these applied science classes, and to explain the BGSA's breadth of provision:

> Engineers, fitters, mechanics, etc., are instructed in machine drawing and construction, the principles of plane and solid geometry and practical mechanics. Carpenters, joiners, bricklayers, and others engaged in the building trade may learn the principles and details of building construction, the nature and strength of materials, and architectural drawing and design. House-painters, decorators, etc., are taught the principles of decoration, design, colour, harmony, etc. Wood and stone carvers, plasterers, die-sinkers, and others are instructed in modelling, moulding, and casting in plaster. Designers, damask weavers, etc., are taught the principles and practice of ornamental design as applied to various manufactures.[9]

The BGSA wanted its classes to demonstrate and use the relationships between theory and practice. Curriculum design helped to meet that objective, but the recruitment of practising artists and engineers as lecturers was an important factor. For example, in 1875 an expert from the Falls Foundry was used to teach drawing with the object of 'affording to the students instruction in the practical, as well as the purely theoretical aspects of the subject'.[10]

These interactions with the world of industry continued throughout the school's lifetime.

Relationships with the Hastings Street Technical School (See Chapter 7) were cordial, especially in that BGSA's early years. The 1883 annual report described the advantages of collaboration; the Board of Managers was pleased to learn:

> …from the syllabus of the new school, that particular attention will be given to the weaving of the more fancy fabrics, necessarily involving a more intimate acquaintance with the principles of design as applied to textile industries. On this ground the Board feel that the Technical School and the School of Art will be of mutual advantage to each other – the former affording to students of the School of Art the means of acquiring that technical knowledge which is absolutely necessary to enabling them to produce designs which can be practically carried out; while, on the other hand, pupils of the Technical School have at the School of Art the requisite facilities for obtaining a knowledge of drawing and artistic design.[11]

The Belfast Technical School reciprocated those sentiments in its very first annual report in 1884. In order to reinforce the relationship between the two organisations, the Board of the BGSA agreed in 1885 to appoint two new staff to develop the teaching of applied textile design. Unfortunately student numbers did not increase sufficiently to justify that particular development; Trobridge blamed the failure on 'competition of other classes in which the same subjects are taught at merely nominal fee'.[12] The other classes referred to were probably those provided at the Working Men's Institute – a worthy institution that received not a single reference in the pages of the BGSA's annual reports.

Another gesture favouring co-operation rather than competition was the Board's decision to admit students from the Technical School to its classes on any two evenings at half the usual fee. Unfortunately the archives do not provide sufficient evidence to permit an assessment of the success or otherwise of the arrangement. However, the general recognition of the advantages of collaboration helped to pave the way towards the establishment of the Belfast Municipal Technical Institute.

Those attempts to expand the science side of the BGSA's portfolio bore little fruit and it remained a minor component of the school's overall provision. This attracted criticism from the Lord Mayor, W.J. Pirrie, when he distributed the prizes in 1896. Pirrie, having progressed rapidly from an apprenticeship in Harland & Wolff to the Chairmanship of its Board, was clearly in a strong position to voice an authoritative opinion about technical education. He was concerned about its lack of progress in Belfast:

> Technical Education, as understood by many people in this city, was very different from that carried out so successfully on the Continent. They must never attach more importance to what was learned in the School than to the experience gained in the workshop. A good many persons seemed to think that Technical Education had to do with the cultivation of taste in the designing of textile fabrics, decorative materials, tapestries, wallpaper, etc., rather than the acquisition of mechanical skill in the iron and wood trades and engineering. It would be a great advantage when those who held different views upon that subject were able to agree upon a scheme that would be generally satisfactory to all.[13]

Pirrie's remarks were particularly germane at a time when the City Council's attention was being directed towards the establishment of a new Technical Institute for the city.

Interacting with the Community

The BGSA worked hard to convince manufacturers that they would reap benefits if their employees attended evening classes. A major success was achieved in 1874 when a group of influential industrialists agreed to sign the following circular:

> The undersigned manufacturers and merchants desire to express their opinion that a knowledge of drawing is desirable in all who have to do with the manufacture, as well as with the buying and selling, of goods of an ornamental character. For this reason, where persons who, in other respects, are equally suitable, apply to us for employment, with a view of becoming designers, heads of departments, drawing clerks, travellers, foreign agents, salesmen, buyers, etc., we will give a preference to those who have a knowledge of drawing.[14]

In acknowledgement of that support, Lindsay did his utmost to supply employers with appropriately qualified individuals. In 1878 he described how the School was able to help good practical men, with knowledge of building construction and drawing, to achieve positions of trust as foremen and clerks of work.[15] By 1879 he was able to describe the School as 'a sort of Registry office for art workmen'.[16] George Trobridge, who succeeded Lindsay in 1880, took this service even further; in 1882 he had been successful in 'finding means of employment for persons afflicted with maladies which debar them from ordinary occupations'.[17]

Exhibitions provided another mechanism for interacting with the community. Some of these were supported by the DSA. Examples of Indian textiles were lent to the School in 1882, but, displayed in the cramped confines of a classroom, they were not able to make their full impact on students and the public. In the following year the DSA helped Belfast to host a display of prize-winning drawings from the national competition. In that year, there were 1,313 entries to the competition – a distillation of an initial submission of no fewer than 214,182 drawings from 182 schools across the UK. The Belfast display included 350 pieces, but once more, the lack of its own art gallery forced the School Board to use the gymnasium of the RBAI which was an unsatisfactory alternative venue. The press gave particular praise to the local winners: R.Q. Lane's design for a wrought-iron gate, which won a Gold Medal, and his design of a balcony, which won a silver medal, received particular attention. So too did a selection of prize-winning displays of drawings of flowers and still-life groups by the ladies.[18] The Board was happy to report that the exhibition would 'undoubtedly have a beneficial effect, as it brought the Belfast School of Art more prominently before the public'.[19]

The School also took full advantage of the various local exhibitions, including an industrial exhibition in the Ulster Hall in 1876 and a grand event celebrating the 1888 opening of the art gallery and museum in the new Free Library.

Relationships with schools also helped to extend the BGSA's influence in the community. The provision of appropriate classes, both within the School itself and at various schools in the locality, did much to further the development of art education. Classes were also provided for the training of teachers. These could lead to the award of the DSA's Art Masters' Certificates and Art Class Teachers' Certificates, the former entitling their holders to take charge of a School of Art.

Students

The student body fell into three major categories: those attending during the evening, those attending during the day, and those attending affiliated (branch) schools. The numbers in these classes are shown below.

Evening classes, at elementary and advanced levels, were held on Wednesday, Thursday and Friday evenings from 7.30 until 9.30p.m. They were attended, on the whole, by employed persons who wanted to devote their leisure time to personal advancement. The following list shows that for the year 1873/74, that not all evening students could be classified as artisans (i.e. craftsmen or apprentices).[20]

Clerks, 23
Bookkeepers, 3
Plasterers, 2
RIC, 1
Carpenters/Joiners, 13
Druggists, 3
Shopmen, 2
Statuaries, 1
Painters, 12
Errand Boys, 3
Brassfounders, 2
Sextons, 1
Teachers, 11
Fitters, 3
Builders, 2
Shipbuilders, 1
Mechanics, 9
Warehousemen, 3
Engravers, 2
Shoemakers, 1
Architects' Pupils, 8
Publicans, 3

Agents, 1
Taxidermists, 1
Mill Managers, 7
Cabinet-makers, 2
Customs, 1
Telegraphists, 1
Designers' Apprentices, 6
Designers, 2
Flaxdressers, 1
Upholsterers, 1
Linen Trade, 6
Drapers, 2
Farmers, 1
Woodcarvers, 1
Lithographers, 6
Engineers, 2
Blacksmiths, 1
Bricklayers, 1
Draughtsmen 5
Gardeners, 2
Blockprinters, 1
Plumbers, 1

Lithographic Writers, 5	Ironmongers, 1
Grocers, 2	Stonemasons, 4
Printers, 1	Housekeepers, 2
Photographers, 1	Jewellers, 1
Ministers, 4	
Hatters, 2	TOTAL 184

Of these 184 evening students, only 100 could truly be described as artisans, and in the following year, of a total of 206 evening students, only around 126 could be so classified.[21] These relatively small numbers were hardly representative of the needs of Ireland's major manufacturing town, where the population was rapidly approaching the 200,000 mark. Regretting the lack of interest by artisans in 1879, James Musgrave, the Chairman of the Board, gave an interesting explanation, 'I think much harm has been done by calling Drawing an accomplishment, because working men are apt to class it along with music and dancing.'[22]

Artisan classes were always high on the BGSA's list of priorities, and the chart overleaf shows that the effort expended in maintaining the related evening classes produced positive results. Several marketing devices were deployed over the years, including:

Obtaining the agreement of employers in 1874 to give preference to those qualified in drawing (see earlier).

Allowing the school's donors and subscribers to nominate free pupils to the artisan classes. Those donating more than £25 were able, for every £25, to nominate one free pupil; those subscribing more than £5 annually were able, for every £5, to nominate one free pupil. There is no record of the take-up of those privileges, but their existence reaffirmed the school's commitment to its artisan students.

Requesting employers to encourage their workers to attend the classes bore some fruit. In 1882, for example, a flyer describing the various classes was circulated to employers with a request that they distribute it amongst their employees.

The figure on page 128 shows that the number of evening students reached its first peak (342) in 1884. In fact, the school had great difficulty in accom-

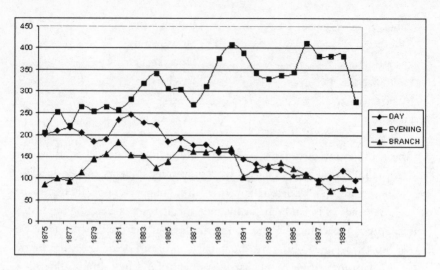

Student numbers in the School of Art, 1875–1901.

modating these numbers, but the generosity of RBAI in allowing the use of the rooms of the Preparatory School saved the day. A period of industrial depression brought numbers down post-1884, but they recovered in 1888, reaching an all-time high of 411 in 1896.

The numbers attending day classes did not fluctuate as wildly as those in evening classes. Gentlemen attended day classes on Tuesday, Thursday and Friday mornings, and ladies on Thursday and Friday afternoons. Provision was made for schoolboys and girls on Tuesdays, Thursdays and Fridays. The number of day students matched those of evening students in the early 1870s, but by the end of the century evening students had grown to outnumber day students by a factor of four. Annual reports show that day classes were dominated by schoolchildren; in 1874, for example, there were 81 adult students in attendance, and 151 schoolchildren. However, the gap in numbers had reduced by 1876 when there were 93 adults and 116 schoolchildren attending day classes. Thereafter, the published statistics do not distinguish between children and adults. It is likely that pupils from the RBAI formed the large majority of schoolchildren at day classes.

Changes in the curriculum of intermediate schools in 1878 held promise of increased attendance by schoolchildren and aspiring school teachers. The Intermediate Education Act had included Drawing amongst the list of examination subjects. Junior candidates (under sixteen years of age) had to take Freehand Drawing, and Practical Geometry; middle-grade candidates (under seventeen) had to take advanced Freehand Drawing, and Practical Perspective;

and seniors (under eighteen) had to take drawing from nature and casts, as well as solid geometry or principles of plans, sections and elevations.[23] The BGSA seemed well placed to provide the necessary instruction, but, in the event, the students did not materialise, and Headmaster Trobridge was regretting in 1881 that the number of schoolchildren was small compared to earlier years. He attributed the decrease to 'the increasing pressure of ordinary school studies; which leaves no time for drawing'. However, substantial contact was maintained with local schools through affiliation arrangements.

Day classes for ladies and gentlemen attracted around 100 students annually throughout the School's lifetime and, at 25s per term, they brought a steady and welcome source of income. There is a shortage of statistics that differentiate male and female students, but early annual reports would indicate that females were the dominant gender in the day classes. In 1874, 62 women and 19 men attended the day classes; in the succeeding two years the figures were 64 and 13, and 79 and 14. Examination results (discussed later) indicate that the numbers of girls and women remained at a substantial level throughout the School's lifetime. They fulfilled an important social function and improved the corporate spirit within the institution.[24] Their influence on the School's ethos far exceeded their numbers. The Ladies' Sketching Club was one of the more popular and effective of the several student societies that sprang up over the years. Concerned with the study of landscape and nature, the club provided an opportunity for exchange of views on art – and on other issues. Evening students set up a similar club in 1875, but both clubs amalgamated in 1882 to form the Sketching Club.[25]

The ladies also provided an indirect spur to the artisan classes:

> The necessity for an increased knowledge of art and improved taste on the part of handicraftsmen must be admitted, when it is found that the upper and middle classes generally throughout the country are becoming more disposed to enter upon the study of such subjects; and the increasing attendance at our own Day Classes would indicate that we are participating in this movement. With the elevation of the taste of the richer portion of the community, who are the purchasers of the higher class of manufactures, articles of a more artistic character will be demanded...[26]

Overall numbers were boosted considerably by students at branch schools. The managers of the BGSA soon realised that there was much to be gained from close collaboration with local schools. As described above, this was achieved to a considerable extent through schoolchildren attending the School's day classes. However, where a school had relatively large numbers of pupils interested in art, it was considered better to take Mohammed to the mountain. Two such mountains were the Methodist College and the Ladies' Collegiate School (Victoria College from 1887). Annual reports also refer fleetingly to branch classes at the Deaf and Dumb Institution[27], and at the Mount Prospect School.[28] The Board of Managers was attracted by the idea of extending the BGSA's influence through affiliation. Indeed some members wanted that influence to extend beyond the boundaries of Belfast: as early as 1877 William Gray had remarked that, 'If they had funds at their disposal they would establish affiliated schools at Lurgan, Portadown, Banbridge, Ballymena and elsewhere.'[29]

The Headmaster and his assistants conducted branch classes in the various affiliated schools on Mondays and Wednesdays at a fee of 12*s* 6*d* per pupil per term. The earlier figure shows that early numbers were well in excess of 100, and, whilst declining from 1887 onwards, they continued to match the attendance at the School's day classes. Many pupils at these branch classes entered for DSA examinations, with freehand drawing, model drawing, and geometrical drawing particularly popular.

The classes at the Methodist College and at the Deaf and Dumb Institution ceased in 1890 when both organisations decided to appoint their own art teachers. The resultant loss of students was offset to some extent by a short-lived affiliation with the Mount Prospect School in 1893, and by increased numbers of girls at Victoria College.

Measures of Performance

Examinations passed and prizes won were the two major measures of success. Candidates across the UK took the same tests organised by the Department of Science and Art (DSA). Elementary examinations were conducted at the various provincial centres, but advanced examinations were initially held at the Royal College of Art in South Kensington, and at the Metropolitan School of Art in Dublin. That arrangement was revised in 1884 when local centres were allowed to host the advanced tests as well as the elementary ones. Members of local committees were required to supervise the examinations, which were

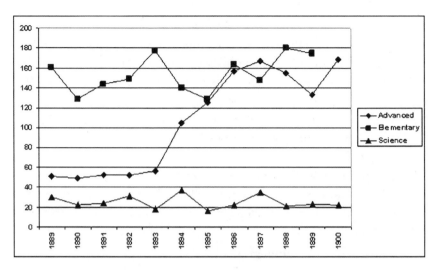

Passes in the examinations of the Department of Science and Art, 1888-1901.

held in May, sometimes spilling over into April and June. The time available varied from subject to subject;[30] in 1900, for example, of thirty-five examinations in twenty-five subjects, the test for Drawing Antique from Memory was allocated 1¼ hours, that for Building Construction 4¼ hours, and that for Casting Models 8¼ hours.

The above figure charts the School's examination successes in elementary and advanced art examinations, and in science examinations from 1889 until 1900. Note that elementary examinations were discontinued in 1899. The relatively large numbers of schoolchildren on the rolls, whilst good news in some respects, tended to impede the BGSA's aspirations to provide advanced work. The School had to wait until 1884 before the pool of students qualified at elementary level had grown large enough to make advanced classes viable. From 1886 onwards, the numbers of elementary and advanced successes more or less matched.

The statistics confirm that, despite much effort and many good intentions, passes in science-related subjects remained low throughout the school's lifetime. However, small numbers of examination successes do not necessarily imply small class sizes – many students attended but did not sit the examinations. It has been estimated that 100 students were attending these classes in 1900.[31]

The considerable impact made by the School's female students has been mentioned. This was evident also in examination statistics. In the 1898 examinations, for example, eighty of the 180 successful candidates at elementary level were women (including twenty-eight schoolgirls from Victoria College). Freehand Drawing was, by far, the most popular choice for women at elementary level, with forty-two women out of a total of eighty-five passing the subject. Female representation at advanced level was less than at elementary level – thirty-seven out of a total of 155. Here the women restricted themselves to only three of the subjects – Outline from Cast, Shading from Models, and Shading from Cast.[32]

Some examination performances were outstanding. In 1895, for example, all forty Belfast candidates for the advanced examination in Shading from Cast passed, thirty-one of them obtaining first-class passes.[33] And at elementary level in the same subject there was a 90 per cent success rate. These success rates have to be compared with the overall UK rates of 68 per cent and 53 per cent respectively.

The relative abilities of the BGSA's students can also be assessed from the numbers of prizes and awards gained in national competitions. In addition to the above-mentioned tests, the best works of the School's advanced students were entered every April for the South Kensington prize competitions. In 1873, for example, no fewer than 1,658 works by 296 Belfast students were forwarded to London. There, a rigorous selection process distilled these to a more manageable fifty-seven, one of which ultimately gained a gold medal, with four receiving bronze medals, and eight Queen's Prizes. But increasing competition from a growing number of schools of art, cramped conditions and lack of resources took their toll; only eleven medals and prizes were earned in the nine years 1889 to 1897. However, the last four years of the School's existence were particularly productive in this respect. Between 1898 and 1901, the local students gained forty-nine medals and prizes in national competition. One prize merits particular mention; S.R. Bolton won a Queen's Prize (see illustration overleaf) in 1898 for high marks in the elementary stage of the examination in Practical Design; he was first amongst 1,903 entries.[34]

National prizes were awarded for submitted works or for examination successes in individual subjects. The award of National Scholarships and Studentships, on the other hand, took into account both submitted works and overall performance in examinations. National Scholarships were the most prestigious awards, providing their recipients with free tuition for three years at the Royal College of Art, along with subsistence grants of £52 10s per annum. Belfast students attracted no fewer than twenty-five of these scholarships over the years – four of them in the year ending 1898. Local Scholarships were also held in high esteem; they provided free tuition for three years at the successful candidate's home school, along with a subsistence grant of £20 per annum. The Free Studentship was the most modest of the three types of national scholarship awards. It provided free tuition at the home school, but there were no subsistence payments. Belfast attracted fifty-one of these studentships over its last ten years in operation.

National scholarships and prizes spurred the Belfast students on to greater things. They were further motivated by a local prize scheme which was introduced in 1871, 'to induce the pupils to apply themselves heartily to the prescribed course of training necessary to attain a knowledge of the Arts of Drawing and Design, and to encourage them in those habits of industry without which the best abilities are often valueless'.[35] Funded by local benefactors,

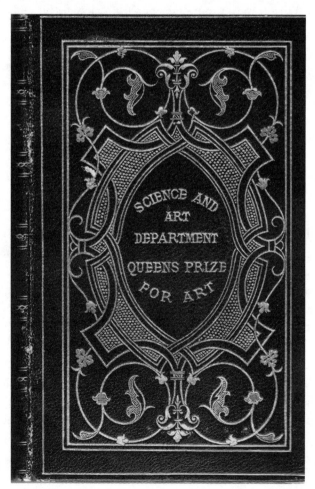

A Queen's Prize,
Department of Science
and Art, 1885.

prizes ranged typically from 10s to 2 guineas. Candidates, whose works were assessed by the Board's Prize Committee, were only permitted entry to the competition if they had 'a fair average attendance, and satisfactory conduct ... for the previous six months'.

The local competition placed considerable emphasis on applied design. In 1871 twelve of the thirty prizes were design-orientated, including prizes for damask designs, for printed goods, for embroideries, and for linen ornaments. There was also a prize for the design of an engraved silver card case. Annual reports show that that emphasis on design was maintained over the years, but the absence of prizes for applied subjects, like building construction, is noteworthy.

Not everyone thought highly of the local prize competition. William Gray felt that it was a major distraction from more useful studies:

> ...it had a pernicious effect when it only encouraged the student's pot-hunting or prize-hunting zeal, and limited the scope of his studies to the special requirements of the local manufacturer offering the prizes, whose standard of excellence is cheap production and quick sale...[36]

The Unending Quest for Resources

Lack of resources had brought the original School of Art to its knees, so the new Board was especially vigilant in financial matters. Income to cover recurrent expenditure like salaries and materials was derived from four sources; fees, annual subscriptions, payments-on-results from the DSA and, over the last ten years of the School's life, contributions from the Corporation. The figure on the next page shows how these amounts varied from 1884 until 1900.

Two compensating trends emerge from these statistics: (a) declining income from fees, and (b) rising income from payments on results. The figure helps to explain the first of these trends. Between 1882 and 1899, the number of students at evening classes increased by around 100, whilst those attending day classes fell by some 150. Since the latter classes attracted substantially higher fees than the former, these movements would have resulted in an overall reduction in fee income. The compensating upward drift in income from payments on results had two underlying causes: (a) increasing numbers of passes, and (b) a growing

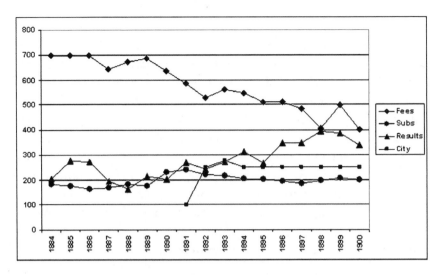

The annual income of the School of Art, 1884-1901.

amount of advanced work from 1883 onwards.

Of the other two income components, annual subscriptions provided welcome and steady amounts around the £200 mark during the School's lifetime, and finally, contributions from a reluctant Corporation commenced in 1881 after an intense period of pressure from the Board, supported by Belfast's other providers of technical education.

The BGSA also attracted one-off donations, which went to ear-marked purposes such as local prizes or were added to the reserve fund. But this was a dwindling feast. Starting at more than £700 in the School's first year, donations had fallen to £62 in 1899. This discouraging trend was interrupted in 1881 by a bequest of £500 from Michael Fitzpatrick, a decorative artist, some of whose work can still be seen displayed on the front of McCausland's Hotel in Belfast's Victoria Street. However, lack of support from Belfast's citizens attracted a degree of criticism, some of it outspoken. W.J. Gilliland, a subscriber, vented his spleen at the annual meeting in 1897, 'There was something wrong in this school when it had not progressed, and a remedy could only be found by those who were influential in such matters putting their shoulders to the wheel and striving to step forward.'[37]

The ongoing small differences between income and expenditure left little opportunity for new developments. Like their counterparts in the original School of Art, the teaching staff were continually complaining about the lack of a suitable art gallery where the best examples of the students' work could be exhibited alongside collections illustrating the application of art to local industries, and perhaps, alongside loans from the National Museum at South Kensington. But funds were not available for such a gallery. Some relief, however, was provided when Belfast's new Free Library permitted the School's students to use its art gallery and museum in 1890.

As the years passed, the Board, staff and students became increasingly disenchanted with the building in College Square North. It was too small, especially for the growing numbers of evening students, and it was in need of decoration and repair. Some effort was made to improve matters in 1896, 'During the last year, the school has been painted, new incandescent gas lamps have been put in the Design Room and Sculpture Room, and new tables for the use of Students of Design.'[38]

In spite of that face lift, the Chairman went on to say how pleased he was that they were meeting that evening in the new Free Library and not in that 'dingy and dreary wilderness in College Square North'. The Board had given consideration to the possibility of constructing a new purpose-built building on the RBAI grounds, but, once again, financial realities were a block to progress. Matters were coming to a head: there was clear need for a major overhaul of Belfast's overall approach to technical education.

As the end of the nineteenth century approached, the Belfast Government School of Art could claim a number of successes. Whilst the number of students always seemed too small for a growing city like Belfast, their performance in national examinations and competitions showed that their abilities, and the quality of their education and training could match, if not exceed, those in other parts of the UK.

Unlike the preceding School of Art, funding, though never sufficiently generous and was always just enough to keep heads above water. The Board could not claim success in fundraising, however, and most members, many of them immensely rich and extremely influential, made little personal contribution either in cash or kind. The Board seemed to be at its strongest when badgering the Corporation for funds.

On the whole, the Board was an ineffective body – surprising when one notes the number of very distinguished members. But many Board members were poor attenders, and rarely put their shoulder to the wheel. In 1883/1884, for example, the annual report showed that only three members had appeared at more than half of the meetings. Indeed, the record shows that several local dignitaries had not put in a single appearance *viz*. James Henderson, E.J. Harland, Sir John Preston, C.H. Brett and J. Workman. On the whole, the burden of governance fell upon the professionals and the middling ranks. William Gray was a particularly assiduous member; he, along with Sir James Musgrave, John Vinycomb and Robert Young served on the Board throughout its lifetime.

The Board's ineffectiveness was demonstrated in other areas. For example, it was unable to convince local employers of the value of education and training – surprising when many board members were themselves local employers. That failure was a major factor in the School's continuing inability to extend its work beyond the confines of the fine and decorative arts. Science classes attracted relatively few pupils, and attempts to improve the situation through collaboration with the Hastings Street Technical School proved a failure. It is surprising that the School appears to have ignored entirely the existence of the Working Men's Institute, which was itself very active in this area.

Despite those weaknesses, the BGSA was in a relatively strong negotiating position as it prepared itself for a role in the city's new scheme of technical instruction. Whilst some shortcomings had been exposed, the Corporation's new scheme of technical instruction would provide ample opportunity for their correction.

7

The Belfast Technical School

Making the Case for a Technical School

The Working Men's Institute's contribution to technical education in Belfast in the late nineteenth century has already been described. However, whilst that Institute had run some classes on textile-related subjects, there was a groundswell of opinion from the textile industry that more had to be done to meet its specific needs. The industry was facing difficult times. With some 90,000 employees in the mid-decades of the nineteenth century, textiles had formed the dominant core of Belfast's manufacturing industries at the time. But foreign tariffs, changing fashions, and, most significantly, foreign competition, had conspired to reduce the industry's share of the market. The first signs of decline were evident at the Paris Exhibition of 1867 when Belfast's textiles attracted less admiration and awards than expected. The situation was to deteriorate further: the export of linen yarns dropped from £37 million in 1869 to £16.5 million in 1880, and this over a period when the number of spindles was growing rapidly and the number of power looms had practically doubled.

The Royal Commission on Technical Instruction (RCTI) highlighted these various concerns. After their visit to Belfast in 1883, the Commissioners concluded that,[1]

It is generally admitted that … the Belfast industry is not so advanced as that of France or Belgium. Even in the higher class of damasks, the Irish production is hardly holding its own, while in fancy and coloured goods, where a knowledge of design and of the chemistry of dyeing come most into play, the superior attractiveness of many Continental productions is placing the Belfast makers at a serious disadvantage, especially in large markets like America where the Irish goods once enjoyed almost a monopoly.

It was clear that the relevant technologies were not being used to good effect, and marketing was not up to scratch. New products to meet new fashions were needed; and they had to be produced efficiently. In their quest for improvement, managers began to take a more enlightened view of technical education. How else were they and their employees to get to grips with the latest technologies and their underpinning sciences? Foreign competitors clearly appreciated the need for technical education; in 1877 the Clothworkers' Company reported that there were forty weaving technical schools in France, Germany and Austria, with others about to be opened in Munich and Zurich.[2] And other major textile-producing parts of the United Kingdom had already taken action. Technical schools, focusing on weaving and dyeing, had been established in Glasgow and Bradford in 1877, and Leeds, Huddersfield, Keighley, and Sheffield followed suit in 1881. All without support from the Government.

However, some of the more influential employers were still not convinced that technical education was the answer to their problems. Many of them were scientific philistines: Robert Barklie informed the Royal Commission that 'you could hardly find in the Belfast linen trade, commencing with the master and coming down to the humblest working men, a man who possesses anything like an accurate knowledge of the scientific principles of the trade in which he is engaged'.[3] Called before the RCTI in June 1883, Sir John Preston denied that there was any advantage to be gained from technical instruction. He blamed the workers for the falling markets; foreign workers put in a seventy-six hour week, but the recent Factory Act ensured that his own employees could only clock up fifty-six hours a week. When asked if he thought that Continental working people had a superior education to their British counterparts, he replied, 'I am not aware that they are better educated. I have said already that they are industrious, sober, and frugal, and attentive to their work; they do what they are told. And there are no strikes, and I think that that is of vast advantage to them.'[4]

A later section will show that Preston's response to the RCTI was somewhat at odds with the enthusiasm he had expressed the previous year, for the establishment of a technical school tailored to the needs of the Belfast linen trade.

The idea for such a school had been triggered by J. Loewenthal, President of the Belfast Linen Merchants' Association (BLMA), who wrote to W.H. Ward, the Secretary of the Association on the matter in June 1881. Following lengthy discussion within the BLMA it was decided that a deputation should raise the matter with the Belfast Chamber of Commerce (BCOC). The deputation met the Council at its quarterly meeting on 11 August 1881. The trade crisis, and the need for appropriate technical education were explained, and it was noted that, whilst the design work at the Belfast Government School of Art was valuable, there was a need for instruction in ways of converting the designs into saleable products. The Chamber resolved that, 'the establishment of a technical school for Belfast was most desirable for the purpose of enabling the manufacturing industries of the North of Ireland to keep pace with the advance in skill and science being made in foreign countries'.[5]

Thus encouraged, the promoters of the scheme gave further thought to its detailed operation. Interested people were invited to a meeting in the BCOC on 12 January 1882, when a Provisional Committee of influential businessmen was set up. Sir James Corry MP and James Musgrave were elected as Chairman of the General Committee and Chairman of the Executive Committee respectively.

F.W. Smith, proprietor of the *Irish Textile Journal*, played an important role. Appointed Secretary to the Provisional Committee, he was authorised to visit leading technical schools in Britain and to report back. In the event he visited schools in Bradford, Glasgow, Huddersfield, Keighley and Leeds. His report identified technical schools as a critical means of regenerating local industry, 'Apart from the benefits which the establishment of technical schools would confer on the linen trade in its several branches, the prospect of the foundation of other textile industries being laid and successfully carried on, is in itself a very tempting inducement to take up the matter here.'[6]

This further encouragement persuaded the Provisional Committee to place the matter before the public. An inaugural public meeting was held in the BCOC on 15 December 1882. The audience received a paper describing Smith's visits to other textile centres, and his recommendations that a technical school should be set up in Belfast.[7] The need for such a facility was confirmed in a letter from P. Haynes, an examiner for the City and Guilds of London Institute (CGLI), who reported that ten candidates from Belfast had been awarded certificates in mechanical engineering, tools, and telegraphy at the last examination, but none had obtained certificates related to textile manufacture. Several speakers supported the proposal, including W. Ewart who felt that 'the report speaks of the weaving school as a beginning, but no time should be lost in adding other branches, such as engineering, bleaching, dyeing…'

The euphoria of the occasion was dampened somewhat by the testy William Gray, who reminded the audience that much of the work described was already being carried out in Belfast 'in schools which were deserving of their support, but which (like the Working Men's Institute) were allowed to remain in debt'. His intervention generated much heat and a rebuke from the Vice-chairman that he was 'endeavouring to thwart us in the attainment of the object for which the meeting had been called'. But Gray's comments had touched a sensitive spot, and later in the meeting Sir John Preston (who was to adopt a different stance before the RCTI the following year) thought it wise to clarify the matter:

> …the proposed institution would not in the slightest interfere with the schools now in progress, and in themselves no doubt doing good work. The technical school which was about to be established would be altogether different to any of those Mr Gray had referred to, and it would be carried on in a way that would not possibly interfere with other educational interests.

Robert Barklie, the manager of the Working Men's Institute, could see which way the wind was blowing and decided to side with Preston rather than Gray. He repudiated any suggestion that his Institute was opposed to the proposed technical school. He claimed, in fact, that the idea of such a school had first been advocated from the platform of his institute. Unlike Preston, Barklie maintained a consistent stance when he met the RCTI the following year; he agreed that the science classes at the institute could form a foundation on which a thoroughly equipped technical school might be laid.

Gray himself accepted the rebuff graciously. In later years he wrote, 'Difference of opinion might reasonably be entertained as to the nature and extent of what should or should not be undertaken, but there could be no question as to the desirability of this step towards furthering technical instruction in Belfast.'[8]

Gray's comments had struck home, however, and they ensured that proper attention would be given to the complementary nature of the total provision of technical education in Belfast. But the practical outcome of such consideration would take some time. When the RCTI visited the School of Art in June 1883, the question of collaboration with the planned technical school was raised. John Jaffe, President of the Belfast Chamber of Commerce, informed

the Commissioners that, in his view, the new school would not address drawing and art, but would rely on the School of Art for instruction in the relevant
skills. However, William Gray, in his capacity as a Vice-chairman of the Board,
continued to express his concern about complementarity:

> The movement as to technical education in Belfast is up to the present inde-
> pendent entirely of the School of Art or the Working Men's Institute. As a
> matter of fact, we have had no overtures whatever from the promoters of
> the technical school with reference to the co-operation of the School of Art,
> which I think is rather unfortunate.[9]

Formal Opening of the Belfast Technical School

With the exception of Gray's interventions, the organisers must have considered the public meeting of December 1882 a resounding success. With formal
public approval to establish a technical school, the business of finding the necessary funds and resources was able to get underway. An appeal for funds attracted
£1,541 in donations, along with a further number of subscriptions amounting
to £274 per annum over various periods.[10] Interest in the scheme was stimu-
lated by the aforementioned visit of a deputation from the Royal Commission
on Technical Instruction in June 1883. The vigorous representations made by
local witnesses to the RCTI, and their evident intention to proceed to establish
a technical school in Belfast must have helped to attract further support from
the Drapers' Company of London. That worthy body visited Belfast in August
1883 and, convinced of the viability of the new scheme[11], agreed to offer £250
per annum for three years, 'towards the cost of maintaining in Belfast a school
for the teaching of science as applied to spinning and weaving and the manufacture of linen'.

With money in the bank, and the prospect of more to come, the Technical
Committee turned its full attention to the procurement of staff and premises
for the new venture. B. Ashenhurst was appointed Chief Instructor. A brother
of T.R. Ashenhurst, Head of the Textile Department at Bradford Technical
College, Ashenhurst himself had had several years' experience as an instructor
at Keighley Technical School[12]. It seems likely that F.W. Smith had made his
acquaintance during his visit to the north of England the previous year.

After a search for affordable accommodation, the Committee decided to take a lease on part of the buildings of Messrs Richardson's old distillery in Hastings Street, off Divis Street. This was not the ideal home for the new school, but it was the best that circumstances would allow at the time. The press described it as follows:

> There is a long building of very great width, and over it a roof chiefly of glass has been erected. This shed has been divided by brick walls into four spacious compartments, the first of which contains the power looms and a ten horse engine, by which they are to be driven. Some of the looms are erected ... In the next room are the handlooms, while the third department has been fitted up as a lecture hall, and for that purpose it seems very well adapted, should its acoustic properties be found suitable. At the upper end is a neat desk for the lecturer, and appliances are being provided for diagrams &c. The hall is supplied with school benches, and is a plain but very comfortable structure. Adjoining is the apartment for bleaching, dyeing and printing. In it operations will not commence just now...[13]

The Belfast Technical School (BTS) was formally opened on 11 February 1884. Stirring speeches were delivered by James Musgrave, Chairman of the Executive Committee, Professors Everett and Letts, E.J. Harland, J. Glass and R.H. Reade. The declared objective was, 'to teach in a complete and thorough manner the principles of weaving and designing, leaving the student to apply the knowledge obtained to whatever branch of manufacture he may afterwards be engaged in'.[14]

Remembering the concerns expressed about complementarity at the public meeting the previous December, it was no surprise to find the Committee adopting a generous approach to the matter:

> Pupils attending art classes in town, and studying designing as applied to textile fabrics, will have special advantages at the Technical School in learning how these may be worked out in the loom, as it is not the intention of the committee to form science or art classes so long as those which are already established in the town afford the necessary instruction. They have also decided that a considerable reduction shall be made in the fees to those who are already attending classes in the School of Art and the Working Men's Institute.[15]

Work Gets Underway

An initial enrolment of 176 students was an encouraging start to the School's
activities. The first classes were restricted to weaving and were set at three levels
– first, second and third. First level required two terms of study, second level
two, and third level, the most advanced, three terms. Evening classes ran from 7
to 10p.m. on weekdays, and a few day classes – for the sons of mill owners and
other well-to-do persons – from 3 to 6p.m. on two days of the week. The following syllabus for the first-level course gives an idea of the range of material
covered:

> PART I: The loom, its parts and appliances; elementary principles of weav-
> ing; single cloths, plain, twilled, and simple effects; arrangements of simple
> patterns upon paper, such as twills, simple stripes, checks, etc; calculation of
> quantities, etc.

> PART II: Mathematics used in the manufacture of cloth viz., flax, cotton,
> jute, wool, mohair, alpaca, silk, and their adaptation to the manufacture of
> textile fabrics; the principles of construction of cloth; draughting, designing,
> calculating, and colouring plain, twilled, and other single cloths; combination
> of effects on single cloths capable of being produced by tappits, with instruc-
> tions for the arrangement and construction of tappits.[16]

As well as lectures and practical work at the loom, Ashenhurst set his students
homework problems. The following question illustrates the level of arithmeti-
cal dexterity required by the first-level course:

> If you have a loom with a slay or going part measuring 35 inches from centre
> of fulcrum or rocking shaft to point of contact with the cloth, and 28 inches
> from centre of fulcrum to centre of connecting pin, the throw of the crank 3
> inches radius, the shuttle 1¼ inches deep and 1½ inches broad, the distance
> from the cloth to front heddle measuring 11 inches, the length of the treadle,
> from centre of fulcrum to centre of connecting rod, 32 inches, and 22 inches

from centre of fulcrum to centre of treadle bowl, what stroke of tappit will be required?[17]

The reasonably large initial intake of students was a source of satisfaction to the School Committee and staff, and this was reflected in an optimistic first annual report. The Chairman, J.P. Corry, looked to a bright future with a greatly expanded role for the BTS:

> The growing interests of this great manufacturing centre will, for the full development of a complete system of technical teaching in connection with the textile, engineering, building, mechanical and other industrial trades, require a building such as those lately opened in Bradford and Huddersfield, where all engaged in skilled labour can have ample facilities for acquiring an intimate knowledge not only of the principles which underlie their work, but be practically trained in their application.[18]

As a start towards that wider role, it was agreed that a department for instruction in bleaching, dyeing, and cloth-printing would be added as soon as possible. Indeed, Professor Letts of Queen's College was drawing up plans for the achievement of that particular objective, but he indicated that, with income a mere £200 in excess of expenditure, the School's finances would not be able to support such a development. Undeterred, nevertheless, the Committee went on to agree yet another innovation; funds permitting, the School would introduce classes in the art of working in iron, wood, porcelain, and other materials.

Unfortunately, early euphoria and visions of expansion were soon dashed by the harsh realities of the marketplace; whilst 176 students had enrolled for the inaugural session, only sixty-seven entered for the second session, which commenced in September 1884. Besides this, the trade itself was showing little interest in the School.

Promoting the New Technical School

It soon became clear to all concerned that the financial viability of the BTS was in jeopardy; increased support from the trade and from the public was

BELFAST TECHNICAL SCHOOL.

CLASSES, Elementary and Advanced, are now being formed. Pupils are invited to join immediately. The Weaving School is in full working order.

For terms and particulars apply at the SCHOOL, in HASTINGS STREET, or at 7 DONEGALL SQUARE EAST. 4776

An advertisement for the Belfast Technical School in the *Belfast Evening Telegraph*.

essential if it were to develop as planned. Realising that relatively few people were aware of the School's existence, the Committee decided to put greater effort into publicity. A visit to Belfast by the Lord Lieutenant of Ireland on 18 June 1884 provided an early marketing opportunity.[19] Besides the usual array of distinguished people, the audience in the Ulster Hall included representatives from trade societies – ship carpenters, sailmakers, tenters, carpenters and joiners, pipemakers, tailors, housepainters, engineers and mechanics, and plumbers. The Viceregal party's tight schedule left no time for a visit to Hastings Street, but Earl Spencer was pleased to meet a deputation from the School Committee on the premises of Marcus Ward's Royal Ulster Works on the Dublin Road. There, the Secretary, F.W. Smith, read a short address in which he referred to the School's co-operation with other providers of technical education. He concluded by asserting that 'The Technical School supplies a connecting link in the education of our artisans which cannot fail to be of great value to them.' In response, Earl Spencer congratulated the School on its achievements to date. When laying the foundation stone of the new Free Public Library earlier that morning, he had expressed the hope that the general education available to the working man in that institution would be complemented by the technical knowledge now available in the BTS.

The organisation of a major seminar on technical education was another example of marketing enterprise. Held in the Chamber of Commerce building on 25 September 1885, the main objective was to hear the views of Swire Smith, who had been a leading member of the Royal Commission on Technical Instruction.[20] Covering the whole gamut of technical education here and abroad, Smith turned his attention to the specific circumstances of the north of

Ireland. Acknowledging the work of the embryonic BTS, he identified some problem areas:

> With regard to appliances, your school – although in every way commend-able as far as it goes – is much behind the best schools of other countries and of England, and your students – your raw materials – have not as a rule in Belfast enjoyed the same advantages of artistic and scientific training in your day schools which they would have had in the advanced Continental countries.

Smith argued that Belfast's system of technical education would be greatly improved if the various contributory institutions were to collaborate more regularly and effectively:

> I have not come here to minimise the great work that you are doing in art and science teaching. You have in Belfast one of the best schools of art in the United Kingdom, and it has done great and signal service to your indus-tries in many ways. You have also some of the most flourishing science classes in connection with the Working Men's Institute, and other good work is being done. These educational agencies are scattered; they are under separate organisations, having no direct connection with each other. Possibly there is no likelihood of these organisations being united, and, indeed, with your population there is room for them all; but I would advise you as commercial men to use your united influence in promoting the affiliation of these agen-cies, so that as far as possible systematic technical instruction may be supplied to all classes in Belfast with the least possible waste of resources.

Smith was aware that local industry – especially the textile industry - had been less than generous to the BTS, both in attitude and in financial support. He placed the ball firmly at their feet:

> Now it may fairly be asked, if the above are the requirements of an educa-tional institution suited to the wants of an important textile industry such as yours, do you consider that you are up with the times in the provision which you have made or in the individual interest which you take in its practical success? Do you consider that you are doing your best for Mr Ashenhurst (your head teacher) in apparatus and material?[21]

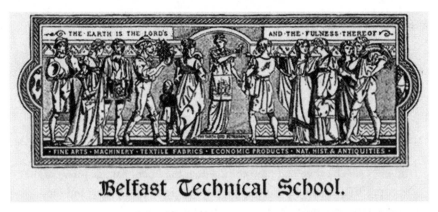

·THE·EARTH·IS·THE·LORD'S· AND·THE·FULNESS·THEREOF·

· FINE ARTS · MACHINERY · TEXTILE FABRICS · ECONOMIC PRODUCTS · NAT. HIST. & ANTIQUITIES ·

Belfast Technical School.

Detail from the 1893/94 *Annual Report of the Belfast Technical School*, 12 September 1884.

Smith knew that the answer to his question had to be a resounding 'NO', but he hoped that his personal chastisement would encourage a more enlightened attitude from the industry. Unfortunately, even his renowned persuasive powers were to no avail, and, if anything, the situation deteriorated even further.

Financial Challenges

The question of funding dominated the second annual meeting of the BTS, held in the Hastings Street premises on 25 January 1886. The students had recorded some excellent performances in the examinations of the CGLI (discussed later), but this good news was overshadowed by concerns about the school's sorry financial position.[22] The accounts for the year showed that income had exceeded outgoings by a mere £4. The lack of funds had prevented further progress with plans to introduce a department of bleaching, dyeing and printing, and the Committee was concerned that the Worshipful Company of Drapers would withdraw the grant which they had provided in August 1884. This amounted to £250 per annum for three years, but it carried the condition that matching funds had to be found from private and public sources. Unfortunately, subscriptions from local sources had 'amounted to hardly anything worthy of mention'.

James Musgrave, the meeting's Chairman, expressed his personal concern and frustration about this lack of support:

> There was one subject which, though a delicate one, he thought it necessary
> that it should be touched, and it was this – that in the committee regulating
> this school there was – he would not say strong – but an impression that
> many of the local manufacturers, and amongst them some of the most suc-
> cessful in designing original methods of procedure, were somewhat adverse
> to [this] school; at all events they had failed to be present to exhibit sympathy
> and help … The time had now come when the linen manufacturers of the
> North of Ireland should make up their minds to come forward and support
> [this] school, or at least say that it ought to be discontinued.[23]

The support that Musgrave was seeking could have taken several forms; donations and active participation were welcome, if not essential, but a more positive
attitude from industry was crucial. The students present at the first annual meeting in January 1885 had touched on this issue. They suggested that manufacturers
and merchants should encourage their staff to attend classes, and should contribute to their fees, and they looked for further personal encouragement in the
form of preferences when situations became vacant.[24]

Professor Fitzgerald, Professor of Engineering at Queen's College, deplored
the lack of support from the industry. But, aware that the preservation of trade
secrets was a major bar to active participation by the industry, he suggested that
more requests for financial support should be directed at the general public, on
the grounds that technical education meant increased prosperity that the whole
community could share.[25]

This poor financial outlook did not stifle enterprise or ambition. In addition
to plans to set up a department for bleaching, dyeing and printing, and aspirations to cover a wider range of topics like the processing of iron, porcelain and
wood, the Committee's third annual report stated in 1886 that:

> Without undervaluing in any degree the educational facilities in connection
> with other institutions in Belfast, the Committee think it will be neces-
> sary that science and art classes should be formed in immediate touch with
> the practical departments. In great centres of manufactures, such as Leeds,
> Bradford, Huddersfield, and other places, such systematic completeness as we
> have indicated in instruction has been organised, and with the best possible
> results.[26]

That theme was pursued in the fifth annual report, presented in 1888:

> Is this town with its numerous very important industries, to rest satisfied with
> a Technological School representing one of them only, or will it be seriously
> aroused to the fact that foreign competition is in conflict with many of its
> interests, and that technical training is at present the most powerful weapon
> to wield in this conflict?[27]

But no such expansion could be accomplished without the necessary resources. Most of the initial donations to the School had been expended on the refurbishment of the old distillery premises and the purchase of weaving equipment. Ten power looms and three hand looms had been installed. In order to provide a similar facility for a new department of bleaching, dyeing and printing, Professor Letts had estimated in the first annual report a minimum requirement of £600 for equipment and a further £300 per annum for maintenance.

These hopes were soon dashed on the rocks of penury. In the first three years of operation the School's annual revenue had amounted to some £700, comprising an annual subscription from the Drapers' Company, fees, and subscriptions from thirty-two firms who had pledged their support for three years on the assumption that the School would be well established and self-supporting at the end of that period. The imminent withdrawal of the last-mentioned source of support threatened to bring the School to an end, and worst hopes were realised when the total revenue in 1886/87 fell to a mere £283.[28] Expenditure exceeded income, but two exceptional mitigating factors have to be considered. Firstly, the autumn of 1886 had seen serious rioting in the vicinity of the School; secondly, the Mayor, Sir James Haslett, had decided on his inauguration in 1887 to plan a major new Technical Institute for Belfast. To be named the Victoria Institute, the new establishment would mark the occasion of the Queen's jubilee in 1888. The first of these factors caused a considerable reduction in attendance at Hastings Street; the latter diverted public funds from the school to the new and grander concept.

The Committee was forced into drastic action. The services of Ashenhurst were dispensed with and he was replaced by the less expensive G.R. Begley. In addition, F.W. Smith displayed true public spirit by forgoing his fee as Secretary. With some suggestions in the air about poor management, the Committee was indebted to W. Kennedy (York Street Flax Spinning Mill) and H.J. Nicholson (Greenmount Spinning Company) for their sterling endeavours to turn matters around. These two were ably supported by, in particular, the Queen's Professors

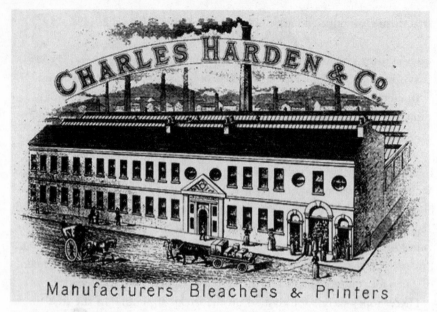

Manufacturers Bleachers & Printers

One of many potential sources of funds for the Belfast Technical School. (Anon, *The Industries of Ireland; Belfast and the Towns of the North*, 1986.)

Fitzgerald and Everett, the former undertaking, gratis, to run preparatory classes in arithmetic and mechanics, the latter actively promoting the BTS. Their combined efforts rescued the School from impending closure and returned it, at least, to its former precarious state of financial equilibrium.

There was some cheering news on the financial front in 1888 when the Drapers' Company agreed to increase their annual subvention of £250 (which they had been threatening to withdraw) by £50 as a contribution towards the costs of employing a chemistry teacher to teach dyeing. But the School's finances continued to operate on a hand to mouth basis. An analysis of the seventeen annual reports[29] reveals that, in addition to grants from the Drapers' Company, annual voluntary subscriptions typically amounted to £200, fees from the CGLI brought a further £40, and from students about £20, and in later years the sale of items woven on the School's looms added about £10. The critical importance of local subscriptions is evident from these figures.

The implementation of the Technical Instruction Act in 1889 brought a more promising financial prospect (see Chapter 8). It empowered local authorities to impose a penny-in-the-pound rate for the maintenance of technical education, but Belfast's municipal authorities stubbornly refused to adopt this provision, which would have amounted to £2,987 per annum in 1890. They chose, instead, to allocate small amounts to the various providers of technical education. Of these the BTS received a paltry £75 in 1891, but continuing pressure from the School and its sister institutions brought an increase to £200 in 1892, and a further increase to £250 in 1893. The BTS received a total of £2,275 from this source over the decade 1891-1901.

This municipal grant, relatively small and inadequate for the School's needs, actually exacerbated the School's poor financial position. It tended to stem the flow of private donations, since individuals were reluctant to subscribe to an institution that they thought should be supported by the entire community; they were also hesitant to direct their hard-earned money to purposes which could well bring direct benefit to already wealthy manufacturers. Worse still, it prompted the Drapers' Company to reconsider their position. An extract from their letter of July 1894 follows:

> The Drapers' Company have had under further consideration the question of continuing their annual subscription to the Spinning and Weaving Classes of Belfast Technical School. When the subscription was first granted, the Company anticipated that the Classes would form a nucleus of a large Technical School, in which instruction would be given to the people of Belfast in the theory and practice of the various manufacturing industries carried on in the city. It is a disappointment to the Company to find that this result has not been achieved, and that the provision made for Technical Education in Belfast, falls very much below that in many places of much less importance. The Company understand, however, that there is reason to hope that in the course of another year or two matters will be put on a better footing, and in this hope they have resolved to continue their subscription for this year and for the year 1894-95. It is to be understood that the subscription will absolutely cease when these two further payments shall have been made, unless in the meantime the Technical Instruction Act, 1889, shall have been put in force in Belfast, and adequate provision made for Technical teaching in the city...[30]

Unfortunately the Town Council's ongoing refusal to implement fully the provisions of the 1889 Act obliged the Drapers' Company to implement their threat of withdrawal in 1895. Overall they had given the School considerable assistance over the years. Their total grant over the School's lifetime amounted to £3,300, compared to £4,975 from the general public.[31]

That loss of income was offset to some extent after 1894 by the receipt of an

annual grant of £250 from the Department of Science and Art. This had originated in the Technical Instruction Act of 1889, which made dispensation for a
grant from the Department equal to that contributed by the local authority.
That sum helped the BTS to maintain a precarious existence until its dissolution in 1901.

Students and Classes

Financial difficulties affected classes and curricula, and enterprising plans for
the development of the School were frustrated by lack of resources. However,
staff and students performed remarkably well under trying circumstances, and
annual reports soon included growing lists of successful students.

Classes in the early years were restricted to weaving, and were supported by
an initially impressive array of technical equipment including ten power looms
and three hand looms. Early attempts to diversify beyond weaving proved
unsuccessful; for example, Musgrave reported in 1886 that they had introduced
'with not much success, teaching of the preparation of flax and the yarns which
supply the weaver with his materials'.[32]

The School Committee was aware that collaboration with other providers
of technical education could well increase their own student numbers, and that
the School's status, and its potential for serving the needs of a much wider
range of industries, could benefit. Indeed, the founding Technical Committee
had envisaged a close link with the School of Art whereby students studying
the design of patterns for textile fabrics in the School of Art would have, in
the Technical School, facilities for bringing their work to practical fruition. It
was further suggested that students studying chemistry in the Working Men's
Institute could have similar opportunities for applying their knowledge, but in
the BTS's departments of bleaching and dyeing. Musgrave was to go further in
1888 when he proposed that students attending the School's bleaching classes
should 'attend also the very admirable lectures in elementary chemistry given
in an allied institution by that very successful teacher, Mr Barklie'.[33]

So the Committee made much of the concept of collaboration during the
School's formative years. In the end, however, there were few real examples
of collaboration. If anything, the School's aspirations for expansion militated
against constructive work with others. For example, the potential introduction

of classes in the art of working in iron, wood, porcelain, and other materials was debated at the very first annual meeting,[34] and the third annual report (1885/86) expressed a desire to introduce science classes:

That same report went even further down the route of unilateral development by proposing a new building – to cost around £12,000 and to accommodate classes in engineering, textiles, building and other trades.

Lack of resources strangled these grand ideas at birth. Nevertheless, the School did introduce some innovations. A modest museum and library was opened in 1886, and the portfolio of classes was gradually increased from two to eight over the first four years of operation. Instruction in Dyeing, supported by the Drapers' Company, commenced in 1888. Plumbing was introduced in 1889, Carpentry, Joining and Woodcarving in 1890, Dressmaking in 1893, and Electric Lighting in 1894.

The classes met with varying degrees of success. Enrolments in Weaving were consistently high in the early years, and the weaving equipment, a matter of some pride at the outset, was enhanced in 1888 by the gift of an additional power loom from the Bloomfield Factory of Ross Brothers.[35] However, the onward march of technology, and poor conditions in the School's workshops, conspired to ensure that the equipment was soon outdated and badly in need of maintenance. In 1894, the School Committee was complaining in its eleventh annual report that, 'The looms in the workshop at present are in a great measure antiquated in construction, and unsuitable for carrying out the more modern ideas which constant and ever-widening competition render requisite in all fabrics which appeal to public taste.'[36]

Whilst facilities for weaving had deteriorated, they were always superior to those for spinning. Some spinning frames had been installed, but the School could not afford an engine to put them to work! The ninth annual report deplored the fact that 'the frames, etc., to illustrate the lessons in spinning are standing idle for want of motive power'.[37] In his 1894 report, the CGLI examiner attributed the weak answering in the spinning paper to this shortcoming; he suggested that the weakness might be remedied by the use of models, or, better still, of the actual machinery itself. In an early attempt to mitigate the effects of this deficiency, classes were started in 1886 on the premises of the Wolfhill Spinning Company,[38] and, in the following year, on alternative Saturdays in Durham Street Spinning Mill.[39]

The spinning classes managed to survive despite these difficulties, but the dyeing and bleaching classes were less fortunate. Dyeing classes commenced with fifteen students in 1888/89, and Bleaching followed in 1889/90 with the same number. With support from the Drapers' Company assured for three years, their futures looked bright. The numbers in the Dyeing class increased to nineteen in 1889/90, including managers and owners of dyeing establishments around Belfast, some of whom had travelled some thirty miles for the privilege. But lack of resources took its toll. Examiners commented in 1890 that 'the appliances at the disposal of the teacher are still of the humblest description'.[40] Funds did not permit the purchase of the necessary equipment, so in 1892, by which time Dyeing and Bleaching had only managed to attract three and four enrolments respectively, the School Committee decided to suspend the classes 'until suitable apparatus has been provided for practical illustration on the subject of the lectures'.[41]

Like dyeing and bleaching, the design classes also failed to establish themselves. Commenced in January 1890, the initial enrolment of thirty-one was encouraging. Basically an adjunct to the weaving classes, lack of suitable accommodation and equipment forced the withdrawal of the classes in the mid-1890s.

Other successes were able to offset the depressing effect of these failures. Plumbing classes, started in 1887, established themselves quickly and continued to draw reasonable numbers of students throughout the lifetime of the institution. At their inauguration, R.H. Reade argued that these artisans required 'a knowledge not only of pipes and valves, but of the laws that regulate the flow and pressure of liquids and gases'.[42] The plumbers recognised that need, but saw themselves in the wider and more important role of saving the health of the 250,000 citizens of Belfast who were in great need of an effective system of public sanitation. A working committee of the school, mostly master plumbers, co-operated with the Worshipful Company of Plumbers in drawing up a suitable programme for recognition by the CGLI.

The plumbers took themselves very seriously. The School Plumbing Committee arranged annual meetings at which progress was reported, prizes awarded, and lectures given. On 2 November 1892, the annual meeting in connection with the plumbing classes reported[43] that the number of students attending classes had grown from an initial twenty-eight in 1888 to forty-one in 1891. With Professor Fitzgerald in the Chair, Dr J. Strahan was then invited to deliver a lecture on 'Plumbing and Healthy Homes'. The Plumbers' Committee had its own auditor and treasurer and presented a separate financial statement in the School's annual reports. In the eleventh annual report, for example, the Treasurer is named as Harrison McCloy (the author's second cousin, thrice removed).

	1893/94	1899/1900
Weaving	81	38
Spinning	32	42
Plumbing	38	39
Designing	19	–
Carpentry (Theory)	27	20
Woodcarving	13	30
Dressmaking	55	18
Carpentry (Practical)	14	–
Electric Lighting	–	28
TOTAL	279	235

Dressmaking classes were started in premises on Royal Avenue in 1893. They were aimed at female students, but it is interesting to note that woodcarving classes, started in 1890, were also dominated by women. Unfortunately for these latter ladies, however, their classes had to be held in Hastings Street in an open shed with an asphalt floor.

The above table shows how the School's curriculum had drifted towards instruction in practical skills, and away from the scientific principles underpinning the various trades. This growing trend drew some criticism at the eleventh annual meeting in 1894, when R.L. Patterson questioned the wisdom of teaching trades like carpentry and dressmaking, both of which could be better taught in the ordinary workshop. Musgrave, the Chairman, put this down to lack of resources:

> We were obliged to contract our operations, and now, I regret to say, the School is confined to teaching trades, such as spinning, weaving, plumbing, carpentry, and woodcarving, just as they are taught in ordinary factories. We are debarred from teaching that practical application of science to manufactures which constitutes the highest aim of technical education…[44]

Despite those shortcomings, Hastings Street students still managed to record good examination performances which matched, and often excelled, those of other centres in the United Kingdom. The second annual report[45], for example, recorded thirteen passes in the May 1885 examinations of the CGLI, with students obtaining six first-class certificates, seven second-class certificates and one bronze medal. Numbers of entries and successes grew, and by 1888, of a total of 181 students, those who had sat examinations achieved fifty-three passes, including thirty-five first-class and eighteen second-class certificates. A particularly outstanding achievement was recorded that year, with students from the BTS winning all seven prizes offered by the CGLI in subjects connected with the manufacture of linen. Honours and prizes continued to arrive; in 1894, of the thirty-two students who passed, four achieved first honours, five bronze medals and two silver medals. By 1896 the CGLI had awarded the school's students more than 350 first- and second-class certificates, thirty silver medals, forty-one bronze medals and £140 in cash prizes.[46]

Twilight Years

The state of the buildings and equipment continued to present insuperable problems. By 1894, of the initial donations to the School, £445 had gone towards adapting the premises, £964 to looms, a gas engine, and other equipment, and £244 to furniture and fittings. But a decade's use, with little money for maintenance, had dissipated that initial investment. Shortage of suitable spinning equipment had attracted damning comment from examiners, and the sorry state of the accommodation was summarised in the Secretary's comments in the 1894 annual report:

> With no prospect of leaving the present premises, the temporary measures to exclude the rain, resorted to for the past two to three years, may be given over, and the roof, which in several places is now unsafe, must be renewed. Additional space is also required, as a second lecture room has long been wanted. Some classes have to be held at present in the corner of an open shed...[47]

This state of affairs had a depressing effect on staff and students alike. The fifteenth annual report (1898) noted that 70 per cent of the students were so indifferent to the advantages of thorough training that they did not return to the School after their first year.[48] Professor Fitzgerald was moved to remark that the School was a disgrace to the city, and John Malone added that he was glad that they were about to be relieved of their duties as the responsibilities for technical education passed to the City Council. The general gloom of the occasion was deepened when S.F. Milligan informed members that the

Working Men's Institute had done particularly well that year, enrolments in the Institute having increased by 360.

Sir James Musgrave, the Chairman, brought some cheer to the proceedings. He looked forward to the city's new Technical Institute, and suggested a model where students would have,

> ...large and wholesome classrooms, where they would be taught from examples of the most improved machinery and appliances; where every engineering novelty would be explained to them, where they would be enabled to pursue the charming study of art, and taught to originate themselves designs for application to manufacture, where also they would have free access to a museum containing copies of the best examples of ancient and modern art, and where they could examine samples of British as well as foreign goods, and ascertain with what amount of success the competing countries have applied science and art to enhance the beauty or the utility of their productions...[49]

The planning of Belfast's new Technical Institute accelerated in the last few years of the century (Chapter 9). All the existing organisations were to be subsumed in various ways, and each had to be formally terminated before the new institution could be launched. The Technical School's final annual meeting took place in the Ulster Minor Hall on 14 November 1900. It was a particularly depressing affair: besides the impending closure, the most recent batch of students had fared poorly in the CGLI examinations. Of the 235 students in attendance (see table, p.157), only forty-five sat examinations, and of these only twenty-three passed. J. Stitt, an examiner of the CGLI, expressed his disappointment that not a single prize in weaving had been secured in such a centre of the linen industry. The only good news was that the spinning workshop had at long last been equipped satisfactorily, thanks to gifts of a new spinning frame and a reel, and the purchase of a hackling machine, a drawing frame and a roving frame.

Sir James Musgrave concluded by referring to the great new Technical Institute that would shortly grace the grounds in front of the Academical Institution. He had reason to believe,' that when such an institution was established they would be able to hand over that Technical School in full working order, together with all the property belonging to it, to such gentlemen as the Corporation might appoint to manage their new Technical Institute'.[50]

Thus ended seventeen years of struggle, and some success, in Hastings Street. The meeting closed by acknowledging the contributions of all concerned, in particular Sir James Musgrave, R.H. Reade, Professor Fitzgerald, R. Kyle Knox, H.J. Nicholson, J. Malone, Sir W.Q. Ewart, Professor Letts, J. Loewenthal, W.R. Young and W. Kennedy.

A good idea, the Belfast Technical School had been strangled by lack of resources and poor recognition and support from industry. Starting off in second rate accommodation in 1884, the School's overall facilities had already deteriorated to an unacceptable level by the end of the century.

Driven ahead by an enthusiastic and committed School Committee, the School had focused on the more practical aspects of technology, and preferred to prepare its students for the examinations of the City and Guilds of London Institute rather than for those of the more science-biased Department of Science and Art. Attempts to collaborate with other providers had met with little success, but they had emphasised and confirmed the need for a co-ordinated system of technical education in Belfast.

In the end, the Belfast Technical School was relieved to find itself an integral part of Belfast's new coordinated system of technical education.

8

Brighter Prospects for Technical Education

Nurturing a Spirit of Collaboration

The fragmented nature of Belfast's technical education was a source of weakness. As early as 1852, Frederick Richard Chichester, the Earl of Belfast, had tried to persuade the various local scientific and technical bodies to combine their resources. He identified a long list of such bodies including The Museum, The School of Design, The Fine Arts Society, The Belfast Library, The Social Inquiry Society, The Diocesan Rooms, The Queen's College Literary and Scientific Association, etc. His proposed Athenaeum was intended to bring them all together, ideally under one roof:

> The universal fault of all and each of these small societies appears to me to be exclusiveness, and an unwillingness to work together in the cause which each have in view ... Unity is strength in learning as in other things, and therefore do I specially desire to impress this conviction on all the members and promoters of the separate local societies, which will much more readily and effectually attain their end if they work together. Instead of soliciting funds and contributions for this Society, that institution, and the other association, let them join in one petition that contributions be liberally made to the advancement of science collectively.[1]

The Earl's proposal was a first step towards a collaborative scheme of technical education in Belfast. But he may have been expecting too much from the struggling providers of the time. For example, he made a special plea to the Belfast

Government School of Design, suggesting that the £700 already collected for a much-needed statue gallery be redirected to the proposed Athenaeum where it would find much better accommodation than 'the concealed locality in which it was proposed to build it'.[2]

However, his proposal generated some interest and some support – indeed, John Mulholland of the York Street Flax Spinning Company promised a donation of £200. But tragedy intervened the following year when the Earl died from scarlet fever when only twenty-six years of age. Without his drive and influence the project faded away. However, as explained in Chapter 4, his plan had done little for the struggling Belfast Government School of Design; by diverting public attention to another initiative, it had helped to bring that school to an early demise. Nevertheless, the notion of unity in strength had been accepted by many.

A spirit of collaboration resurfaced in 1882 when the Belfast Government School of Art (BGSA) extended a hearty welcome to the new Hastings Street Technical School. There seemed to be clear links between the design-based work of the former and the applications-based work of the latter, and students at the School of Art might well see their designs brought to fruition at the Technical School. Both schools were happy to offer concessionary fees to the other's students. Unfortunately, good intentions on both sides produced few concrete examples of fruitful collaboration.

Belfast's leading citizens were urged further down the road of collaboration when Swire Smith, a member of the Royal Commission on Technical Instruction, addressed the friends of the Belfast Technical School in the Chamber of Commerce on 25 September 1885. Urging a more intensive development of technical instruction in Belfast, he added,

> You have in Belfast one of the best schools of art in the United Kingdom, and it has done great and signal services to your industries in many ways. You have also some of the most flourishing science classes in connection with the Working Men's Institute, and other good work is being done. These educational agencies are scattered; they are under separate organisations, having no direct connection with each other. Possibly there is no likelihood of these organisations being united, and indeed, with your population there is room for them all; but I would advise you as commercial men to use your united influence in promoting the affiliation of these agencies, so that as far as possible systematic technical instruction may be supplied to all classes in Belfast with the least possible waste of resources.[3]

Smith's remarks, reinforced in the Commission's Report of 1884, struck home. Three years later, in 1887, the golden jubilee of Victoria's accession provided an opportunity to put such ideas into practice. The plan was centred on the new Free Library which was due to open in 1888.

The Proposed Victoria Institute

The Public Libraries Act of 1855 had authorised boroughs with populations in excess of 5,000 to raise a penny-in-the-pound rate towards the establishment of libraries. However, the adoption of the act was slow in Ireland, with Dundalk being the only town to respond (1858). There were some early rumblings in Belfast; William Shepherd, the Secretary of the BGSA, was a strong supporter of libraries. His letter to the press in 1871 reminded the public that the town had only two libraries – The Linen Hall Library, and the Belfast People's Library Institute, neither of which allowed free access to the books.[4] Displaying, perhaps, a rather one-sided approach to collaboration, he proposed that the Working Men's Institute should hand over its new building in Queen Street for use as a free public library. Whilst that proposal had little chance of success, Shepherd's suggestion that any new library should include a museum seemed more viable, and attracted more support.

Encouraged by the more generous provisions of the Public Libraries Amendment Act of 1877, the Town Council started to take the matter more seriously. The Mayor, John Preston, recommended an early start on the construction of a library, but the Council, claiming there were much more urgent needs, put the matter aside for future consideration. However, the public continued to press for action. Seeing the new library as a solution to its own space problems, the BGSA proposed that it should contain both a museum and an art gallery. The press decided to jump on the bandwagon, 'what have we done for science and art? Where is our free public library? Our town museum with its art and economic branches? Where is our art gallery and our public lecture hall? Simply nowhere'.[5]

Public outcry for a new library reached a peak in 1881. Two petitions to the Council in the early summer resulted in a poll of ratepayers which confirmed that around 80 per cent of them were prepared to use the rates to pay for the new facility. The Council had little alternative but to proceed with the planning of a library. A Library Committee was established in December 1881, and the wheels began to turn, albeit extremely slowly. Architect W.H. Lynn, who included Belfast Castle amongst his many projects, designed the building in Royal Avenue. The foundation stone was laid on 18 June 1884, and the building was officially opened to the public on 13 October 1888.

William Gray was a tenacious proponent of the scheme throughout. His persistence and persuasive skills were largely responsible for the art gallery and museum that graced the top floor of the library. However, when the building was finally completed, the professional artists of the town concluded that the available area was insufficient.

Looking to the future, the Council had decided in 1883 to acquire land at the rear of the new building. The sight of the slowly growing building on an extensive site persuaded some that this could be the nucleus of something even bigger and grander. And the imminence of Queen Victoria's golden jubilee provided further motivation for the launch of such a scheme. J.H. Haslett, the Mayor at the time, recognised the opportunity and used his inaugural speech to propose that the memorial to the Queen's jubilee year should be of an educational character. The idea was grasped by the town's educationalists, and a planning committee was set up post haste. It consisted of representatives from the BGSA, the Royal Belfast Academical Instituion (RBAI), the Working Men's Institute (WMI), the Natural History Society, the Belfast Technical School (BTS), and the Naturalists' Field Club.[6] After several meetings, the views of the committee were presented to the public in the Town Hall on 20 April 1887.

Not wishing to upset the existing providers of technical education, the Mayor made it clear at the outset that he had no wish to 'put aside or supersede completely the existing establishments'[7], but he believed that there should be 'some other form – some other concentrated form – from which educational establishments throughout the town should radiate'. His system would involve a large central institution at the centre of a town-wide network of smaller organisations. For example, the schools affiliated to the BGSA would be extended considerably to deal with the bulk of elementary art work, and this would allow the BGSA to concentrate on the more advanced aspects. The following resolution was adopted:

> That we cordially approve of the wise suggestion made by the Mayor of Belfast
> on the occasion of his installation, and are of opinion that the best form which
> the commemoration of Her Majesty's jubilee could take in our town would
> be the establishment of a central institution for the teaching, in a combined

form, of art, science, and technology, as applied to the trade and manufactures of the district, utilising and combining, as far as possible, for the purpose the School of Art, Schools of Science and Technology, and Technical School.[6]

A second resolution added flesh to these bones:

That, to make the instruction in trades and manufactures complete and effective, rooms and workshops shall be provided, comprising a museum for works of art and industrial products; rooms for preparing, spinning, weaving, designing, bleaching, dyeing, and printing textile fabrics; and trade workshops furnished with suitable collections, machinery, and appliances for giving instruction; as well as with practical teachers for the several trades and manufactures.

James Musgrave, an old campaigner, was only too aware that sensitivities were likely to be offended by the proposed merger. Treading warily, he reminded his audience that the intention was not to interfere with the existing schools, but to cooperate with, and assist them. He suggested that it should be left to the existing schools to decide when they were ready to join the scheme. But

The Belfast Central Library today. The top floor was originally reserved for a museum and art gallery.

A.H. Reade was not so subtle. He asserted that the proposed institution was necessary because of the shortcomings in the existing provision. He argued that the Belfast Technical School was in a state of gradual decay, the Working Men's Institute was poorly equipped, and the School of Art 'was an institution on which much energy was dissipated and to a great extent misdirected'.

A third resolution addressed the financial aspects of the scheme. Funds were to be gathered from the Public Libraries Act, the Department of Science and Art (DSA), the City and Guilds of London Institute (CGLI), and from public subscription. The audience was pleased to learn that John Jaffe, a former Mayor, had started the ball rolling with a generous donation of £250.

Before the meeting closed an Executive Committee was set up to carry the various resolutions forward. After several meetings that committee agreed that the necessary new buildings should be constructed on the grounds at the rear of the new Free Library, and those buildings, the Library, and the existing school buildings should be affiliated under the name of the Victoria Institute. Management of the Institute would be the responsibility of a composite committee appointed by the Town Council. A deputation from the Executive Committee persuaded the Council's Library Committee of the worthiness of the scheme, and that body, in turn, recommended in June that the Council carry it forward. However, even with £2,000 promised in subscriptions, the scheme was quietly shelved. It can be surmised that other pressing schemes, such as sanitation works and the asylum, had first call on the Council's resources. There is also the possibility that the various interested organisations failed to see eye-to-eye on the structure and funding of the venture. And, with growing support for technical education in Great Britain paving the way for greater support from the State, the Council may have been persuaded to play a waiting game.

Technical Education
Recognised by Government

Changing attitudes to technical education in England brought some hope of helpful knock-on effects in Ireland. The British Government's interest in technical education was still strongly influenced by economic concerns – particularly the fear of foreign competition. Those concerns were further enflamed in 1881 when the CGLI published a small book on *Technical Education in a Saxon Town*.[9] Its author, H.M. Felkin, described in some detail how the productive efficiency of the German town of Chemnitz – a rival to the British in the manufacture of lace and hosiery – was assisted by a well-organised system of technical education. The book provided sufficient additional motivation to persuade the Government to establish a Royal Commission on Technical Instruction (RCTI) in 1881 with the brief, 'To inquire into the instruction of the industrial classes of certain foreign countries in technical and other subjects for the purpose of comparison with that of the corresponding classes in this country; and into the influence of such instruction on manufacturing and other industries at home and abroad.' The Commissioners were basically a small freelance pressure group, whose members were content to pay their own expenses. Bernhard Samuelson, the Chairman, was one of the country's leading industrialists and an active founding member of the Iron and Steel Institute, so he was well placed to contribute to the debate. The other members were Philip Magnus (Director and Secretary CGLI), Henry Roscoe (Professor of Chemistry at Owens College, Manchester), Swire Smith (a wool manufacturer), John Slagg (a cotton manufacturer), and William Woodall (a manufacturer of china). Roscoe was largely responsible for the team's work on research and its industrial applications, Magnus for curricula and school organisation, and Smith for manufacturing industry.[10] William Mather, another distinguished industrialist, focused on education in the United States.

The Commission conducted exhaustive inquiries over a three-year period, including a visit to Belfast in June 1883. Its voluminous report was a monument of thoroughness. Evidence from a multitude of sources confirmed the Government's concern about foreign competition; Germany, for example, was profiting from work originally carried out in England. These developments were linked back to the lack of an effective system of technical education in Britain, 'Our industrial empire is vigorously attacked all over the world. We find that our most formidable assailants are the best educated peoples.'

The Report was published in 1884. Largely supporting those of earlier Government commissions and select committees, the recommendations included;[11]

Local Education Authorities should establish State secondary and technical schools, and rate-aid should be available for the purpose;

Elementary and secondary education should be radically improved; especially with a view to providing adequate preparation for scientific and technical education;

More technical colleges should be established;

More science should be included in the curriculum of teacher-training organisations.

There was a danger that these recommendations would be approved and noted, but no concrete action would follow. Henry Roscoe, one of the Commissioners, was especially aware of this possibility. He had entered Parliament in 1885 as a Manchester radical[12], and now, using his influence in the House, he persuaded forty fellow MPs to meet with a delegation from education, industry and commerce to discuss how they together could press for an early implementation of the recommendations of the RCTI. They established a National Association for the Promotion of Technical Education (NAPTE), and that Association, presided over by the Duke of Devonshire until its demise in 1906, agreed to supply relevant information to local authorities and, more importantly, to press for legislation on technical education. NAPTE's agitations were rewarded when an all-night sitting in the House saw the passing in 1889 of The Technical Instruction Act.

The 1889 Act empowered county and borough councils to subsidise science teaching in secondary schools and, crucially, to establish technical schools for teaching 'the principles of science and art applicable to industries, and in the application of special branches of science and art to specific industries or employments'.[13] Local authorities could support technical instruction by raising a penny in the pound from the rates, and curricula and classes, subject to the approval of the DSA, would be administered by local Technical Instruction Committees. This was a remarkable victory for the proponents of technical education.

Local rates, however, did not produce the expected riches. By 1898 the 160 local authorities in England had together allocated a mere £39,000 from the rates for technical education.[14] That lack of generosity can be attributed largely to a windfall deriving from the implementation of the Local Taxation (Customs and Excise) Act of 1890. The residue of monies, originally set aside to compensate publicans when the Government decided to reduce the number of public houses, was directed to local authorities, either to relieve the rates or to subsidise technical education. In the beginning most local authorities used these

Some members of the Royal Commission on Technical Instruction (1883). From left to right: G. Redgrave, Swire Smith, P. Magnus, H. Roscoe. (Magnus, *Educational Aims and Efforts; 1880-1910*, 1910.)

unexpected riches ('the whiskey money') to relieve the rates, but allocations to technical education gradually increased, and, by 1898, £740,000 of an available £807,000 was being used for that purpose.[15] However, these grants were under the control of the DSA which, as has been demonstrated, was pushing for a strong scientific bias in technical education.

The Irish Dimension

The implementation of the Technical Instruction Act of 1889 was a relatively straightforward process in England and Wales. There, new county councils had been set up in 1888, and it was their responsibility to put the act into practice. Ireland, however, did not have such an underpinning administrative system: there were no county councils to act as local authorities and take the scheme forward. The Regulations had foreseen this difficulty, stating that, in applying the act to Ireland, 'the expression local authority shall mean the urban or rural sanitary authority ... within the meaning of the Public Health (Ireland) Act of 1878'.[16] So the development of technical education in the towns of Ireland would have to rely on their urban sanitary authorities, and the country districts would have to look to their rural sanitary authorities. Such an arrangement attracted a deal of criticism in the House of Commons:

> The whole of the existing law as to the purposes for which the Local Sanitary Authorities are appointed shows how absurd it is to invest the powers of this Bill, as to Technical Instruction, in the hands of a body charged with the supervision of such matters relating to sewage, common lodging houses, water supply, nuisances, and other odoriferous subjects...[17]

It was, indeed, unlikely that the people associated with these authorities would have the expertise, or even the interest and motivation, to organise and finance systems of technical education in Ireland. The municipal authorities in the cities – and Belfast was a city by this time – were better organised and resourced to deliver, so there were high expectations that they would take the lead in the establishment of Ireland's new system of technical education. However, by 1898, the Irish local authorities combined could only muster a grand total of £5,649 from the rates.[18]

The Irish proponents of technical education were greatly disappointed by this response. And, unlike their counterparts in Great Britain, they did not have the compensation of substantial amounts of whiskey money. Ireland's share of those funds, estimated at £78,000 per annum in 1898, was handed over to the Commissioners of National Education and to the Board of Intermediate Education who used it to upgrade facilities and to improve teachers' salaries.[19]

Persuading Belfast Corporation to Support Technical Education

Belfast's supporters of technical education continued to urge the City Council to find the much-needed resources for their various schools from funds generated from the implementation of the Technical Instruction Act (TIA). The last decade of the nineteenth century saw much support from the press, in whose pages the general tenor of editorial comment was sympathetic to the cause, and readers' letters – especially the many from William Gray – chastised the Council for its apathy. A procession of deputations wended their way to the Town Hall where they pressed for resources and for a fresh new approach to technical education. But this was, on the whole, a thankless and fruitless task, and, in the end, it was the promise of parliamentary funds that persuaded the Council to throw its weight behind technical education.

The first of many deputations argued its case before the Council's Finance Committee on 10 November 1890, but the Committee explained that the rate for next year was just about to be struck, and it was too late in the year to give the matter of technical education adequate consideration. Nevertheless, it was agreed to give a grant of £300 for the year 1891, with £100 going to the School of Art, £75 to the Working Men's Institute, £75 to the Hastings Street School, and £50 to the Science and Engineering School in the Model School. That £300 has to be compared with the £2,987 which could have been raised from a penny rate. Rubbing salt in the wound, the Council stipulated that the Corporation should be represented on the boards of management of the various schools.

This pittance of a grant inflamed, rather than encouraged, Belfast's providers of technical education and, just a week later, representatives of the BGSA, the Technical School and the Chamber of Commerce were back again, snapping at the Finance Committee's heels.[20] They informed the Committee that Sheffield's Council had allocated £4,534 under the TIA, and that grants had been made by the authorities in Birkenhead, Macclesfield, Stockport, Shipley,

York, Rotherham, Bingley and Wakefield. Manchester's Special Committee had proposed expenditure of £4,000 under the Act, and large schemes were being contemplated in Bolton and Nottingham. But the Finance Committee was not moved to increase its grant.

In October 1891 a group of ninety ratepayers appealed to the Lord Mayor to call a public meeting to consider the desirability of taking full advantage of the TIA. The meeting, which took place in the Town Hall, elected a deputation which met the Finance Committee in November. However, the relevant Council minute shows that only some small headway was made:

> A large representative deputation appointed at a public meeting waited on the Committee to request that they would recommend the Council to levy a special rate of one penny in the pound, under the Technical Instruction Act; but, having regard to the many demands on the rates and the heavy undertakings in which the Council is at present engaged, the Committee are of opinion that they would not be warranted now in so doing. They, however, recommend that the grant to schools coming within the provisions of the Act be increased for 1892 from £300 to £700.[21]

The £700 was distributed as follows: BGSA, £250; WMI, £175; Technical School, £200; School of Science and Engineering, £75. The grant was increased to £800 the following year, and that small amount continued to be distributed annually up to 1901. A total of £7,400 was so distributed over the decade 1891–1901.

Despite these pressures, the Belfast City Council steadfastly refused to implement the provisions of the TIA. There seemed to be several reasons for this parsimony and lack of resolve. Firstly, the problems of a rapidly growing city were already placing many demands on the rates; in his speech at the School of Art's prize-giving in March 1894, the Lord Mayor remarked that, 'Immense and costly drainage, and other works absolutely essential to the health of the community, had to be undertaken.'[22] A second reason for the Council's lack of action could be attributed to the ongoing concerns of industrialists. Some of these industrialists saw no benefit from educating their workers, some thought their apprenticeship schemes were more than adequate for the purpose, and some were wary about trade secrets leaking out at evening classes. It is noteworthy that the textile industries were usually well represented on the various deputations, whilst engineering and shipbuilding employers rarely put in an appearance. James Musgrave probably understated the case when he informed the RCTI in 1883 that 'there is amongst some of our best employers a slight

William Gray; formidable adversary and thorn in the flesh of the Belfast Council. (Gray, *Science and Art in Belfast*, 1904.)

prejudice against the introduction of technical education'.[23] A third reason for the Council's doggedness in the matter was an awareness that the Government was developing a growing respect for technical education, and there was an increasing likelihood that central government funds would ultimately come to the Council's rescue.

Several joint deputations from the city's providers of technical education met the Finance Committee over those crucial years, mainly to plead their own cases, but, sometimes to present outline plans for a new all-embracing Technical Institute. Perhaps the most significant and rewarding encounter took place on 19 January 1898 when a newly elected and enlarged Council was confronted by a widely representative and influential body of men. By that time public opinion had become very much alive to the importance of technical education, and that awareness was reflected in the membership of the deputation which comprised eight representatives from the Chamber of Commerce, seven from the Technical School, eight from the School of Art, three from the Working Men's Institute, four from the Linen Merchants' Association, four from the Power Loom Manufacturers' Association, three from the United Trades Council, two from the Flax Spinners' Association, and one from the Bleachers' Association. The lack of formal representation from shipbuilding and engineering interests is noteworthy.

R. Kyle Knox, President of the Chamber of Commerce, opened the case for the deputation. He pulled no punches;

> There was one thing which he deeply felt, and that was the comment of some English papers upon those engaged upon the promotion of this techni-cal education movement to the effect that Irishmen were ready enough to unite when they thought they could get anything from the Exchequer, but that they were not so ready to put their hands in their own pockets and do something for themselves at their own expense. Now, that large deputation was there to press upon the Corporation the desirability of preventing any such charge being brought against the city of Belfast in the future. The miser-able support which had been given to the gentlemen who now for several years had been exerting themselves to foster technical skill in Belfast appeared to him very little short of a scandal.[24]

Major General Geary, representing the Working Men's Institute, proposed the establishment of a committee, representative of the Council and the existing providers of technical education, and briefed to draw up a compre-hensive scheme of technical education for Belfast. But the Lord Mayor, James Henderson, was able to parry that thrust by informing the deputation that the Council had already agreed – on the third of that very month – to set up a special committee for that specific purpose. It would also consider the striking of a special rate under the TIA.

The Lord Mayor concluded the proceedings by offering full support to the establishment of a new and comprehensive system of technical education in Belfast, and he hoped that a penny rate – generating £4,500 at the time (worth around £350,000 today)[25] – could soon be struck for that purpose. It was agreed that the General Purposes Committee would appoint the afore-mentioned Special Committee at its next meeting, and it would be asked 'to consider the advisability of establishing a municipal technical school in the city of Belfast, and to formulate a scheme with the view of striking a special rate in accordance with the Technical Instruction Acts'.

The Special Committee had fourteen members, chaired by the Lord Mayor, Alderman James Henderson. It was agreed that representatives of the four local providers would be invited to help. The Committee's members soon became aware of their ignorance of activities in this field elsewhere in the Kingdom, so it was decided to despatch a deputation to England to see what could be learnt from existing practice. A report was presented to Council on 22 September 1898:

The deputation is thoroughly confirmed in the opinion that Belfast should follow the lead of municipalities and other large centres of population in their efforts to impart the highest class of education in the several trades, with the use of the latest and most improved machines and tools, in order to train students, as well as fit them to excel, in the various branches of science and art for positions they may be required to fill in practical industries.[26]

Here, at last, was evidence that at least some of the city fathers recognised the need for an effective system of technical education in Belfast. However, the Council continued to procrastinate, and no immediate steps were taken to implement the recommendations of its Special Committee. In the absence of government funding, the Council seemed resolutely opposed to the implementation of the TIA in Belfast.

Horace Plunkett to the Rescue

The foresight and persuasive powers of Horace Curzon Plunkett MP did much to attract that government funding. Born in England in 1854, the third son of Baron Dunsany, Plunkett studied at Eton and Oxford before health reasons sent him to Wyoming where, over a period of ten years, he ranched in the summer and wintered in Ireland. The death of his father in 1889 brought him back to Co. Meath where he established himself as a well-known public figure. He had a keen interest in cooperative creameries – an interest which led to his establishment in 1894 of the Irish Agricultural Organisation Society which embraced no fewer than thirty-three creameries.

Plunkett became MP for South Dublin in 1892, but he did his utmost to remain aloof from party politics and sectarian squabbles. His wide experience of Irish agriculture, and his awareness that an associated system of technical education was needed, persuaded him that these were matters that required Irish solutions – not English ones. Initially opposed to Home Rule (although he later became a strong advocate for the cause), he was unhappy with London's central control of local affairs; he felt that the DSA, in its South Kensington offices, was too remote, geographically and culturally, to determine the most appropriate and effective system of technical education for Ireland. His letter to the *Irish Press* in August 1895 started the ball rolling. It proposed a committee of Irish MPs to look into these matters, and to call on appropriate experts as and when required. This committee – called the Recess Committee because it met during the parliamentary recess – held its first and subsequent meetings in the Mansion House in Dublin. There were twenty-two members in all, including the five founding MPs. A fourteen-strong Ulster Consultative Committee, chaired by James Musgrave, provided a northern perspective on the various issues.[27]

The Recess Committee worked intensively and with remarkable harmony and good will. Its report recommended in 1896 that a new department should be established to deal specifically with agriculture and technical instruction in Ireland, and those powers that the DSA exercised in these matters should be transferred to said department. In 1896 a Bill was drafted for the creation of such a department, but its passage through the House was delayed in order to give time for the proper consideration and enactment of the Local Government (Ireland) Act 1898. By setting up county councils in Ireland, this Act provided the infrastructure necessary for the delivery of the provisions of the new department.

The Agriculture and Technical Instruction (Ireland) Act (1899) came into operation on 1 April 1900. It called for the establishment of a Department of Agriculture and Other Industries and Technical Instruction in Ireland (DATI). This substantial body, with £166,000 at its disposal annually (worth around £13 million today),[28] and 300 employees, was housed in Dublin's Upper Merrion Street. Its President (G. Balfour, Chief Secretary of Ireland), was supported by a Vice-President (Plunkett), a Secretary (T.P. Gill) and two Assistant Secretaries, one for agriculture and one for technical instruction. There were two boards, Agriculture (twelve members) and Technical Instruction (twenty-one members), and further advice and guidance was provided by a Council of Agriculture (102 members) and a Consultative Committee (five members). There were three Belfast representatives on the Board of Technical Instruction – Alderman James Dempsey, Sir Otto Jaffe, and Alexander Taylor.[29]

The Chief Secretary decided to tour the country in order to explain the significance and complexity of the new Act. His visit to Belfast on 19 January 1900 included an address to a large audience in the building in Wellington Place belonging to the Young Men's Christian Association (YMCA).[30] The new Department would have wide-ranging powers, including some formerly exercised by the DSA. For example it would take responsibility for the Royal College of Science of Ireland, the Science and Art Museum, the National Library, the Metropolitan School of Art, and the Royal Botanic Gardens at

Glasnevin. It would also administer grants for science and art, and technical instruction in Ireland.

The Chief Secretary was warmly applauded when he indicated that Belfast was likely to attract around £10,000 annually (worth around £780,000 today)[31] under the new arrangements. But he emphasised that the City Council would have to establish a Technical Instruction Committee which would, in practice, be the executive authority in all matters related to technical education in Belfast.

The Board of Technical Instruction would determine the precise amount that Belfast would receive. £55,000 of an available £166,000 had been allocated to technical instruction and, at its second meeting in June 1900 the Board decided: (1) to hold £15,000 of this amount in reserve; (2) to distribute £20,000 to the six county boroughs; (3) to use £20,000 for technical instruction in other parts of Ireland. The initial sum allocated to county boroughs was later raised to £25,010, and its distribution was based on population and rate of population increase as follows,[32]

BOROUGH	1891 POPULATION	1901 POPULATION	ALLOCATION
Belfast	273,079	349,180	£10,943
Dublin	245,001	260,247	£8,289
Cork	75,345	76,122	£2,436
Limerick	37,155	38,151	£1,219
Londonderry	33,200	39,892	£1,257
Waterford	26,203	26,769	£866

These were considerable sums of money, and it seemed that at long last technical education was beginning to receive the respect it deserved. It was important, however, that local authorities were aware that funds would only be provided for schemes approved by the new DATI, and already supported financially by local benefactors; the principle of helping those who helped themselves remained. Plunkett visited Belfast to explain the Department's expectations.[33] At a meeting of the city's Technical Instruction Committee and representatives of the relevant schools, Plunkett built his address around three important points,

(1) Belfast's technical instruction scheme would have to be co-ordinated with, and complementary to, the city's scheme of general education. The Department's

funds ought not to be applied solely to any new technical college; they should be available also to those existing institutions which are providing science and art teaching. Also, scholarships should be provided to assist and encourage the transfer of pupils from these schools to any new technical college.

(2) The work of any new technical college must be closely related to the needs of the chief industries of Belfast. These would include, of course, the linen industry and the engineering industry, but Plunkett, noting that 'Belfast runs rather more on horse-power than electrical power just at present', made a strong plea for a greater emphasis on the new and growing electrical industries.

(3) The work of any new technical college should be coordinated with the educational system of the whole country. Here Plunkett was attempting to justify the DATI's decision to strengthen the Royal College of Science in Dublin. He pleaded, 'if you could … postpone the question of providing the highest scientific education until you see whether your requirements are met in Dublin, you would be doing great service to the general education of the country.' The next chapter examines Belfast's response to those points.

9

Planning a New System

Establishing a Committee Structure

The new Department of Agriculture and Technical Instruction, with its promise of untold riches, provided a much-needed stimulus to a procrastination-prone Belfast Corporation. But the allocation of £10,000 to the city had many strings attached. A general scheme of technical education, driven by a Technical Instruction Committee, had to be put in place, and the Council had to contribute at least one penny in the pound from the rates. The scheme would require coordination of the work of the existing national and intermediate schools, and of the several providers of evening classes in science and technical subjects. Of great significance, those latter voluntary agencies that had struggled for years to deliver technical education in Belfast, were about to come under municipal control.

The Technical Instruction Act of 1899 made it a condition that Councils establish Technical Instruction Committees if they were to be eligible for the various grants available under the new legislation. The establishment of the relevant committee in Belfast was a protracted and complex business. Chapter 8 described the preliminary steps taken in January 1898, prior to the establishment of the act, when the Council finally yielded to public pressure on the question of technical education. The Council agreed to appoint a committee to consider the advisability of establishing a municipal technical school in Belfast, and this Special Committee was to include fourteen members of the Corporation alongside representatives of the existing science and art schools.[1] However, the Council was slow to appoint the latter members, and a confrontation between the Special Committee and a joint deputation from the School of Art and the Technical School on 11 November 1898 brought the matter to a head. A compromise was agreed; the schools would not be represented on the

Special Committee, but they would be consulted. It was resolved that,

> Governing Bodies of each of the Schools in receipt of grant in aid of Technical Education from the Corporation be invited to nominate two of their members to consult with the Committee in regard to any points which may arise during the progress of the undertaking where their special knowledge would be of public advantage.[2]

Eight representatives, elected by their respective schools, formed a Schools' Representative Committee (SRC) whose membership was as follows (note that the titles Engineering School, and School of Applied Science and Engineering were used interchangeably at the time):

School of Art: J. Stevenson, W. Gray.

Technical School: Prof. M. Fitzgerald, J. Malone.

Working Men's Institute: W.J. Alderdice, S.F. Milligan.

Engineering School: R. Graeme-Watt, W. Weir.

The SRC met the Technical School Committee (the renamed Special Committee) frequently, but there were those who complained that they had never been seriously consulted on any issue.[3]

Tentative Steps Towards a New Scheme

The impending implementation of the Technical Instruction Act focused minds. Time was slipping away and the Council could no longer afford to be indecisive. In William Gray's words, 'The light of the twentieth century exposed their lassitude and compelled them to fall into line with municipal progress in industrial education.'[4] The Lord Mayor, Sir Otto Jaffe, realised that Belfast had to move quickly if full advantage were to be derived from the Act's provisions. To this end, he arranged a conference of the Technical School Committee and the SRC to consider the planning of the new municipal technical school. The meeting took place in the Reform Club on the 9 January 1900. The major outcome was the decision to recommend the establishment of a Consultation Committee, 'to prepare and submit a scheme for technical Instruction, including the necessary buildings, etc., for the consideration of the Technical School Committee and the several bodies interested'.[5] Chaired by the Lord Mayor, the Consultation Committee had four members from the Corporation side, and the existing science and art schools were represented by Professor Fitzgerald, J. Stevenson, R. Barklie, and W. Weir.

This development prompted Gray to write to the press[6] about the earlier unsuccessful attempt to establish a city-wide system of technical education in 1887. Then, plans for a proposed Victoria Institute, based on the Free Library and the grounds to its rear, were mysteriously abandoned at an advanced stage. Gray outlined his own views on a new technical institute: it would require eight schools – Art, Science, Engineering, Manual Instruction, Modern Languages, Health, Commerce, and Music. And it would complement the rest of the city's education system with scholarships facilitating movement into the technical institute from the intermediate schools, and movement onward to Queen's College and other higher education institutions.

Those ideas may or may not have influenced the Consultation Committee's recommendations, which were considered by the Technical School Committee at its meeting on 29 January 1900. Various amendments and additions were made, such as training for teachers, an increased focus on women's work, and preparatory classes. The agreed scheme was as follows:[7]

Both day and evening classes to be held, and to comprise:

A School of Art
A Technical or Trade Subjects School
A Chemical Subjects School
A Commercial Subjects School
A Domestic and Women's School
Training for Agricultural Technical Teachers (except in practical agriculture, if
desired by the Agricultural Board)
Training for Manual Teachers

Preparatory Classes, sometimes called 'continuation classes', to be provided for in the building, and the departments of the school enumerated below are recommended accordingly. The Departments of the School to be:

Art
Pure and Applied Mathematics and Physics
Mechanical and Electrical Engineering and Naval Architecture
Chemistry, Pure and Applied
Textile Fabrics, including Bleaching and Dyeing
Building Trades and Sanitary Engineering
Training for Agriculture, Technical, and Manual Teachers
Botany, Zoology, and Geology
Commerce and Preparatory Classes
Domestic Economy

How such a scheme would be delivered had yet to be considered, but that required a clearer definition of the roles of the various players – i.e. the existing providers, the intermediate schools, and the Queen's College. And further thought had to be given to the physical arrangement of the new buildings, bearing in mind that they together would have to provide easy access to technical education across the city.

The Library and Technical Instruction Committee

The SRC held its last meeting with the Technical School Committee on 20 July 1900. Its demise was the result of a Council decision to reorganise its committee structure. The Library Committee merged with the Technical School Committee to form a new, fifteen-strong Library and Technical Instruction Committee (LTIC). The LTIC met for the first time on 2 August 1900, when James Henderson was elected to the Chair. Two consultative committees were set up – a Manufacturers' Consultative Committee (MCC) and a Scholastic Consultative Committee (SCC). Of these, the MCC was by far the more dominant body; its fifty-two members were all influential (mostly wealthy) citizens of Belfast, and it went about its work in a focused and professional way. Instructed to meet at noon every Thursday, the MCC managed its work by dividing the members into six vocational groups covering art, building, chemistry, engineering, textiles, and bleaching and dyeing.

The SCC, on the other hand, had fewer numbers and carried much less clout. Its twenty-four members represented: Belfast Royal Academy (one member), Christian Brothers' Schools (two), Methodist College Belfast (two), Royal Belfast Academical Institution (two), St Malachy's College (two), Queen's College (two), National Schools (one), and teachers (four). To these were added the eight members of the already established SRC, but with one difference – William Gray, now clearly *persona non grata* in Corporation circles, was replaced by J. Vinycomb.[8]

The LTIC's predecessor committees had been composed entirely of members of the Corporation, albeit advised by various consultative committees. But pressure had been growing for formal representation on the LTIC of employers and existing providers of technical education. (Those pressures had been initiated as far back as 1883 when a deputation of rate payers had demanded the establishment of a composite managing committee.) The Corporation finally yielded on the matter in October 1900 when the LTIC agreed to co-opt five members from the MCC.[9] The members chosen initially were J. Horner (Clonard Foundry), W.H. McLaughlin (Castleton Building Works), R.H. Reade (York Street Spinning Company), R. Thompson (Mulhouse Works), and W.H. Wilson (Queen's Island).

The SCC was ignored in all of this, indicating the Council's clear intention to use a new broom to sweep the old technical education system clean. Feeling slighted, the academics put pressure on the LTIC to co-opt three members representing existing providers, but the proposal was turned down by a vote of seven to five. Some recognition of local achievement was achieved, however, when J. Stevenson (of McCaw, Stevenson and Orr), the Chairman of the BGSA, was co-opted in January 1901.[10]

Looking for a Site for the New Institute

Thoughts turned from curriculum to bricks and mortar. Several sites were proposed for the new technical institute. Even the Old Town Hall, which would shortly become redundant with the completion of the new City Hall, was seen by some as a possible contender. Lord Mayor Otto Jaffe made such a suggestion at the annual meeting of the BGSA on 25 March 1896, but a member of the audience drew attention to the building's general lack of suitability for the purposes in mind, and the difficulties which the many surrounding buildings would place in the way of expansion.

The strongest runner appeared to be the St Anne's Market site (sometimes referred to as the Carrick Hill site), which lay to the rear of the recently constructed Free Library in Royal Avenue, and which had been a central feature in the defunct plans for a Victoria Institute. In August 1899, the Technical School Committee resolved, 'That the Council do authorise the Town Clerk to proceed to acquire the unbuilt piece of ground next Carrick Hill which will be required as an addition to the site for the Technical School.'[11] Further support for this site was provided by the Special Committee, which had been appointed to visit and report upon technical schools in Great Britain.

So planning seemed to be moving inexorably towards the acquisition and development of the Carrick Hill area. However, an unexpected and somewhat sensational interjection by Lord Mayor Otto Jaffe introduced yet another strong contender. The Marcus Ward business had struck hard times, and its Board had taken the decision to sell off its Royal Ulster Works on the Dublin Road. Jaffe, for whatever reason, made a personal intervention and purchased the buildings for £25,000. He informed the Technical School Committee of the purchase in November 1899,[12] and stated that he was prepared to give the Corporation one week to decide whether or not it would wish to avail of the buildings for the proposed technical institute.

Jaffe argued that the purchase would bring great overall savings, 'The premises are most extensive and have boiler engines and shafting with large rooms suitable for machinery, art work and the holding of classes, and there is ample ground for extensions.'[13] Intrigued, the Technical School Committee met on the site the following day and, following a brief tour, it was agreed that a surveyor should be asked to estimate the costs of conversion to an educational facility. The business moved ahead at great pace, and only four days later,[14] the City Surveyor was able to present his thoughts on the matter. He listed several good points, including the site's central position, its glass-roofed buildings, its suitability for workshops, and the northerly aspect, which provided good lighting for art classrooms and galleries. But a lot of refurbishment would be necessary: all the rooms would need to be soundproofed; a system of ventilation was needed; lifts were needed; a main front staircase would have to be installed; lavatory facilities needed improvement, etc.

Having digested the surveyor's report, the Technical School Committee decided in November 1899 to recommend that Council purchase the Marcus Ward buildings.[15] There were mixed reactions to the proposal from those who were likely to have to work in the new Institute. The BGSA[16] considered the proposed site 'ideal as to central position, light and quietness for the art sections with buildings almost perfectly adapted to the requirements of the combined schools'. The BGSA was aware that the lease on its College Square accommodation would expire in a year's time, so the possibility of a relatively quick move into the Marcus Ward buildings held many attractions. The Working Men's Institute also offered its support:[17] S.F. Milligan argued that the rooms could, at little cost, be subdivided to provide accommodation for science classes, and he was also attracted by the possibility of early occupation of the premises. But the Board of the Belfast Technical School opposed the proposal, Professor Fitzgerald arguing that 'it would entail a larger initial expense to carry out the new scheme of utilising Marcus Ward's buildings than to erect a school on the site originally proposed'. No doubt, the experience over many years of living and working in rehashed industrial premises had influenced the decision of the School's Board to prefer a new build at Carrick Hill.

In the end, the tide turned against the proposal, and the Council agreed with the following resolution of the Technical School Committee:

> That this Committee having considered the public spirited and generous offer of the Lord Mayor in regard to the premises lately occupied by Marcus Ward and Co. Ltd for a Technical School are of opinion that those premises would not be nearly so suitable as a new building to be erected upon the site already adopted by the City Council.

The Carrick Hill development now seemed a certainty. However, a late contender was about to enter the competition. Rumours that the Trustees of the Royal Belfast Academical Institution (RBAI) were interested in renting a part of their grounds in College Square persuaded the Technical School Committee to make a formal approach to the Institution early in December 1899. The next meeting of the Committee[18] welcomed a deputation from RBAI, and the ensuing discussions indicated that both sides were willing to pursue the matter further. The fact that the Technical School Committee deleted a recommendation for the Carrick Hill site from its Consultative Committee's report a few weeks later indicates that background negotiations with RBAI had been progressing satisfactorily. Formal negotiations began in earnest in February 1900 when RBAI proposed an annual rental of £1,600 for the 5,400 square yards (4,514 square metres) of ground fronting their property.[19] The Corporation responded by setting £1,200 as an upper limit. The final settlement in February committed the Council to an annual rent of £1,350, and to a sum not exceeding £1,000 for the development of College Square East.

Helping the Providers

The Department of Agriculture and Technical Instruction (DATI) had made it very clear that Belfast had to produce a comprehensive plan for technical instruction. The plan would have to include the intermediate schools that would provide students for any new technical institute, and the higher education institutions like Queen's College and the Royal College of Science in Dublin who might, in turn, receive the graduates from the new institute. The Technical School Committee therefore instructed R. Meyer, the Chief Clerk of the Belfast County Borough Council, to circulate the following letter to all schools and technical institutions in the city on 23 June 1900:

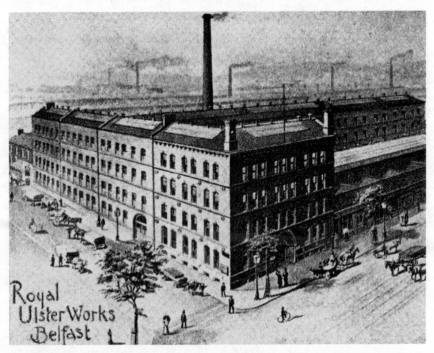

Marcus Ward's Royal Ulster Works on the Dublin Road (completed 1874). (Dixon, *Marcus Ward and Company of Belfast,* 2004.)

In order to take advantage of the grants and make them available for schools, the Committee will be prepared to consider schemes drawn up by school authorities, with the view of recommending grants in aid of salaries and science and art teachers, and for instruction in technical subjects, and for provision for suitable laboratories, workshops, equipment, and apparatus, and provision of scholarships and exhibitions tenable local or otherwise; but it must clearly be understood that a comprehensive and definite plan must be arranged, so that all establishments, whether elementary, secondary, or advanced will prepare students for the technical college which will take up the studies where the others leave off.

Schools were reminded that the new technical institute would be ready in about two years. They were urged to have their technical classes in place so that, when the institute opened, 'there may be a crop of pupils sufficiently advanced to be able to take advantage of it'.[20] The letter prompted some considerable activity in Belfast's educational circles, especially with its prospect of grant aid.

Whilst schools and others were preparing plans and requests for financial aid, Mr Blair, the DATI's Inspector, brought an air of reality to proceedings. He visited Belfast in late September 1900 in order to see for himself what was on offer in the field of technical education.[21] The following examples of his findings paint, on the whole, a sorry picture. In the National Schools, the Belfast Model School, with 123 pupils, had no special rooms for drawing or for science; there was a cookery room, but the manual instruction room was poorly equipped. Of the intermediate schools, most provided classes in science subjects under the Intermediate Regulations in science subjects. However, many of these classes were small, e.g. BRA could only muster six pupils in its chemistry class. Facilities were generally inadequate: RBAI, with 200 pupils, had a serviceable chemistry laboratory, but there was no physical laboratory, and the few manual instruction benches were gathering dust. In St Malachy's College, all 198 pupils took drawing, but the apparatus in the natural philosophy rooms was out of date. BRA, with 116 pupils, had a special drawing room, but there was no physical laboratory, and the workshop was a 'most unwholesome place'. The Methodist College, with 334 pupils, had a chemistry laboratory, but there was no drawing room, no manual workshop, and no other science lecture room or laboratory. Campbell College was the only school to receive a glowing report, its 160 boys having access to excellent science lecture rooms and a well-equipped chemistry laboratory. There was, in addition, a physical laboratory, a woodwork shop and a metal shop that included two lathes and a gas engine. Blair considered

Preparing to build the Municipal Technical Institute on the lawn of the Royal Belfast Academical Institution, 1902. (Hogg Collection, Ulster Museum.)

Campbell College the best-equipped school in Ireland.

Blair also spent some time on the premises of the various specialist providers of technical education. Here, also, he found much to criticise. At the BGSA he attended a Design Class and 'was not greatly impressed by the system of teaching'. At the Belfast Working Men's Institute he found that, 'This place has been so poorly managed in past sessions it would hardly be safe to estimate the numbers of students during the coming session.' At the Belfast Technical School, he found the premises poor and the roof weak.

These findings were an indictment on the city's schools and on the city fathers. Blair concluded that 'The state of things existing in Belfast is, from a Technical Instruction point of view, deplorable; and no parallel to it could be found in any such industrial centre in Great Britain.' This obloquy was expanded in a lengthy report, part of which follows:

The character of the instruction: Literary, bookish, almost without qualification, so far as Day Schools are concerned. That is to say, in a centre the existence of whose inhabitants depends on (a) the hand skill of the workers (b) on the capacity of the manufacturers and businessmen to deal with practical questions which come before them in a concrete form, the pupils devote the greater part of their waking hours at the most impressionable time of their lives to a form of Education in which practical work has no share, and which is said to be opposed to practical life.

And why? Because the want of funds, the previous training and the tastes of the teachers, the Intermediate and University Regulations shape the curriculum of all according to the wants of the few, presumably the best. The few are those looking forward to a University or possibly a professional or Civil Service career. This also means that presumably the best brains turn aside or are directed from industry and commerce – on which the existence of their town depends.[22]

Belfast's educators must have been stung by these criticisms, but they would have taken some solace from the fact that lack of funds had been included as a mitigating factor. They would have also been pleased to note that the provisions of the Agriculture and Technical Instruction Act would give them access, through the Corporation, to grants for apparatus and equipment. These were interim grants pending the implementation of the city's new scheme of technical instruction.

The month of October 1900 saw a stream of deputations knocking at the doors of the LTIC in pursuit of this money. Each institution was required to provide assurance that its grant would be used for the stated purposes. Methodist College's response follows:

> Gentlemen,
> On behalf of the Board of Governors of Methodist College, I beg to give you the required guarantee that Technical Instruction will be made an integral and permanent part of our curriculum, also that we will provide suitable Laboratories and Lecture Rooms, wherein Chemistry and Physics may be taught practically.[23]

After much deliberation and further consultation with Blair, the following equipment grants were agreed in November 1900:[24]

Christian Brothers' Schools: £400
Royal Belfast Academical Institution: £400
St Malachy's College: £400
Methodist College: £400
Belfast Royal Academy: £200
Hastings Street Technical School: £150
School of Art: £220

Following a challenge from the DATI, an application for £250 from the School of Applied Science was allowed to lapse. BRA, the only day school not to get £400, made representations to have its grant raised to match that of RBAI, but the LTIC turned the appeal down on the grounds that there were insufficient pupils attending relevant classes at BRA. The school's governors were asked to prepare new plans for the LTIC's consideration.

The total sum of £2,470 for equipment may not seem much by today's standards, but, in terms of purchasing power, that sum would be worth around £180,000 today.[25] The matter of maintenance grants for the year ending March 1901 also required attention. These were:

School of Art: £250
Hastings Street Technical School: £250
Working Men's Institute: £200
School of Applied Science: £75
Royal Belfast Academical Institution: £25

RBAI was a newcomer to this particular list. The Technical School of Science (TSS), whilst based in RBAI, was described by Francis Forth as a 'separate and distinct school'. The TSS used two lecture rooms and a chemistry laboratory, and the ninety-seven pupils on its register were attending classes in Mechanics, Mathematics, Telegraphy and Telephony, and Chemistry.[26] The maintenance grant of £25 was found by reducing the grant to the Working Men's Institute by £25.

Appointing a Principal

The Belfast Council agreed on 2 July 1900 to appoint a Principal at a salary of £500 per annum. However, subsequent discussions with Captain Shaw of DATI, and Mr Blair concluded[27] that this figure would have to be raised to £600 if they were to be sure of attracting a 'first-class man'. The LTIC made such a resolution to Council, and a special meeting of the Corporation was convened in August to consider the matter. That meeting exposed a breath-taking ignorance of the difficulties and challenge involved in the planning, administration and management of technical education.[28] One Alderman saw the post as a sinecure and stated, 'His reasons for dissenting were that they had no technical school for a man to be principal of.' A Councillor remarked that 'the plans had not even been adopted, and in these circumstances it was surely premature to come to any conclusion regarding salary or regarding the office itself'. However, the Lord Mayor, Sir R.J. McConnell, handled the matter adroitly. He explained that the members of the LTIC were not conversant with the needs of such an institute, and that special expertise and knowledge would be needed to bring together the city's five or six kindred institutions. The LTIC needed a man who had been 'through the mill', to carry all of this forward. The Lord Mayor's arguments won the day and Council voted unanimously to raise the Principal's salary to £600 per annum (worth around £45,000 today).[29]

The Town Clerk was instructed[30] to advertise the post of Principal in the Belfast daily papers and to 'use his discretion as to what English, Scotch and Dublin papers the advertisement be inserted'. There was no shortage of applicants. At the end of October a sub-committee of the LTIC drew up a short-list of fifteen, and in November, a further distillation, directed by the DATI, reduced the numbers to three – an Englishman, a Scotsman and an Irishman. The LTIC interviewed these three on 26 November 1900 when the Irishman, Francis Charles Forth, won the day.

Forth was born in Londonderry on 10 August 1861, but his father Douglas, an upholsterer, decided to move the family to the north of England in the mid-1860s. After completing an elementary education in Lancashire, Forth started an apprenticeship in sign-writing in 1878, but it is not clear whether or not he carried this through to completion.[31] There are records of his working for the Bury Corporation Waterworks, and the London and North-Western Railway Company, but it seems that dissatisfaction with his career prospects persuaded Forth that he needed to improve his education. So in 1884, at the relatively late age of twenty-three, he headed back across the water to Dublin where, aided by a Royal Scholarship, he enrolled on a three-year course in the Faculty of Engineering at the Royal College of Science for Ireland in St Stephen's Green. Forth was awarded his Diploma of Associateship (Assoc.R.C.Sc.I) in 1887.

The Associateship qualified its holders to teach science. Forth recognised the challenges of technical education and the urgent necessity of establishing an effective system, so, having returned to Lancashire after graduation, he moved south early in 1888 to join the staff of the People's Palace Technical School, which Queen Victoria had just opened in London's East End. Marrying Hannah Lawson in August 1888, he and his new wife settled in Bethnal Green for four years whilst he became immersed in teaching engineering to both day and evening students. That experience, including working with the relatively poor of the East End, was to stand him in good stead for the challenges of Belfast.

With a growing reputation as a technical teacher, Forth was attracted back north to Manchester in 1892 where he was to lecture for six years on engineering at the Municipal Technical School – a rapidly growing establishment with roots in the Manchester Mechanics' Institute. Its Director, J.H. Reynolds, soon recognised Forth's talents for management and administration, and he was duly appointed Assistant Director in 1898. Forth applied himself with characteristic vigour to the task, and Manchester's newspapers were soon lauding the achievements of this born organiser and workaholic.[32] As the evidence bears out, Belfast was extremely fortunate to attract this man of many talents. It was hoped that Forth could take up his new post on the first day of the new year, but his duties in Manchester forced him to delay his start until 1 February 1901.

Incorporation

Forth's mettle was soon put to the test. With time running short, it was crucially important that immediate steps were taken to draw together the component parts of Belfast's new scheme of technical education. A first priority was the incorporation into the proposed scheme of the work of the various institutions which were already providing scientific and technical instruction in evening classes. The LTIC appointed a sub-committee in February 1901 to pursue these matters but, as expected, it was left to Forth to drive the business forward.

Of the five institutions concerned, the Belfast Government School of Art (BGSA) was the first to be taken over by the Corporation. But the amalgamation was initiated by the BGSA itself. Concerned that the lease on the property at College Square North was about to expire in December 1901, and aware that new buildings would not be in place for several years, the Board of BGSA despatched a deputation on 7 March to explain their predicament to the LTIC, and to suggest a way forward.[33] They proposed that the BGSA be transferred, lock, stock and barrel, to the control of the City Council. Asked to advise, Forth responded less than two weeks later.

Forth's report, dated 26 March 1901, was marked Private and Confidential; for Members of the Library and Technical Instruction Committee Only.[34]

Forth was of the view that 'the teaching is conducted on sound and artistic lines, and the staff is capable of doing efficient work', but he concluded that management, administration and discipline were defective. Forth argued that the BGSA had not met the needs of the industries of Belfast. He latched on to a public statement by the usually more astute William Gray that BGSA students 'had not been successful in getting employment locally and they had invariably had to leave Belfast and get appointments elsewhere'. Forth concluded that the blame for this state of affairs lay at the feet of the BGSA Board of Management, which had neither effectively influenced the popular view of the applied arts in Belfast, nor demonstrated how art could be applied with effect to Belfast's industries. Reinforcing the latter point, he informed the LTIC that his inquiries had uncovered that 'the School of Art has not produced the class of designs desired by the manufacturers, and that one firm which presented prizes has demurred to continuing them because the work produced not meet with its approval'. All things considered, including the general air of unrest amongst the BGSA staff, Forth recommended that the LTIC should assume responsibility for the future conduct of art instruction given in the Belfast Government School of Art.

Whilst the outcome was welcomed by the Board of the BGSA, some members took exception to Forth's comments about management defects. Principal George Trowbridge complained to the LTIC on 25 April, and William Gray presented a lengthy defence in his book. Gray's argument[35] is an interesting one, and one still central to the relationship between education and industry. Should educators provide fodder – or enlightenment – for industry? Gray was convinced that enlightenment was the *raison d'être* of education, and that the BGSA should 'exalt the limited standard of the practical manufacturer'.

Forth produced a further report[36] on progress towards amalgamation in June. It reminded the LTIC of the advantages of incorporation, including: greater efficiency through improved co-ordination; the combination of small classes into more viable larger classes; the elimination of competition; the reduction or elimination of duplication. Of greater moment, perhaps, was his reminder that other major towns and cities across the United Kingdom had introduced such systems to great effect, and that the DATI was of the view that 'in the interests of Technical Instruction it is most desirable that such an amalgamation as is now referred to should be aimed at, and brought about at as early a date as possible'. A further advantage surfaced at a later meeting of the LTIC in August: more suitable for internal consideration than public discussion, the minute read,[37]

The Committee were of the opinion it would be better to take over all these

COUNTY BOROUGH OF BELFAST.

TECHNICAL INSTITUTION.

THE CORPORATION desires to APPOINT A Qualified Person as PRINCIPAL of their proposed TECHNICAL INSTITUTION, to enter on his duties at 1st October. He must be a thoroughly qualified Educationalist, and it is desirable that he should be conversant with the Technical Requirements of the Textile or Engineering Industry. He will be required to advise as to the Plans for the Building, and prepare a Scheme for the Co-ordination of Education in the City, report on the existing Schools of Technology, and subsequently to take Charge of a Department. Salary, £600 a year.

Applications, stating age, experience, and qualifications, with not more than three Testimonials, to be lodged in my Office on or before 22nd September.

Personal canvassing of members will be a disqualification.

SAML. BLACK, Town Clerk.

The Northern Whig's advertisement for a new Principal, 21 August 1900.

Francis Charles Forth in the uniform of a Captain in the Royal Irish Rifles. (Belfast Metropolitan College.)

existing institutions at once rather than allow them to go on and become so strong that perhaps when the new Institute was completed they could not get control of them at all.

Forth's progress report indicated that, setting aside the BGSA, the other four providers of relevant evening classes had accepted incorporation as unavoidable. Indeed, it seems that several viewed it as a blessing in disguise:

The School of Applied Science: A letter from W.J. Fforde had been read at an earlier meeting of the LTIC meeting on 6 June. It confirmed his willingness to hand over classes.

Technical School, Hastings Street: The Board of the Technical School was content with the proposed incorporation. There was a request that LTIC should pay for equipment, but the School Board would use those monies for scholarships to further the scheme.

Working Men's Institute; The Chairman of the Board, W.J. Alderdice, expressed willingness to hand over classes. Principal Samuel Templeton concurred, but made clear his wish to obtain a suitable post under within the new Municipal scheme.

Technical School of Science (RBAI); Forth anticipated no problems in incorporating this relatively small organisation.

Writing six years later[38], Forth described these negotiations as having been 'carried on in a most harmonious manner by all concerned'. It is abundantly clear that he was a man of considerable ability.

Transitional Accommodation Arrangements

The amalgamation of the five existing institutions provided the new scheme with a substantial accommodation for tuition in art. But much more space would be required if the scheme's aim to meet the needs of all of Belfast's citizens were to be met. Forth arranged for advertisements to be placed in the local press seeking temporary accommodation for evening science and technical classes.[39] In addition to a building in a central position, he sought rooms within easy distance of Carlisle Circus, Shaftesbury Square, Templemore Avenue, and

Falls Road. Any buildings offered would have to be capable of division into at least six classrooms, each able to accommodate forty to fifty students.

Responses to the advertisement must have been satisfactory, since the Technical Institute's first published prospectus[40] was able to include the following list of accommodation:

College Square North
Working Men's Institute, Queen Street
Hastings Street
Royal Academy, Antrim Road
Tennent Street National School
Model School, Falls Road
Raglan Street National School
Montgomery National School, Donegall Pass
Mountpottinger National School, Albertbridge Road
Templemore Avenue Baths
School of Art, North Street

Two of the above merit further comment – College Square North and North Street. After much deliberation it was concluded that the north wing of RBAI at College Square North would no longer be suitable – even on a temporary basis – for the teaching of art. But Forth's advertisement for a central location had drawn a response from the owners of the vacant Merchant Buildings (now 170 Upper North Street). These, with three spacious floors, and the top one particularly well lit, seemed to be more than adequate for the purposes in mind. So the building was rented initially for three years (at £180 per annum) and opened in grand style on 25 September 1901 by the Marquis of Dufferin and Ava. The opening ceremony was chaired by Sir James Henderson, who painted a vibrant picture of the Corporation's initiatives in technical instruction. However, it also gave J. Stevenson a last opportunity to vent his spleen as Chairman of the Board of the BGSA:

Nothing was more depressing than for those engaged in an important work to be without the necessary funds to carry it on as efficiently as they would wish to do, and this had been for a long time their position in the Government School of Art. They would understand this when he told them that their accommodation and equipment were the same as they had been for the last thirty years. They had no Mr Gill to go to for £10,000 a year. All they

The now-derelict Merchant Buildings in North Street.

The old School of Art building in College Square North in 1902. (Hogg Collection, Ulster Museum.)

received was £250 a year from the Corporation and a few small sums given by citizens. The rest they had to earn by results at South Kensington and by fees from pupils. When they compared these resources with the magnificent sums given for the encouragement of art in Birmingham and other cross-Channel towns, it was no wonder they felt dispirited.[41]

The building in College Square North was not lost during the acquisition of the new facility in North Street. The lease on this building was due to expire on 31 December 1901, but RBAI offered an extension at the same rent of £100 per annum on condition that 'the Corporation transferred to the Governors the old railing of the school in the front of the ground taken for the Technical School'.[42] In the early years of the Technical Institute the building housed classes in electrical engineering and in women's work.

IO

A Dream Realised:

The Municipal Technical Institute

Planning the New Building

With the merger of the five antecedent institutions completed in June 1901, and arrangements for temporary accommodation for the new Municipal Technical Institute, Belfast (MTIB) resolved in mid-summer of that year, intense activity was now required to make the Institute fit for purpose on its opening day, 30 September 1901. Central to this was a determination of what the Institute would provide in order to deliver 'instruction in the principles of those arts and sciences which bear directly or indirectly upon the trades and industries located in Belfast and the neighbouring districts'.[1] A secondary, but equally immediate concern, was the acquisition of suitably qualified and experienced staff to provide the relevant instruction. The marketing of this new system of technical education and the role of the new Institute in its delivery was a crucial task. Whilst aimed at potential students, the marketing policy would also have to win the support of employers.

All of this would be going on in temporary accommodation, but the work of planning a new central building would have to forge ahead. Having chosen a site for the new Institute, and having obtained it at a reasonable rent, the Corporation now sought to appoint an architect to design the building. In March 1900, the Technical School Committee agreed to seek an architect through open competition[2], but two weeks later that decision was rescinded and it was quietly decided to invite a local architect to design and superintend the erection of the buildings.[3] This action prompted the editor of *The Irish Builder* to remark that, 'Belfast seems destined to preserve an unenviable notoriety in the matter of questionable architectural methods'.[4]

Samuel Stevenson, of 83 Royal Avenue, Belfast, was chosen for the task. His remuneration would amount to 4 per cent of the total costs, which were initially set at £55,000. The instructions to the architect, published on 4 May 1900, included the following;

> The Architect shall submit the following Preliminary Drawings, drawn to a scale of 8 ft to the inch, on plain white paper, mounted on plain stretchers, without frames, each 38 inches wide and 25 inches high;
> (1) Plan of each floor.
> (2) Such sections as may be necessary to illustrate the general treatment and arrangement of the interior.
> (3) All external elevations.
> (4) One sheet showing details of some portion of the exterior to a scale of ½ inch to the foot.
> (5) A perspective view taken from a point in a street from which the view could actually be had.

The Library and Technical Instruction Committee (LTIC) set down firm guidelines: on style, for example, the instructions stated that 'The Corporation are desirous that architectural character without undue extravagance should be aimed at.' They also suggested that a four-storey building would adequately meet the specification, with the exception of the space required for a spinning room, a weaving shed, and engineers' shops, which were to be accommodated in one-storey buildings on the central parts of the site. It was originally intended to extend Wellington Place right to the front porch of the Academical Institution, and to construct a connecting street, open to the public, at the rear of the new Institute between the extended Wellington Place and College Square North.[6] However, further thought, and objections from various quarters nipped that idea in the bud.

Stevenson submitted his designs to the Corporation in August 1900[7]. In addition to the required drawings, he produced a booklet of eight sketches, including a perspective view. Whilst some members of the LTIC had visited other similar developments in England and Scotland, the Committee was lacking in relevant expertise and experience and found it difficult to comment sensibly on Stevenson's proposals. However, Francis Forth's appointment in November brought great relief. Although unable to take up the post of Principal until February 1901, Forth travelled to Belfast several times to meet the LTIC and to have discussions with the architect and other appropriate persons. For example, he and Stevenson met the Manufacturers' Consultative Committee on 19 December 1900. Forth went further in seeking the professional opinion of Walter H. Wilson of Harland & Wolff, who criticised Stevenson for having allocated too much space to corridors and passages. Whilst he approved Stevenson's proposed third-floor balcony corridor on the College Square South frontage, that particular feature never materialised.[8]

Other critics had their say. Councillor Dr O'Connell, a surgeon and a neighbour of Sir William Whitla (living in numbers 9 and 8 College Square North respectively), asked that the Institute's chimney be moved 'with a view to its position being slightly altered so as to cause the minimum annoyance to the residents in College Square North'.[9] And the indomitable William Gray[10] expressed concern that the new college was to be built from 'the absorbent limestone from the convict stations of Portland, instead of from the granite hills of the County Down, the carboniferous limestone of Armagh, or the sandstone abounding in the North'. If Co. Down could supply the materials for London's Albert Memorial, why, Gray asked, could it not do the same for a major local institution?

Stevenson had adhered rigidly to the guidelines set down by the Corporation. As instructed, he had left a well in the centre of the building, the ground floor of which was to accommodate workshops and weaving sheds, etc. But Forth noted a major omission – that of a central hall where examinations and grand events could take place. Rectification of that omission was a major problem, but well worth the effort. As well as serving an essential facility for large gatherings, the finished hall was to provide a treat for the eye:

> This hall will be finished in Keen's cement, having a moulded and panelled dado about 6 feet high all round, and will be lighted by ten large oriel windows of teak filled with lead lights, the ceiling being of plaster, broken into deeply-recessed panels by heavy beams, and all moulded and enriched, a recessed platform being placed at the end of the hall.[11]

There were other problems. Space was always at a premium, and the surprisingly large influx of students in the Technical Institute's first year brought matters to a head. As originally planned, the building was to have been set back on all

ELEVATION TO COLLEGE SQUARE E.

Stevenson's original front elevation of the proposed Municipal Technical Institute. (LTIC 21/8/1900 and PRONI LA/7/7HD/2.)

sides 12ft (3.66m) from the footpath, but in order to gain some additional space it was decided in late 1901 to cover the whole of the site and to make certain internal additions. This brought the total estimated cost up to £81,000. But even that increase in space was not enough, and burgeoning student numbers in the second year of operation forced the decision in 1904 to add a fifth floor, bringing the cost to some £100,000 (around £8 million today).

Construction, the responsibility of W.J. Campbell & Sons, got underway on 26 May 1902. The foundation stone was laid by the Lord Lieutenant, the Earl of Dudley on 24 November 1902.

Getting a Team Together

Despite of the immense burden Forth had to shoulder in the early months of 1901, he still managed to set the highest standards of diligence and enterprise. In addition to extensive discussions and negotiations with the various providers of technical education in the city, he worked hard to publicise the new venture and to seek the views and support of local employers. On top of all that, he was working closely with the architect to perfect the new building, and, voluntarily, he was delivering a series of Wednesday evening lectures in the new Free Library. This was more than enough for any one man. His many challenges were recognised, but not relieved, when the City Council resolved in February 1901 to extend his duties to embrace the Directorship of Technical Instruction for the city.[12] Forth's achievements received material reward in 1904 when his salary was increased by £200.[13]

With the opening of the new Institute only six months away, Forth was forced to turn his attention to staffing matters. He hoped to call upon the services of those staff who had contributed to the five predecessor organisations, but new contracts of employment had to be drawn up. Advertisements, which were placed in the press towards the end of April 1901, illustrated very clearly the vast range of the Institute's work. Part-time (or occasional) teachers were sought for evening work in Mathematics, Mechanical Engineering, Naval Architecture, Physics and Electrical Engineering, Architecture and Building, Textiles, Pure and Applied Chemistry, Natural Science, Commerce, and Women's Work. Practical knowledge was given precedence over teaching skills, 'A sound practical acquaintance with the subject proposed to be taught is of the first importance, but previous teaching experience is not essential.'[14] One hundred part-time teachers and teaching assistants were in place when the Institute opened its many doors in September 1901.

These staffing matters, along with a growing number of other tasks, constituted a substantial administrative burden – one which even the indefatigable Forth was beginning to find unbearable. So, in May, with the opening of the Institute only five months away, he decided that he urgently required the assistance of a Registrar. The advertisement for the post, at £150 per annum, attracted around forty applicants from whom H.H. Dunlop was appointed late in June.

The teaching staff were on part-time contracts for the first two years of the Institute's operation, but as the curriculum and structure of the organisation developed, Forth was able to identify a need for full-time posts.[15] In August 1903, applications were invited for a range of full-time posts including a Chief Lecturer in Physics and Electrical Engineering (£350 p.a.), and a French and German Master (£200 p.a.). The former of these two posts was filled by Rupert Stanley, chief lecturer in Electrical Engineering at Brighton Municipal Technical School, and a man who was to play a crucial role, including that of Principal, in the Institute's development.

The growing need for full-time posts provided the Institute's part-time staff with opportunities for advancement. S. Templeton, for example, former

Construction of the new building gets underway in 1902. Note the Institute's College Square North building in the background. (Hogg Collection, Ulster Museum.)

Principal of the Working Men's Institute and part-time Chemistry teacher, was transferred to the permanent staff as Chief Lecturer in Chemistry (£300 p.a.) in September 1903. And W.J. Fforde, former Director of the School of Engineering at the Model School, was transferred at the same time.[16] There was some criticism concerning the calibre of the teaching staff in the early years. A letter from the DATI to the LTIC in August 1904 highlighted the issue:

> Workshop training and experience, whilst undoubtedly affording evidence of very creditable work as workmen or foreman, cannot if standing alone, be accepted as implying on the part of the persons concerned, a wide knowledge of the scientific principles underlying the principles to be taught. Moreover, owing to the specialised character and quantity of the work passing through of an individual thus engaged, certain methods of procedure become of necessity customary to him, and it is likely that those methods will find a prominent part in the instruction which he may afford to his classes ... Such individuals may be excellent workmen, they may even excel in looking after men, but those qualifications do not of themselves fit them to become teachers.[17]

Forth's response to this letter admitted that the LTIC had experienced great difficulty in securing fully qualified teachers largely due to the fact that, up to then, the Institute could only offer casual employment in most of the technological subjects. The growing maturity and reputation of the Institute, and the increasing numbers of full-time staff, would together help to improve the overall calibre of the teaching staff. For example, J.H. Smith, appointed Head of the Mechanical Engineering Department in January 1905, was a Whitworth Scholar, and held Bachelor and Doctorate degrees in science.

Staff numbers had grown to 176 by May 1907, by which time, in addition to Forth, there were 36 full-time administrative staff, 36 full-time teachers, and 103 part-time teachers.[18] The distribution of the teaching staff follows:

	FULL-TIME	PART-TIME	TOTAL
Preparatory Course	–	7	7
Intro Science & Art	–	6	6
Mathematics	2	4	6
Mechanical Engineering	6	8	14
Naval Architecture	–	2	2
Physics/Electrical Eng	5	3	8
Building Trades	1	8	9
Plumbing/Sanitary Eng	–	3	3
Textile Industries	4	2	6
Pure/Applied Chemistry	4	5	9
Printing Trades	–	4	4
Miscellaneous Trades	–	6	6
Natural Science	–	4	4
Commercial Subjects	3	12	15
Women's Work	3	20	23
Art	8	8	16
Gymnasium	–	1	1
TOTAL	36	103	139

The Prospectus

What classes should the new Municipal Technical Institute offer? In drawing up a prospectus, Forth was guided by the Corporation's determination that Belfast's system of technical instruction would provide, 'Instruction in the principles of those arts and sciences which bear directly or indirectly upon the trades and industries located in Belfast and the neighbouring districts.'[19]

He also had to bear in mind the Corporation's determination that the system would offer 'not only the better training of the artisan population, but also the provision of specialised instruction which would fit students for the positions of foremen, managers, or employers'.

The Principal had a relatively free hand in the matter of academic structures and classes. He would have been aware, however, of the earlier work of the Consultation Committee, which had made recommendations in these areas before he was appointed. He also would have relied, to some extent, on the experience of the five institutions that the Corporation had now taken under its wing. Nevertheless, Forth was his own man, and he was anxious to ensure that the Institute's classes were relevant and up-to-date. To this end he devoted much time to seeking the views of employers.

The above table demonstrates the wide range of disciplines included in the MTIB's portfolio. In the early years, classes were provided in a variety of locations. The College Square North building (which formerly housed the Government School of Art), sometimes referred to as the Central Building, catered for Physics, Electrical Engineering, and Women's Work; the Queen Street building (the former Working Men's Institute) provided facilities for teaching Mathematics, Mechanical Engineering, Naval Architecture, and Chemistry; Hastings Street (the former Technical School) dealt with textiles and plumbing, and the newly rented accommodation in North Street provided a wide range of art-related classes.

However, the four main buildings together did not provide sufficient accommodation and additional space had to be found. To that end commercial classes were housed in the Queen Victoria School in Durham Street for a while, and, as well as rooms in College Square North, the popularity of women's work classes required the use of Templemore Avenue Baths, where space was provided by covering the second pool during the colder months of the year. In addition to these facilities, Forth argued for out-centres for use as evening continuation schools, where pupils leaving National School at twelve to fourteen years of age and, indeed, adults, might continue their education and training. By this means such students could be brought to a level of proficiency that would allow them to progress to more demanding classes at the MTIB.

In the Institute's first year of operation (1901-1902) courses like Chemistry and Building, which had been well established in the antecedent institutions, continued to be popular, but newer offerings – yet to receive adequate publicity – proved to be only marginally viable; Land Surveying, Physiology and Gas Manufacture fell into this latter category.[20] Forth continued to press industrialists to articulate their needs, and newspaper advertisements reminded the public that, 'Courses of study in science, art, technical and commercial subjects not included in the prospectus will be formed if a sufficient number of applications is received.' That offer seemed to attract a considerable response. At the annual prize-giving on 14 December 1903, Sir James Henderson told his audience that, 'It was a particular pleasure to the committee to receive deputations from the Ballymacarrett district, where that wonderful shipbuilding industry was located, to ask the committee to start new classes in Ballymacarrett'.[21] Sir James was not so receptive, however, to a proposal in 1907 to include the teaching of Irish in the Institute's portfolio.[22] It seems that twenty students had asked for a class in Irish, but Sir James pointed out that a similar class in Cork had failed. He went on to assert that the LTIC 'could only allow such subjects to be taught as were useful, and he would certainly in this category place Chinese, Japanese and Hindustani, which were useful to young men finding employment in the great eastern world, before Irish'.

Forth's proactive approach to marketing ensured that classes were up-to-date and relevant. Student numbers increased year on year. In the MTIB's fourth year (1904-1905), new classes were introduced in strength of materials, pharmaceutical chemistry, material medica and botany, company law and practice, etc.[23] By 1903 the Secretary of the DATI felt moved to comment that 'nothing was too great and nothing was too small for [the Institute]. It dealt with the mighty leviathans of the deep, which were forged with Titanic clangour in their shipyards, and it handled at the same time the delicate and perishable constructions of the confectioner.'[24]

The breadth of provision is exemplified by the range of classes offered in the Department of Physics and Electrical Engineering in 1907:

Classes are held for National School teachers to qualify them for certificates from the National Board of Education as teachers of elementary science, and for teachers of secondary schools to qualify them for similar certificates from the Board of Agriculture.

Classes are held to give young students who are attending the introductory courses of the Institute a general knowledge of natural science. Elementary and advanced classes are held in physics for students wishing to obtain certificates from the Board of Education, Government or other appointments by examination; these classes are suitable for science teachers, university students, etc.

A four years' course of electrical engineering is taught, and students are prepared for the examinations of the City and Guilds of London, and the external degree of BSc in electrical engineering of the London University.

A three years' course for electric wiremen is arranged, and students of this course can obtain certificates as wiremen or foremen wiremen from the City and Guilds of London Institute.

Classes are held in telegraphy, and will be arranged in telephony when sufficient students are qualified for the course.[25]

The work of the MTIB was split into Evening and Day Divisions. The activities of the former dominated in the early years, but day classes ultimately achieved substantial proportions.

Helping Evening Students to Progress

Evening classes fell into three groups: (a) a Preparatory Group; (b) an Introductory Science, Art, Technology, and Commerce Group, and (c) a Specialised Science, Art, Technology, Commerce, and Domestic Economy Group.[26] In the third and most advanced group, students were encouraged to spend up to four years studying their choice of specialisation. In Mechanical Engineering, for example, the Preparatory Section met on two evenings a week, when English, Arithmetic, Geometry, Mensuration, and Freehand Drawing would be taught. In the early years some of these classes were held on the premises of the Belfast Royal Academy and the Mountpottinger National School. The Introductory Section also met on two evenings a week with classes in English, workshop arithmetic, and manual instruction.[27] The definitive, or specialist course in mechanical engineering, had an initial duration of two years, but had expanded to require four years of study by 1907.

Forth was convinced that the Institute's success depended on its students being properly prepared to progress from one level of study to the next. This was particularly important when young people were first embarking upon a course of technical education. Arrangements were made, therefore, for evening continuation classes to be held in English, arithmetic, elementary drawing, and elementary science on the premises of Tennent Street National School, Montgomery National School, Raglan Street National School, and, as mentioned above, at the Belfast Royal Academy and Mountpottinger National School. Fees were one shilling per annum for courses of instruction in English, Arithmetic and Elementary Drawing, but Elementary Science, with its need for specialised equipment, cost participants 2*s* 6*d* per annum. This initiative reaped dividends, and Forth was able to report in 1907 that, 'the wisdom of providing instruction of a preparatory grade for those whose general education was imperfect received ample justification'.[28]

Getting on the roll of the MTIB became an increasingly challenging task. In a letter to students in 1905 Forth declared that, in the near future, all prospective students would have to pass an entrance test.[29] For example, from 1907, all wishing to enrol on the Institute's evening classes had to face an entrance examination lasting three hours and covering English, arithmetic and drawing.[30] The test in English was allocated forty-five minutes, followed by forty-five minutes for Arithmetic, and ending with thirty minutes for Drawing, and the whole examination, which must have been quite stressful, lasted from 7.30p.m. until 9.30p.m. on the first night of the particular class. The English examination in 1908 gives an indication of the levels sought:

The candidate must first attempt Question 1. Any three of the remaining Questions may then be taken.

(1) Write an essay on one of the following subjects: (16 marks)
(a) The Shipyards of Belfast
(b) The Beauty Spots around Belfast
(c) Hospitals

(2) Analyse the following sentence, and parse the words underlined: (8 marks)
'It is an ill <u>wind</u> <u>that</u> <u>blows</u> nobody <u>good.</u>'

(3) Insert in sentences of your own composition, the following words (one in each sentence): frequent, awarded, conviction, generation, unanimous, affect, system, similar. (8 marks)
(4) Correct, where necessary, the following sentences: (8 marks)
(a) This boy is more cleaverer than anyone else in the class.

(b) Was it me who you were talking to?

(c) The boy has went away without no food.

(d) Let him and I settle who we will invite.

(5) (6 marks)

(a) Write the proper form of the indefinite article (a or an) before each of the following words; horse shoe, union, hour, umbrella.

(b) How is the possessive case formed?

(c) Give two examples of each of the following: adverbs of place; proper nouns; transitive verbs; personal pronouns.[31]

Scripts were marked immediately after the examination, and this quick turn-around allowed candidates to report directly to the Registrar's office where they could complete their enrolment for the relevant classes. A candidate could achieve a maximum of forty marks in the English paper, forty in Arithmetic and twenty in Drawing. An overall total of seventy or more would allow candidates to progress directly to the first year of their chosen specialisation; forty to sixty-nine allowed admission to the Introductory Section; and less than forty marks admitted to the Preparatory Section.

Prospective students could claim exemption from the entrance examination if they held qualifications such as the Junior, Middle or Senior Grade of the Intermediate Board. And those of more mature years – twenty-five and over – were automatically exempted, as were students admitted to Art classes only. There was another escape route[32] – exemption could be obtained by paying treble the fee for the class you wished to join!

Day Classes

Evening classes dominated the MTIB's work in the early years. The unsatisfactory nature of the available accommodation contributed to that situation, but as brick piled upon brick in the new edifice in College Square, there were growing pressures to establish a range of courses which would make full use of the new facility.

The establishment of the Trade Preparatory School, with its day classes, was an important step. Forth advised the LTIC in August 1903 that a great deal of evidence pointed towards the need for a form of technical education that young people could follow immediately after National School. At the time, National School pupils with a technical bent were able to progress to intermediate schools – if their families could afford it – but the opportunities for a meaningful encounter with technology were rare in such schools. Alternatively, they could find temporary employment before entering apprenticeships at fourteen to sixteen, but such jobs were often of a menial nature and the time spent tended to dull memories of the basic knowledge and skills they had learned in primary school. The DATI had proposed Trade Preparatory Schools (TPSs) as a solution to these difficulties; they would 'prepare youths to enter in a properly prepared manner upon industrial occupations', and would focus on the mechanical sciences. Entrants would have to be at least twelve years of age, there would be up to four years of study, the fee would be sixpence per week,[33] and scholarships would be available to help pupils with fees, books and instruments.[34]

At first glance an excellent idea, the proposed TPS caused a furore at the following meeting of the City Council. Some members expressed fears about its potentially injurious effects on local intermediate schools, but others were adamant that none of the existing schools covered the work of the proposed TPS. And the non-denominational nature of the proposed school was considered an attractive feature by some. When it came to a vote, eleven members voted for, and eleven against, but the Lord Mayor's casting vote in favour decided the issue.

That acrimonious baptism did not impede the progress of the new initiative. F.M. Saxelby replaced S. Templeton as the TPS's Headmaster in 1906, by which time 124 students were enrolled on the three years of the course – all taught in the Institute's so-called Central Building (the old School of Art building in the grounds of RBAI) in College Square North. Following a tough entrance examination, the pupils faced an even tougher curriculum. The first year, for example, involved thirty hours of classes per week, and included the following subjects, with hours per week in brackets: Mathematics (five), Drawing (one), English (four), German (three), Geography (one), Experimental Physics (eight); Art (three), Woodwork (four), and Gymnastics (one).[35] Students had a choice of progression routes; those leaving for employment at sixteen or seventeen could continue their education in the Institute's evening classes, and others could proceed to the senior sections of the Institute's day classes.

The TPS introduced a number of innovations. Whilst training of the mind was top of the agenda, gymnastic classes ensured that the pupils' physical development was not overlooked. This was accomplished in some style with the school carrying off the National Physical Recreation Society's shield in 1905.[36]

The DATI inspectors were pleased with all they saw, and Forth himself was able to assert that 'this school has been markedly successful in the work which it undertook: indeed no branch of the expenditure of the Technical Instruction Committee has yielded more satisfactory results than this one'.[37]

The DATI developed its own national curriculum for such schools, and, over a short period of time, a limited number of other TPSs had been launched in other parts of the country. Unfortunately the birth of one of them generated a great deal of acrimony, most of it springing from the well-established differences of opinion in the North of Ireland. The Christian Brothers, whose Belfast schools had certainly not neglected the scientific nor the technical, planned to extend those activities through a TPS in Hardinge Street in North Belfast. The managers approached the LTIC for an initial equipment grant of £400 just a few months after the establishment of the MTIB's own school, but the request was rejected on two counts: (1) the school would not be under the control of the Corporation, and (2) the proposed curriculum included religious instruction. The large majority of members – particularly Sir James Henderson – were opposed to the use of rates for such purposes.[38] However, the DATI insisted that the new Hardinge Street TPS receive appropriate support, so it opened its doors to an initial intake of seventy-one students in 1903. Unlike the Institute's TPS, it included commercial subjects in its curriculum.

Even with its TPS up and running, the MTIB's buildings were still practically empty during the daytime. In the years before the new building was opened, a few voices could be heard echoing along the corridors of the old Central Building, where the TPS and a few day classes in women's work were active during the hours of daylight. There was, in addition, some daytime activity in the School of Art in North Street, and student teachers could be found bustling about on Saturday mornings. But these bits and pieces did not amount to much, and the resultant waste of public money attracted comment at the 1906 prize-giving, when the chief guest, Sir William White, former Director of Naval Construction, described his visit to the newly occupied Technical Institute that morning. The reports of his remarks stated, 'That day he had walked through the Institute and found classrooms, drawing offices, and laboratories standing practically empty. That was to his mind waste. In the interests of the community which had built that Institute, it should be used to the fullest possible extent.'[39]

Of course, as far as Forth was concerned, this was preaching to the converted. He had been doing his utmost to attract day students, and he was still drawing the matter to the attention of employers when the LTIC deputation met the Chamber of Commerce the following year.[40] He explained then that it had not

A woodworking class in the Trade Preparatory School (c.1906). (Forth, *Souvenir of the Opening of the Municipal Technical Institute*, 1907.)

been possible to develop the Day Department because 'the young people were not coming forward, and the employers were not giving them facilities such as were given in many other cities'.

So the Day Division progressed slowly. Day courses for engineering apprentices were launched in 1905, and the inspector's report described them as marking an epoch in the history of the school.[41] These courses required apprentices to attend for six hours every Monday for a year. The fee was £1 10s, and employers were regularly updated on the performance of their apprentices.

Self-contained day technical courses took longer to establish than one-day per week apprentice courses. Forth explained that the former were of university standard, and were designed to provide a sound training in the science and technology of Mechanical Engineering, Electrical Engineering, Textile Industries, and Pure and Applied Chemistry.[42] They were intended 'for youths who aim to fill positions of responsibility'. Prospective students had to be older than fifteen and were required to pass an entrance examination covering four compulsory topics – English, Geography, Elementary Drawing, and General Knowledge – and two optional topics (Latin and French). The General Knowledge test was designed 'to test the candidate's intelligence in so far as this can be measured from a knowledge of such current public affairs as receive special newspaper or local attention'. Of three years' duration, each involving thirty hours of classes, students of all disciplines shared a common first year. Interests diverged thereafter, and the final year was devoted entirely to the chosen specialisation. But the day technical courses attracted very few students; in 1907 there were only six candidates for the entrance examination.[43] Nearly ten years had to pass before these courses could be described as viable.

Student Numbers and Successes

Prior to amalgamation, the Institute's five constituent organisations had together mustered 800 students, so it was a reasonable expectation that the new combined body would attract around 1,200 students in its first year of operation. But this turned out to be a gross underestimate, and by the end of the year 1901/1902, 3,381 students had enrolled and had purchased 4,292 tickets to attend classes. Six years later, in 1906-1907, these numbers had grown respectively to 4,625 and 6,973.[44]

Enrolment progressed throughout the year. In 1901, for example, 2,442 tickets were purchased by 31 October, but this figure had risen to 3,038 by 4 December. The following table shows the relative popularity of the various sites, in terms of tickets purchased by 14 November 1901:

Central Building, 769
Royal Academy, 188
Templemore Avenue, 78
Working Men's Inst., 751
Tennent Street NS, 144
Raglan Street NS, 60
School of Art, 304
Hastings Street, 125
Model School, 22
Mountpottinger NS, 210
Montgomery NS, 116

Total, 2,767

The students' ages varied from ten to sixty-seven, but most lay in the age range of fifteen to twenty. Students aged eighteen and over outnumbered those below eighteen by a factor of 2.5, and female students made up approximately one quarter of the total.[45]

Large and growing numbers of students were encouraging signs, but examination performance would be the real test of the Institute's effectiveness. Not all students entered for examinations, but those who did could choose from several alternatives. The Institute conducted its own examinations in a number of subjects, and awarded certificates to successful candidates. But the prestige of national examinations attracted increasing numbers of candidates. These were conducted by the Board of Education (which, by 1901, had taken over the examining role of the Department of Arts and Science), by the Society of Arts (which examined in commercial subjects), and by the City and Guilds of London Institute (CGLI), which covered the technological subjects.

Examination results revealed that progress in the scientific and technical areas was less than satisfactory in the MTIB's early years. Admitting to this shortcoming at the Institute's second prize-giving ceremony in the Ulster Hall in December 1903,[46] Forth attributed it entirely to the lack of adequate accommodation for classes. The situation improved marginally the following year, but an inspector's report noted that:

> While the numbers enrolled for the elementary classes were very large, the numbers in the advanced classes were comparatively few. This was particularly noticeable in the classes in Machine Construction and in Building Construction- and the instruction in these classes was little more advanced than that given in the elementary classes.[47]

These criticisms were noted and acted upon. Forth was able to report in 1905 that, whilst in former years science students had qualified in the first (elementary) stage and in the second (advanced) stage of the science examinations, a fair proportion were now entering for examinations in the third (higher) stage.[48] Passes were now being obtained in the third stage in Magnetism and Electricity, Applied Mechanics, Chemistry, etc. He also pointed out that the MTIB attracted more than one quarter of the Science and Art grant awarded to all technical and art schools in Ireland.

But, whilst performance in science was improving, Forth was still concerned about the technological subjects, which he felt were of central importance to Belfast's industries. He looked for very high standards in this area, but was frank enough to admit in 1905 that that standard had not yet been reached by the

Institute as a whole or by individual students[49]. It was noted, however, that there were twenty-one Irish technical schools at the time and, of the 383 students who had passed the CGLI examinations that year, 170 (44 per cent) were students at the MTIB.

With the acquisition of better-qualified staff, with Forth's insistence on rigorous underpinning preparatory work, and with the attraction of increasing numbers of bright, motivated students, the examination performance of the Institute's students improved steadily. Amongst the more famous alumni from those days are Frederick (later Sir Frederick) Rebbeck, who was to become Chairman and Chief Executive of Harland & Wolff, and Harry George Ferguson of tractor fame. Rebbeck was awarded a Whitworth Exhibition in 1902 and Ferguson enrolled on classes for Machine Drawing, Applied Mechanics, and Practical Mathematics in 1906.[50] By the close of the Institute's sixth year of operation, a considerable number of high-level national medals and scholarships had been obtained. These included twelve silver and fourteen bronze medals from the CGLI, a Drapers' Company Scholarship, a National Scholarship in Art, eight National Bronze Medals from the Board of Education, and the aforementioned Whitworth Exhibition.

Marketing the New Institution

The DATI was making a special effort to arouse interest and support for technical education at the time of the Institute's launch. A series of four promotional lectures – the Pioneer Lectures – was arranged and delivered in Belfast's Grosvenor Hall in the early months of 1901. They attempted to explain how building, art, the machine trades and building would benefit from technical education. Unfortunately, the LTIC was forced to complain to the Department that the first two lectures in the series had not been resounding successes, neither in content nor in delivery. Forth's own attempts at the podium were more effective, however, and his presentation to the Natural History and Philosophical Society in December 1901 explaining the aims and aspirations of the new Institute, was well received by a large audience.[51]

That lecture was part of an ongoing series of public lectures which Forth used to explain the importance of technical education and the role of the MTIB in its delivery. Activity on this front reached a peak in 1903 when the records show that at least five major public lectures were delivered. These ranged from Forth himself on 'Sir Joseph Whitworth; Engineer, Inventor and Philanthropist' to 'Stained Glass' by James Taylor. Exhibitions of artworks in the North Street Building also helped to generate public interest in the Institute's work. The inauguration of a series of annual prize-giving ceremonies provided further opportunities for spreading the gospel. Held in a packed Ulster Hall, and preceded by an organ recital, each session was addressed by an important guest speaker who added special gravitas to the proceedings. At the first ceremony on 12 December 1902, Forth took the opportunity to invite his former boss – J.H. Reynolds, Principal of the Manchester Municipal School of Technology – to do the honours.[52]

If the Institute were to succeed, it was clear that employers would have to recognise the advantages of technical education, and would have to encourage their employees to attend the Institute's classes. Forth worked hard to gain the support of both employers and workers. There are records of early visits to firms[53], such as Gallagher's, the Belfast Ropeworks, and Workman Clark, where Forth addressed the workers on the benefits of technical education. In addition, much effort was devoted to ensuring that the Institute's courses were immediately relevant to the needs of local employers. It was reported in May 1901, for example, that Forth, 'had an interview with the Postmaster of Belfast relative to the establishment of courses of Technical Instruction for telegraph clerks, and further that he had been in communication with the Honorary Secretary of the Ulster Society of Architects relative to the establishment of courses for Architects' pupils.'[54] The same set of minutes report Forth's success in persuading Davidson and Co. to offer prizes to its boys. Trades unions – or trade societies as they were sometimes called – were also consulted, and Forth's charisma soon persuaded them to back the Institute. At the formal opening in 1907, he commented on the 'enlightened view' of the trade societies concerning the MTIB's trade classes, and how they had encouraged apprentices and journeymen to attend.

In spite of the presence of several co-opted employers on the LTIC, the overall support from industry remained modest in the early years. Forth sent a circular around the major industries in Belfast in February 1904, urging them to allow their apprentices to attend the Institute's day classes, but positive responses were few and far between. The need for stronger support from industry was a regular theme at prize-giving addresses. In 1906, the address of the chief guest, Sir William White, contained a mild rebuke which was reported as follows:

> He was delighted to hear from the Principal that many of those who repre-
> sent the leading industries in the city had given real and active support to that
> Institute. He hoped that support would go on and increase. It was essential
> to those who were employers of labour and captains of industry should show
> sympathy. He knew that they did in Belfast, but they ought to do it to a
> greater extent, for from experience he could say that generous treatment on
> the part of employers towards the employed did not fail of its reward.[55]

Employers, however, continued to be slow to respond, especially in such matters
as day-release and the payment of fees. Their apathy persuaded the LTIC to send
a five-man delegation to meet the Chamber of Commerce in November 1907
– just three weeks after the formal launch of the Institute.[56] The deputation's
objective was to bring the Chamber's attention to 'the relations of Technical
Instruction with industrial concerns'. Members suggested that employers could
help by (a) persuading their employees of the benefits of technical education,
(b) requesting a certificate from anyone applying for a job, (c) paying half the
fees, (d) exempting students from overtime on class evenings, and (e) recognising technical education as a formal part of apprenticeship.

There was a frank exchange of views. Forth did not hesitate to complain that
local employers were not giving their workers facilities such as were given in
many other cities; Manchester, Glasgow and Birmingham were named. John
Horner, one of the deputation, pointed out that, 'In nearly every city in Great
Britain there existed a very great amount of sympathetic consideration between
employers and technical schools, but in Belfast this was represented simply by
two hundred pupils in their various classes belonging to various trades, the fees
being paid by those who employed them.'[57]

These exchanges, and the various promotional lectures previously mentioned,
gradually brought positive results. By 1906, prizes and scholarships were being
offered by companies like York Street Flax Spinning Company, McLaughlin
& Harvey, Musgrave & Company, and McCaw, Stevenson & Orr. Trade and
professional bodies were increasingly generous. For example, at the local level,
the Master Grocers of Belfast and the Operative Bakers' Society both offered
prizes.

The operation of the various classes also brought employers closer to the
MTIB. The large majority of the Institute's students were in employment and
were able, therefore, to make their own contribution to promoting the MTIB

to their workmates. In addition, as day classes increased in number, there were growing opportunities for field visits. In November 1906, for example, plumbing students were invited to inspect the steam, water and sanitary plants at the new Purdysburn Hospital. The press records that 'a start was made from the new Institute at 2.30 in a four-in-hand, and in less than an hour Purdysburn was reached'.[58]

Transition to the New Building

Forth was impatient to be rid of the dilapidated buildings in which his colleagues were struggling to maintain morale and achieve results. With the building contractors making good progress, the LTIC was able to persuade them in 1903 to release a suite of five rooms on the ground floor of the unfinished building. Forth used these rooms for classes in commercial subjects. As well as relieving congestion elsewhere, the use of the rooms allowed Forth and his colleagues to experiment with the layout of the rooms – their furniture, lighting systems, fittings, etc. The results of those experiments were later applied throughout the whole building.

There was steady progress in the planning of laboratories and workshops. Members of the LTIC, Forth and some of his newly appointed heads of department visited similar institutes in Britain where they learned much about what was required and what was available in laboratory and workshop equipment. Forth's visits extended to Germany, and the results of all this planning are discussed in the next chapter.

Forth continued to put pressure on the contractors and, although the building was still in their hands in September 1906, he was permitted to transfer practically all of the Institute's classes into the new premises.[59] This allowed all save one of the branch schools to be abandoned. Most of the necessary equipment was in place in the new building at the time of its formal opening in October 1907. With a brand new building and a wide range of equipment in place, the Institute was ready to show its paces.

11

Technical Education Recognised

The New Building Complete

The matter of the title of the new Institute is of interest. The 'Royal' qualifier had been sought early in 1901,[1] but impenetrable political reasoning caused the Home Office to procrastinate to such an extent that the LTIC decided in the end not to pursue the matter further. However, that set back did not diminish the grandeur of the formal opening ceremony, which took place on 30 October 1907.

The opening was a splendid occasion graced by the presence of many local dignitaries, including James Craig, later Northern Ireland's first Prime Minister, Lord Pirrie, Chairman of Harland & Wolff, and Thomas Andrews, later to design the *Titanic*. (Three of the Institute's alumni were lost in the *Titanic*, and students and staff together contributed some £50 towards the Lord Mayor's *Titanic* Relief Fund.)

The ladies were not to be outdone by the gentlemen:

> …Lady Shaftesbury was dressed in the faintest shade of mauve, and tulle hat of the same colour, and she had a stole of ermine … Mrs O'Connell, the wife of the High Sheriff, had on a gown of a light shade and a hat with feathers at the side to match. Lady Kilmorey was dressed in mole-coloured cloth, with large hat trimmed with pelican plumes … Mrs Forth, the wife of the Principal of the Technical Institute, had on a green dress and very stylish hat with green and terra-cotta wings…'[2]

CITY AND COUNTY BOROUGH OF BELFAST.

The Chairman (Alderman Sir Jas. Henderson, D.L.) and the Members of the Library and Technical Instruction Committee have much pleasure in inviting

Professor & Mrs Bradbury

to be present at the Opening of the New Municipal Technical Institute, at noon, on Wednesday, the 30th October, 1907, by His Excellency the Lord Lieutenant of Ireland, who will be accompanied by Her Excellency the Countess of Aberdeen.

Please reply to
The Principal,
Municipal Technical Institute, Belfast.

SCIENCE · TECHNOLOGY · INDVSTRY · ART

An invitation to the formal opening. Professor Bradbury was Professor of Textile Engineering in the Institute. (PRONI, ref LA7/7HD/9.)

The Lord Lieutenant of Ireland, the Earl of Aberdeen, officiated. The ceremony, conducted from a specially built pavilion at the front of the building, commenced at noon and was followed by a sumptuous lunch for some 150 guests in the Central Hall. After lunch, the Countess of Aberdeen unveiled a stained-glass window commemorating the occasion, and each guest was presented with an illustrated booklet describing the history and present state of the Institute.[3] Forth's booklet provided the guests with a wealth of statistics, including, for example, the fact that 2,756 piles had been driven, that there were 4½ million bricks in the structure, and that the corridors, in total, stretched to half a mile.

Whilst the opening was an undoubted marketing success, it had been directed, on the whole, at a limited selection of the great and good. The LTIC recognised that the ordinary people of Belfast also deserved an opportunity to join in the celebration, and a conversazione, held two days later, was the first step towards that end. Some 2,000 people visited the Institute on the evening of 1 November 1907, when they were entertained by a military band and were able to view 'quarter-hour cinematograph entertainments' in the Central Hall. Light refreshments were provided, and guests were taken on tours of inspection where they were able, amongst other treats, to see the spinning and weaving machinery in action. The press reported that 'many who had seen the interior only for the first time were literally bewildered with its magnificence, as well as the extent and variety of its equipments'.[4] As a sequel to this event, Forth opened the building for inspection by the general public on the following Wednesday and Saturday afternoons; there was an enthusiastic response, with around 1,000 visitors enjoying a personal introduction and tour by the Principal.

Admired by many in its early years, the new edifice also attracted considerable criticism. It had met the Corporation's stricture that appearance should not be unduly extravagant, but, an example of the French Renaissance style,[5] *The Irish Builder* rated the building's utility higher than its beauty.[6] It received only faint praise at the formal opening in 1907, when it was described as not presenting 'any notable architectural features, but ... is commodious, airy and well-planned for its purpose'.[7] Criticism became more acerbic in later years when personal attacks on Stevenson accused him, indirectly, of having copied the designs of the War Office in London – a building which was opened the same year as the Technical Institute.[8] And there were those (not only architects) who deplored the building's impact on the stately Academical Institution. Even in the 1950s the building was being described as an 'outrageous piece of philistinism – an incongruous building',[9] which had half destroyed 'the lovely prospect of a gracious late Georgian building'. Even later, in the 1960s, it was described as 'the largest and most ornate cuckoo's egg ever laid in songbird's nest'.[10]

Students and Classes

The opening and its associated publicity helped to attract students. Starting at 4,625 in 1906/07, student numbers steadily increased to 7,001 by 1913/14.[11] But the Great War stifled growth, and numbers dropped to 5,934 in 1915/16 before rising to top the 7,000 mark again in 1918/19. The figure below shows that the Institute continued to cater for a wide spectrum of ages, but there was clear evidence that the numbers of younger students were increasing. This trend was encouraged by a positive campaign by Forth to encourage youngsters to come to the Institute as soon as possible after leaving the National Schools.

Students were offered an increasing array of classes; in 1910 the local press expressed bewilderment at the breadth of provision:

> From a room where girls are grappling with the mysteries of how to make blackberry jelly or busy with mysterious paper patterns, one passes into a class of apprentice painters, absorbed in the art of lettering, or of students drawing from the antique. In one department textile machinery is clattering like a mill; in another one sees a row of heads bent over Bunsen burners, stirring weird concoctions and waving test-tubes in mystic circles. Lower down the corridor cake ornamentation is being taught; further on students are deep in French, wrinkling brows over book-keeping by double entry, or wrestling with shorthand symbols. It seems less a school than a model in miniature of the various activities of a great industrial community.[12]

Students were not evenly distributed across all departments. The most popular departments were Commerce, Women's Work, and Mechanical Engineering. In 1913/14, numbers registered on the class rolls (not the numbers of actual individuals) of these departments peaked, respectively, at 2,900, 2,000, and 1,800.[13] Other departments did not fare so well. The class rolls in the Department of Physics and Electrical Engineering, for example, averaged around 350 per annum between 1913 and 1918, and the Textiles Department could only muster 300.

Day Classes

Most students attended in the evenings, but day classes soon began to grow in popularity. The Department of Women's Work consistently attracted relatively large numbers of day students. Indeed, this department proved so popular, and made such large demands on the available accommodation, that a decision was taken in 1912 to move some of its classes to out-centres. The College Square North building (on the grounds of the RBAI) housed a comprehensive range of related equipment. Cookery demonstration rooms and practice kitchens were fitted with coal ranges and gas fires, the housewifery centre comprised a suite of furnished rooms, and the sewing rooms housed an ample supply of sewing machines and all the appliances necessary for instruction in dressmaking, blouse-making, plain needlework and millinery. Day classes in Women's

A brand new Municipal Technical Institute in 1907. (Hogg, Belfast Metropolitan College.)

A modern-day view of the ceiling of the Institute's entrance hall.

Work, including some on Saturdays, were provided in cooking, sewing, laundry work, housewifery, etc., and students were encouraged to enter for City and Guild's Certificate examinations in Household Sewing, Dressmaking, Cookery and Millinery. There were also special Saturday morning classes in cookery, laundry work, and household knowledge for National School teachers.[13]

The School of Art occupied the Institute's fifth floor (E Floor), where it ran a wide variety of day classes ranging in challenge from elementary, through advanced section I, to advanced section IV of the syllabuses drawn up by the Department of Agriculture and Technical Instruction (DATI). Its work was arranged in five divisions – a lower division, an upper division, a teachers' special division, a postgraduate division, and public lectures and art exhibitions. Classes catered both for prospective artists and for members of the public who had recreational interests in art. There were special weekday elementary classes for school pupils and for National School teachers, the latter attending on Saturday mornings when they learned how to teach freehand drawing, elementary design, brush work, model drawing, geometry, perspective, light and shade, elementary modelling, and blackboard drawing.

Day classes in industrial subjects were slower to make their mark. The Day Technical Course, established in 1906, was renamed the Day Technical College in 1915. Aimed at youths of fifteen years of age and over, it provided instruction in Mechanical Engineering, Electrical Engineering, the Textile Industries and Pure and Applied Chemistry. It prepared youths for positions of responsibility in these different fields of endeavour. Applicants had to pass an entrance examination covering English, Geography, Mathematics, Elementary Science, Elementary Drawing, and General Knowledge.

In Mechanical Engineering the instruction was described as thoroughly practical and of university standard; indeed, many of the subjects formed part of the engineering degree course of Queen's. The course, costing students £10 per year, extended over three years, with forty weeks of instruction in each year. The first year, which was common to all departments (Electrical Engineering, Textiles, etc.), required a student to attend thirty hours of classes per week, including two hours devoted to the study of German. After first year, students focused increasingly on their chosen specialisms. The third year of the Mechanical Engineering course included Practical Geometry, Mechanical Drawing, Mechanics, Machine-shop Practice, Theory of Structures, Theory of Machines, Strength and Elasticity of Materials, Theory of Heat Engines, and Hydraulics.[14]

The future of the Day Technical Course hung in the balance for a while. In 1911 the LTIC was of a mind to close it down, but it decided to review the

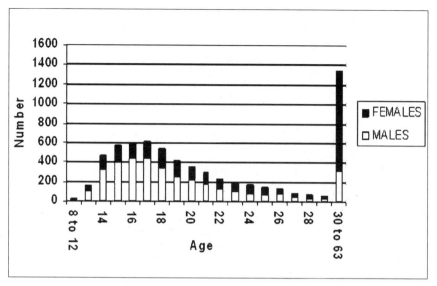

Age distribution of the Institute's students in 1912. (Belfast Metropolitan College Archive.)

position in a year's time. The DATI was also concerned, its annual report for 1911/12 stating, 'The Day Technical School was again disappointingly small ... and it can only be inferred that its advantages have not yet been made sufficiently widely known.'[15]

Day classes were also provided on Mondays for engineering apprentices and apprentice draughtsmen nominated by employers. Initially attracting only small numbers of engineering students, these classes were gradually extended to cover other trades. In 1912, for example, courses were arranged for apprentices in the printing trades, and in 1916 for painters.[16] Numbers attending these classes and the Day Technical Course increased as employers and Government began to take a more positive view of technical education. In 1914, the DATI reported that certain industries were offering inducements to staff to attend classes, and the Day Technical Course and the Day Apprentice Classes were both increasing in numbers.

The Trade Preparatory School (TPS) continued to be a strong component of the Institute's Day Division. The total numbers attending the course annually between 1906 and 1914 hovered around the 140-150 mark. However, very few students completed the full three-year course. Around 60 per cent returned to attend second year, but only 12 per cent of the initial enrolment carried on to the third year. They were being snapped up by local employers. The Hardinge Street

THIS DAY.

MUNICIPAL TECHNICAL INSTITUTE BELFAST.

SESSION 1908-1909 (Eighth Session).

EXHIBITION

OF

STUDENTS' WORK.

THE OPENING CEREMONY WILL TAKE PLACE AT NOON TO-DAY (FRIDAY), when the EXHIBITION will be declared OPEN by Alderman Sir JAMES HENDERSON, M.A., D.L.

The Exhibits will be on View Daily from 12 noon to 9 p.m. until Saturday, 19th June.

ADMISSION FREE.

Students of the Institute and the General Public are cordially invited to visit the Exhibition.

The Northern Whig advertises an exhibition in the Municipal Technical Institute, 3 June 1909.

MUNICIPAL TECHNICAL INSTITUTE, BELFAST.

ANNUAL EXHIBITION

OF

ART STUDENTS' WORK.

THE ART WORKS SUBMITTED for the 1911 NATIONAL COMPETITION by the STUDENTS of the SCHOOL OF ART of the MUNICIPAL TECHNICAL INSTITUTE will be ON VIEW DAILY in the CENTRAL HALL of the INSTITUTE.

The EXHIBITION will be OPENED TO-DAY (Friday), at 2.30 p.m., by Alderman Sir JAMES HENDERSON, M.A., D L., J.P., and will REMAIN OPEN DAILY from TWELVE noon to NINE p.m. until SATURDAY, 28th October.

ADMISSION FREE.

Art Students and the General Public are cordially invited to visit the Exhibition.

Yet another exhibition advertised in *The Northern Whig* (20 November 1911).

TPS was also flourishing; with around fifty-five enrolments to first year each year, it managed to maintain a viable third year of twenty to thirty students.[17]

By 1914, the Institute's Day Division had grown to include Art and Women's Work, the TPS, and the Day Technical Course, as well as courses for engineering apprentices, printing trades apprentices, commercial apprentices and shop assistants. Meanwhile, numbers studying for the QUB degree in engineering were growing slowly.

Evening Classes

The Institute's evening classes fell into three groups: (1) a Preparatory Section; (2) an Introductory Science, Art, Technology and Commercial Section, and (3) a Specialised Science, Art, Technology, Commercial, and Domestic Economy Section. As described earlier, performance in the entrance examination determined which of these three levels would be the most appropriate starting point for a particular student. Students in the Preparatory Group received instruction in English, Arithmetic, and Elementary Science on two evenings a week, from 7.30 to 9.30p.m. In the 1909/10 year, there were twelve preparatory classes in operation.[18] These classes were particularly popular; in 1913/14 for example, some 1,600 students attended in the early weeks of the teaching year, although numbers had fallen to around 900 by the end of the year.[19] In 1915, pressures on accommodation forced the LTIC to remove all preparatory classes to out-centres.

Students in the Introductory Section also attended two evenings a week. In the 1909/10 year, seven introductory classes were needed to cater for students following courses in commercial subjects. Classes covered English, Commercial Arithmetic, and Drawing. In Engineering and Technology, six introductory classes covered the various Engineering disciplines separately. Each addressed three subjects – English, Elementary Science (including Drawing), and Practical Arithmetic. Surprisingly, these carefully considered classes attracted few students, only some 100-150 per annum attending between 1914 and 1918. Art students were exempt from the entrance examination and required, therefore, neither preparatory nor introductory classes.

Specialised courses provided the ultimate challenge for evening students. Requiring, in some cases, up to four years of evening study, they demanded

Students at work in an art class in 1908. (Hogg Collection, Ulster Museum.)

a level of commitment that only the most able and dedicated could pro-
vide. Students could pursue many subjects to advanced level. In Commerce,
for example, there were classes in commercial English and Arithmetic,
Bookkeeping, Shorthand, Company Secretarial Work, Commercial Law,
Money, Exchange and Banking. Modern languages were popular, with
classes in French, German and Spanish. In 1912, 772 students sat the Royal
Society of Arts commerce-related examinations.[20] However, the Commerce
Department, which was one of the largest in the Institute, was criticised in
1914 for a lack of focus in its course provision. Unlike Engineering, for example, the Commerce Department did not offer integrated programmes that
drew together related aspects of the curriculum. The DATI insisted that 'It
is … highly desirable that a number of well-designed courses in Commerce
should be arranged which will meet the requirements of the chief types of
business employees in attendance.'[21] The Commerce students, nevertheless,
seem to have been an enterprising group, setting up an Economics, Statistical
and Commercial Society in 1913.

Satisfactory completion of some of the specialist courses was acknowledged
by the award of a certificate by the Department of Agriculture and Technical
Instruction. An ordinary certificate required at least two years of study, and an
honours certificate at least four years.

Millinery students in the Department of Women's Work in 1909. (Hogg, Belfast Metropolitan College.)

Meeting New Needs

Whilst meeting a wide variety of needs, the Institute's classes were also establishing new reputations. The skills of cake ornamentation, for example, used to be in short supply locally and had to be imported from Britain, but the Institute's classes turned the tables, and by 1909, members of the local bakery trade were providing these services to customers 'over the water'.[22] And in bookbinding, instruction in 'marbling' encouraged several Belfast firms to pursue the technique on a commercial basis. Forth and his colleagues were ever on the *qui vive* for new opportunities, although some of their ideas never got beyond the drawing board. In 1910, for example, the DATI rejected a bid to allow Latin to be taught in the Institute. On the subject of languages, external pressures attempted yet again to persuade the LTIC to run Irish classes, but, despite the earlier enthusiasm for Latin, the motion to teach Irish was defeated by twelve votes to three in 1911. Forth's proposal to introduce classes in horticulture was more successful; the DATI approved the appointment of a teacher in 1912, and the annual inspection report of 1913/14 was able to refer to the fact that 'a number of helpful lectures have been given to allotment holders and others anxious to improve their methods of gardening'. Forth publicised this development in a paper on 'Horticultural Instruction in an Urban Area' which he presented in Bangor in 1913 at a Conference of the Irish Technical Instruction Association.

Staffing the Institute

The Institute's expanding portfolio demanded more resources. The staffing complement increased as student numbers grew. Between 1905/06 and 1913/14, the number of individual students grew from 4,960 to 7,000, and the number of full-time and part-time academic staff increased respectively from 36 to 42, and from 103 to 157.[23] Whilst the growth in staff numbers seems considerable, the absolute numbers were small by today's standards. There were those who thought that the Corporation was being particularly frugal with its resources. When Professor Perry opened the mechanical engineering laboratories in 1911 he remarked, 'A city puts up a magnificent building with well-arranged laboratories full of expensive apparatus, and it economises in the most important item – the teacher.'[24]

An analysis of the staff in post in 1914 shows a total of 284 persons of whom (excluding the Principal) 228 were involved in teaching, sixteen in clerical matters, thirty-seven in maintaining the building, and two in running the Textiles Testing House. Of the teaching staff, forty-two were employed full-time, and 157 on a part-time basis. There were a further twenty-nine full-time teaching assistants including draughtsmen, mechanics, laboratory and workshop attendants, and labourers. In the year 1912/13 the salaries and wages of all full-time staff – teachers and others – came to £12,814, and the bill for part-time teachers amounted to £2,857.[25]

The number of teachers may have been small, but their quality was improving steadily. Five professors were in post by 1909:

Professor F. Bradbury: Head of Department of Textile Industries
Professor J. Earls, BA: Head of Department of Mathematics
Professor J. Hawthorne, BA PhD: Head of Department of Pure and Applied Chemistry

Professor J.H. Smith, DSc, WhSch, ARCScI: Head of Department of Mechanical Engineering

Professor R. Stanley, BA AMIEE: Head of Department of Physics and Electrical Engineering

Professor F. Hall, MA BCom FCIS, was appointed Head of the Department of Commerce in 1910, and was succeeded in 1915 by Professor F.T. Lloyd-Dodd, MA BSc. Professor H. Wren, MA DSc PhD, replaced Professor Hawthorne in 1914. Other senior academics in 1914 were:

Miss E Myerscough: Head of Department of Women's Work

T.R. Hampshire: Head of Department of Building Trades

W.J. McCracken, BA BL: Headmaster, Trade Preparatory School

R.A. Dawson, ARCA: Headmaster, School of Art

Local secondary schools, as well as the Institute, were looking for people qualified to teach scientific and technological subjects at the time, and with local experts short on the ground, it was not surprising that the majority of the Institute's

Classes are advertised in the *Northern Whig*, 23 September 1912.

new appointments came from England and Scotland. Salaries were reviewed occasionally. Forth's salary had reached £1,000 by 1910, and a review in 1913 raised Professor Smith's salary, for example, from £400 to £500 over four years. Professor Earls was appointed Assistant to the Principal in November 1910.

Learning Lessons

As the Institute moved from aspiration to reality, some of the early approaches to teaching and curriculum design needed review. The operation of the entrance examination was a case in point. In 1909 Forth was re-emphasising that the majority of students would continue to progress from the Preparatory Course to the Introductory Course to the First Year of Specialisation, and the entrance examination would determine which of these three levels would be a particular student's starting point. Forth was confident that the entrance examination had proved effective in securing an improvement in the classification of students, but he was concerned that it was having a deterrent effect on those wishing to pursue trade courses, At the time this was felt to be due to ' a proportion of such students being unable to reach the entrance standard required for admission to Trade Classes, as well as to the circumstances that a number of these

Advertising for staff in *The Northern Whig* on 3 June 1909.

students were unwilling to go through the preliminary study necessary to pre-pare for the entrance test.'[26] Indeed, it could be argued that the skills demanded in the English test (as seen in Chapter 10) had only a tenuous relevance to the needs of apprentice joiners and their like. Forth, however, remained convinced that every student needed an adequate foundation of general education.

Some employers did not fully appreciate the niceties of this pedagogical ideal. Herbert Johnson, from the Highfield Factory, complained that several of his apprentices and experienced employees had failed the entrance examina-tion and had been asked, as a result, to attend additional classes on this, that and the other subject – most of them bearing little significant relevance to the specialised technical topics in which his staff had requested instruction. Many had subsequently lost interest in technical education as a result. He confronted the Institute on the matter, 'Evidently the framers of the system were as defi-cient in their knowledge of both the education and requirements of the artisan as our artisan is deficient in "elementary" education.'[27] He also asked, 'Do these theoretically based rules and regulations work satisfactorily in actual practice?'[28] In an aggressive series of letters to the press he accused the Institute of set-ting unnecessarily difficult entrance examinations in order to fail students who would then have to attend additional corrective classes – all of this increasing the number of students in class and, in turn, the Institute's income. The press carried an interesting exchange of views that extended over several weeks. The LTIC could not avoid being drawn into the debate; Forth was quizzed by the Committee and was asked to make a press statement. However, after all the huffing and puffing, it was clear to all that Johnson had made a valuable point, and the Institute would have to do something about it. The Inspector's report on the Institute (1909-1910) included the following:

> For some time it has ... been felt that the entrance test has exerted a more deterrent effect upon trade students than on others whose preparation for the work has been better. Difficulties have also been experienced in inducing these students to take an introductory course to fit them for advanced study. In these circumstances it has been decided to relax the regulations to some extent, and permit trade students to take their trade subjects in the first year of entering.[29]

In the end, all the Highfield men were admitted after subsequently passing 'a more suitable' entrance examination. From 1910 onwards, apprentices and jour-neymen were admitted to trade classes without sitting an entrance examination

– provided they attended a parallel class in rudimentary English, arithmetic, and drawing.[30] However, Forth and his successors continued to believe in the advantages of a well-designed system of entrance examinations.

That exchange of views affected other aspects of the curriculum. The Introductory Course was given a more practical slant, with the inclusion of practical drawing and an introduction to the materials used in particular trades. The practicality of Forth's concept of a 'course' was challenged. Intended to direct a student towards a balanced programme rather than a group of disparate subjects, the imposition of courses often required students to study subjects which they considered to be of little direct use to their employment. A careful reconsideration concluded that such a concept might not be appropriate in all circumstances.

New Developments

By 1907 it was clear that the new building was struggling to cope with the rapidly increasing numbers of students. The demand had become so great that storerooms and cloakrooms were being used as classrooms.[31] In 1908 the Corporation agreed to provide more space by raising the rear of the building from its original one storey to six, and with Samuel Stevenson as architect and Robert Curry as contractor, the extension was ready for formal opening on 3 June 1910. It provided much-needed accommodation for printing and allied crafts, bleaching and dyeing, woodwork, baking, and for a Textile Testing House, and it was topped by a splendid gymnasium.

The formal opening of the extension provided an opportunity to unveil a plaque commemorating the opening of the Institute on 30 October 1907 – and that plaque can still be found in the entrance hall. The occasion also moved the Lord Mayor to predict that 'so much additional accommodation would one day be required as would render necessary the erection of another building...' It seems that plans were already afoot to raise another large building on a site directly facing the Institute. Sir James Henderson informed the assembly that the Corporation had recently granted an extra halfpenny rate to meet the demands arising in connection with the extension of the building, and this would add around £3,000 per annum to the Institute's income that year.[32] The additional halfpenny rate was not available in subsequent years, however.

The extension to the building did little to placate the long-suffering staff at the Royal Belfast Academical Institution (RBAI), where further offence seems to have been caused by the fact that, whilst the Institute was faced on three sides by Portland stone, the rear, facing the RBAI, had been finished in plain red brick. The building was accused, therefore, of 'turning a raspberry-coloured backside' on the school.[33]

Forth wanted the Institute's laboratories to bring maximum benefit to the local industrial community, so, in addition to the primary teaching function, he encouraged their use for research and development. He wanted the Institute to be a hub of industry and technology in the city. For example, research on fatigue was carried out on a machine constructed by Combe Barbour, and the Adie cement tester was regularly used by the local building industry.

The textile laboratories were highly regarded. The annual report (1909/10) of the City and Guilds of London Institute (CGLI) stated that, 'The Textile Department of the Institute at Belfast has become, in equipment and organisation, the first in the country for linen manufacture. In these respects, it compares favourably with some of the best schools for flax spinning and linen designing and weaving on the Continent.'[34]

Textile employers made increasing use of these facilities. They supported the Public Testing and Conditioning House, which was introduced when the building was extended in 1910.[35] With its suite of rooms, including a reception area and waiting room, the Testing House could test textiles for weight, length, condition and strength, and the Institute could, if required, issue a certificate of accreditation. The Institute's prospectus made much of this facility, emphasising the great care taken to protect trade secrets. Unlike the main body of the building, the Testing House was closed to the general public.

The building itself was sometimes used as a laboratory. A house-draining test rig was laid out on the Institute's roof, and the accompanying picture of that equipment includes the various aerials that were part of the wireless telegraphy installation. Forth reported with pride to the LTIC in June 1913 that 'through the medium of the Wireless Telegraphic Installation on the Institute, a complete series of messages giving correct time, weather conditions and other data had been received this morning from the Eiffel Tower'.

When the Mechanical Engineering Laboratory was formally opened in November 1911, Professor John Perry, the guest speaker from Imperial College, remarked that 'the machinery installed in the new laboratory was such that in every case two or three students would be competent to take charge of any unit, and they would run little risk of doing themselves any injury'.[36] Of the original equipment fund of £40,000 (approximately £3 million today), more than half had been allocated to laboratory facilities in mechanical engineering, naval architecture, physics, electrical engineering, and textiles. The Mechanical Engineering and Naval Architecture Laboratories together attracted £9,700[37]. The records show that the completed facilities were showpieces of international standard. Engineering equipment, representative of the state of the art, was designed on a reduced scale so that students would have easy access, and claims on staff supervisory time would be minimised.

Collaboration with Queen's

The birth and early growth of the Municipal Technical Institute Belfast (MTIB) coincided with a period of great turmoil in the history of Queen's. The first decade of the twentieth century saw the development and implementation of plans to change the status of the Queen's College – a process that culminated in the establishment of the Queen's University of Belfast in 1908.

Since the MTIB's foundation in 1901, the Senate of Queen's College had foreseen the possibility of considerable gains accruing from a close working relationship with the Institute. In early 1902, a memorandum from the College to the Commissioners, who were reviewing the provision of higher education in Ireland, commented, 'It is eminently desirable, in order to provide a complete Technological curriculum for university degrees etc, that an arrangement should be made between this college and the Belfast Municipal Technical Institute, whereby complementary courses and joint examinations might be established.'[38]

The equipment and facilities of the MTIB must have been a source of envy to an ambitious, but under-funded and poorly equipped college, and this was particularly so in the field of engineering and technology. The Senate of Queen's College had taken the initiative of setting up a Better Equipment Fund in April 1901, and there was hope that this would help to provide some of the much-needed resources. But the fact that many of the necessary facilities were already in place in College Square was an irritation. Various pressures were brought to bear to persuade the Institute that co-operation with the College was the next logical step in its development. At the laying of the MTIB's foundation stone in 1902, the Lord Lieutenant, the Earl of Dudley, had argued that no

An experimental house-drainage rig on the roof of the Municipal Technical Institute (*c.*1912). (Hogg, Belfast Metropolitan College.)

Some newly installed equipment in the Mechanical Engineering Laboratory (*c.*1909). (Hogg, Belfast Metropolitan College.)

scheme of technical instruction was complete until it included opportunities to learn all that science had to tell. He suggested, 'the most obvious course would be to make your scheme culminate in the Queen's College; to link that College to your Institute'.[39]

That suggestion was a persuasive one, and before the year was out a twelve-man Joint Committee had been set up, with the Chamber of Commerce, Queen's and the LTIC providing four members each. The Committee had the almost impossible task of drawing up a system of collaboration acceptable to all concerned. The proposed scheme, circulated for comment in January 1903, recommended the establishment of three faculties at Queen's – Commerce, Engineering, and Manufactures – each awarding diplomas to successful students. The MTIB would work with Queen's to deliver courses and research in these faculties, and both organisations would require increased resources in order to do this effectively. But the crucial recommendation – and a step too far – was that the power of regulating the arrangements should be placed in the hands of a common board:

> This common board shall act as a board of co-ordination for the College and Technical Institute, and ... direct – (a) the courses given in higher technical classes at the Institute and in complementary technological and commercial subjects in the College; (b) the facilities given for technological investigation and research in both establishments; (c) the specification of the courses to be pursued and the examinations to be passed by students seeking diplomas...'[40]

This all-powerful board was to consist initially of twelve members – four from Queen's, three from the LTIC, the Principal of the MTIB, two from the Chamber of Commerce, and two appointed by the Crown. Its proposal, however, raised a furore at City Hall. The LTIC considered the proposed scheme carefully and seeing some sense in the elimination of overlapping areas of work, it was agreed that collaboration could well generate opportunities for attracting increased resources for higher technical education. But the Committee was strongly opposed to the formation of 'any new co-ordinating board in Belfast'. The subsequent debate at the City Council was a lively one, with the outcome summarised aptly in the press, 'Co-operation Accepted, Co-ordination Rejected.'[41] The Belfast City Council was firmly opposed to any form of co-ordination; the MTIB would continue as a self-contained and complete organisation. As Alderman O'Connell remarked, 'The Institute was ower young to marry yet.' Whilst not opposed to some form of co-operation, the Council declared emphatically that 'nothing shall take place or be done that shall impair the absolute independence of the Technical Institute'.

That outcome was a douche of cold water on aspirations at Queen's. The Council seemed to lose interest in the business thereafter, and when the DATI sought to raise the issue again in May 1903, the LTIC deemed it 'inadvisable to take any action at present with regard to the suggestions proffered'. However, Queen's maintained an optimistic outlook: responding to the City Council's concerns, the Senate reported in November that the scheme would safeguard the independence of both Institute and College.[42] But other developments were diverting the Senate's attention. The Government had set up a Royal Commission in 1901, under Lord Robertson, 'to inquire into the present conditions of the higher, general, and technical education available in Ireland'. Whilst its final report, published in 1903, was a disappointment and made little impact, the whole business had raised doubts about the wisdom of pursuing the Belfast scheme of collaboration until the Government's views on the matter had been clarified.

So the question of collaboration remained in abeyance until 1908 when the Irish Universities Act gave Queen's the status of a free-standing university. A team of Belfast University Commissioners was charged with the tasks of arranging the transfer of property and staff, and organising the structure and constitution of the new Queen's University of Belfast. The Commissioners had also to ensure that any formal arrangement between the new university and the MTIB was adequately covered in statutes. So the spotlight was once again on collaboration, and the issue soon found a prominent place on the Commissioners' agenda. The Belfast Chamber of Commerce and the LTIC both raised the matter within a few weeks of the establishment of the Commission, but the problems of earlier years resurfaced and, in an attempt to move quickly, the Commissioners proposed a temporary arrangement which would allow the engineering facilities of the MTIB to be made available to university students in the 1909-1910 academic year. However, the LTIC wanted 'fundamental preliminary details' resolved before they would commit themselves.

Having made little headway, the Commissioners decided in September 1909 to seek the assistance of Queen's Senate. The Senate, in turn, delegated the matter to a sub-committee which, in addition to considering the best way forward, had the unenviable task of negotiating with the hard-nosed representatives of the LTIC – Sir James Henderson, R. Trimble, J. Horner and Principal Forth. At the first joint meeting (February 1910), the LTIC representatives suggested that Queen's was only concerned with filling a gap in its own curriculum by making use of the equipment and staff of the Institute, without giving anything in return[43]. Francis Forth was more constructive, however, and he proposed a model of collaboration similar to that practised in Manchester where the University and Technical Institute worked together in a Faculty of Technology. That model was accepted initially by Queen's, but after further consideration the University decided that a Faculty of Technology and Commerce would be preferred as the collaborative device, since it would also allow for collaboration in the latter area. By March the model had been changed yet again to encompass two Faculties – a Faculty of Technology and a Faculty of Commerce.

The prospect of agreement seemed bright at this stage, but yet again Queen's raised the Corporation's fears that the MTIB would lose its autonomy; Queen's proposed that it should have a role in the appointment of the Principal of the MTIB, and of the teaching staff on the relevant courses. So, in June 1910, the LTIC resolved that it 'was unable to recommend the Council to agree to the proposals for co-ordination made by the University Authorities; that the University Authorities be informed accordingly and invited to reconsider the proposals'.[44] All seemed lost for a while, but the timely intervention of T.P. Gill, Secretary of the DATI, saved the day.

Gill's letter to the LTIC in late May proposed an alternative scheme, the central features of which were: (a) the MTIB would be recognised by the University, (b) the Principal of the MTIB would be a member of the Faculty of Science, and (c) A joint advisory committee would be set up. The Commissioners were relieved to accept these terms as the basis for an agreement, and work commenced immediately on a draft. In July the LTIC was able to report progress towards 'a basis on which it would be possible to formulate a scheme of co-operation'.[45] Further meetings with the two sets of representatives resulted in a draft agreement which was circulated for comment in October. The Belfast Corporation put its signature to the document in November 1910.

In essence, the agreement stated that the MTIB would be recognised by the Senate as a college in which the University's students might study for degrees or diplomas of the University.[46] Six areas of study would be involved: Mechanical Engineering, Electrical Engineering, Chemical Technology, Textile Technology, Architecture, and Naval Architecture. The relevant courses would come under the regulations of the University's Faculty of Science. The relevant professors and lecturers in the MTIB would become recognised teachers of the University, and the Principal of the MTIB would become a member of the Faculty of Science. An advisory committee to the Senate – the Committee of

Technology – would represent the interests of both University and Institute, and would provide appropriate checks and balances.

Detailed planning proved time-consuming, so the collaborative scheme did not come into full operation until October 1912, when twelve students enrolled. The records show that Henry Taylor, the first to graduate under the new scheme, was awarded a BSc in Mechanical Engineering in 1913. The story of higher technical education does not end there, however, for the LTIC was anxious to obtain permission for part-time students to sit for university examinations. The matter was raised in 1912, and considered by the University's Technology Committee in 1913. But, while that was under consideration, another development offered students an alternative route to a degree: the Government announced in 1914 that external or unattached students would be given access to the examination of a reconstructed University of London.

12

War, Politics, and the End of an Era

The Impact of War

The Municipal Technical Institute, Belfast, was launched in difficult times. As it struggled to establish itself, political tensions were intruding into all aspects of Belfast life. The Ulster crisis was top of the political agenda: Nationalist aspirations for Home Rule clashed with Unionist ambitions to remain part of the United Kingdom. This wide gulf of opinion brought injury and death, demonstrations and rioting in the streets. Unionists arranged mass meetings and signed a Solemn League and Covenant in the City Hall in 1912, and an armed Ulster Volunteer Force (UVF) threatened civil war if Home Rule were implemented. The Technical Institute had been set up to serve all the citizens of Belfast, but there is evidence of more than tacit support for the Unionist cause. Forth, for example, addressed a meeting of Young Citizen Volunteers in the Central Hall of the Institute in December 1912.

However critical these local troubles, they were forced to take a back seat as the great European States clashed in 1914. The Great War did not leave the Municipal Technical Institute (MTIB) unscathed. Many of its staff and students decided to serve their country. Forth reported in November 1914 that 523 students and staff had joined up;[1] one had the rank of Captain, seven were Lieutenants, fifty-six Second Lieutenants, and sixty-seven Non-Commissioned Officers. In June 1915, the Principal himself 'considered it his duty at this critical juncture to place his services at the disposal of the Crown'.[2] He was appointed Captain of a Company of the 18th Battalion of the Royal Irish Rifles, based at Clandeboye, Co. Down, where he was placed in charge of training recruits, and remained so until his return to civilian life in 1918. The serving staff and students brought great honour to the Institute. Professor Stanley's record is particularly noteworthy: appointed Captain, and later Major, he was awarded the Legion of Honour by the French Army for services at the front related to telegraphy and electrical work.[3] Of the students, Forth reported that former pupils of the Trade Preparatory School had won a Victoria Cross and a number of Military Crosses, and many had received Mentions in Dispatches.[4] The Victoria Cross was awarded posthumously to Private William Frederick McFadzean, whose heroism is still commemorated on a plaque at Cregagh in Belfast.[5]

The MTIB offered a warm welcome to the serving forces. In May 1914 Forth arranged a tour of facilities for a representative body of officers led by Brigadier General Count Gleichen,[6] and later that summer the College Square building served as a temporary barracks for troop detachments.[7]

Staff and students who did not enlist were also able to make substantial contributions to the war effort. The Institute set up a special organisation for the manufacture of munitions, and specially trained women were employed to assist the Institute's staff in the mechanical engineering workshops. Hand grenades, as well as flanges, ferrules and other components of munitions, were produced in their thousands. Classes were arranged in drawing and machine operation for women munitions workers employed by Coates & Sons, and in domestic economy for girls and women who were out of work due to the war. In the MTIB's workshops and laboratories, inspection gauges, used to check shell primers and fuses, were manufactured and assembled in great numbers. Sand bags were woven in the Textiles Department, and the Textile Testing House carried out many tests for the War Office.[8] The profits generated from the sale of equipment, ammunition and weapons financed Munitions Prizes that are still being awarded today.

Of direct local benefit, around 700 women students attended classes in Red Cross work, including first aid to the injured, home nursing, and hygiene.[9] The Bakery School on C Floor provided bread and cakes for the Somme Hospital at Sir James Craig's Belfast home, Craigavon, and the Institute's experts in carpentry helped to make surgical appliances for wounded soldiers in the UVF Hospital.

Day Classes

Student numbers may have fallen, but the Institute still remained a hive of activity during the war years. Day classes maintained, and in some cases increased their enrolments. The Trade Preparatory School (TPS) preserved its excellent reputation and attracted, on average, around 120 new students each year from 1914 to 1921. However, the earlier patterns of student attrition persisted; in 1919/20 for example, there were 130 students in first year, but only thiry-nine in second year, and none at all in third year.[10] In 1916 the Belfast Suffrage Society proposed to the LTIC that the TPS should accept girls, but when this was put to the vote, the Committee was divided, and it decided[11] to drop the matter *pro tem*. Fifteen years were to elapse before girls were admitted. Growing demands on the TPS persuaded the LTIC in 1920 to add a teacher in Science and Mathematics and an Instructor in Wood to the staffing complement.[12] The graduates of the TPS were much sought after by employers; in 1921 for example, Harland & Wolff agreed to take twelve of the best boys annually.[13] It is interesting to note that Belfast's other Trade Preparatory School – that in North Belfast's Hardinge Street – was also flourishing. Total numbers there regularly exceeded 100 from 1911 onwards. In 1921/22, first, second, and third years had respectively fifty-nine, forty-one, and twenty-five students. Hardinge Street received substantial support from the LTIC; by 1913, £1,109 had been granted for equipment, £1,874 for working expenses, and £401 towards scholarships.[14]

War had put a spotlight on the importance of technical skills, and by demonstrating its ability to provide those skills, the MTIB's credibility was increased in the eyes of employers. Attendance at day classes was encouraged by an increasingly supportive attitude from employers and trade associations. In 1917, the Old Bleach Linen Company at Randalstown paid its apprentices' fees and railway fares, as well as providing the necessary books and materials.[15] Major Rupert Stanley, Forth's successor, described the schemes of support that employers were offering apprentices in 1921:

> The members of the Bleachers' and Dyers' Association allow their apprentices
> to attend courses of instruction on two full days per week; the Belfast Society

of Architects allow their pupils to attend on two full days per week. The members of the Printing Trades Association have decided to send their apprentices to classes on one full day per week. The scheme has also been adopted by Messrs Workman, Clark and Co., Ltd, and they have made a commencement during the past session by allowing all their plumbing and painting apprentices to attend on one full day per week, besides offering prizes and otherwise encouraging the scheme in every way. In each case wages are paid for the time spent at these classes.[16]

University classes added a few more day students, but the grand total of only twenty-nine such students in 1921[17] would have been seen as a poor return for all the effort that had gone into the establishment of the collaborative scheme with Queen's.

Evening Classes

Evening classes were hardest hit by the reduction in student numbers during the war years. The surprising decision in 1915 to abandon preparatory evening classes brought a substantial drop in student numbers[18] – around 1,500 – but the reduction was largely matched by increases in numbers in Mechanical Engineering and in Commerce, under the leadership, respectively, of Professor Smith and Professor Lloyd-Dodd. In Mechanical Engineering, students and employers were particularly enthusiastic about classes in machine shop practice, pattern making, turning and milling, boilermaker's work, fitting, engine repairs, etc.

Whilst the Commerce Department did not have such an impressive array of equipment as the engineers, its classes, nevertheless, showed the greatest growth during the years of conflict. The press remarked,

> Too much attention cannot be paid in any large industrial city to the provision of facilities for a sound commercial education. The rooms of this Department in the Institute are specially adapted for this purpose, so that students may acquire that technical knowledge and specialised education so necessary for present-day commercial administration. Last year a very special successful course for grocers was established, and numerous successes were obtained by the students at the national examinations of the grocers' Institute.[19]

Post-war, the MTIB turned its attention to rehabilitation classes aimed at giving demobilised soldiers a variety of opportunities to learn new skills. For example, Stanley's *History of the Scheme; Municipal College of Technology, Belfast* was printed by students attending ex-servicemen's training classes.[20] Classes in boot and shoe repair were provided for disabled former soldiers, and the Appointments Department of the Ministry of Labour funded courses in flax culture and preparation for demobilised officers.[21]

Mechanical Engineering and Commerce were flourishing, but the Textiles Department, originally a jewel in the Institute's crown, was struggling to keep its head above water. A large slice of the Institute's resources had been devoted to this area, which, springing from Hastings Street roots, had been central to the Institute's *raison d'être*. However, despite an impressive array of facilities, the number of students attending Textile classes rarely exceeded 300. In 1921, Stanley referred enigmatically to 'the unsatisfactory conditions under which the Textiles Department was being run'.[22] He arranged the help of an Advisory Committee consisting of three representatives from the Spinners', Weavers', and Bleachers' Associations in a review of the diploma courses in weaving and spinning.

The development of new courses continued to compensate for those that had lost momentum. Forth had always worked hard to ensure that the MTIB was part of a 'seamless robe' of educational provision in Belfast. At one end, he wanted to facilitate access from National Schools and intermediate schools; at the other, he wanted to give the Institute's students ample opportunity to progress to university studies. The DATI provided an opportunity to develop the former in 1915, when it sought ideas for improvements in National Schools. The Institute's proposals for encouraging primary schoolchildren to remain in the sixth standard for an additional year were well received.[23] Such children would sit a special examination for a higher-grade certificate, which would cover subjects taught in the MTIB's introductory classes, and success in that examination would permit students to enter specialised courses directly. Unfortunately, no evidence has been unearthed concerning the success or otherwise of that particular initiative.

During the war years, the MTIB's students started to organise themselves into representative groups. Commerce students had done so as early as 1913, when they set up an Economics, Statistical and Commerce Society. The LTIC was wary, however, of these developments and insisted that such societies could not be established until their objectives and regulations had been approved.[24] The Committee appeared hostile to any manifestation of independence from students. When Forth informed members that some classes had been displaying their gratitude to staff in a concrete way, the minute recorded that the LTIC, 'did not look with approval on the presentation of gifts to teachers by classes of students at the close of courses of instruction, nor of the giving of gratuities by classes to attendants or other employees'.[25]

Higher Technical Education

The demand for degree-level studies in technical subjects grew slowly. The scheme of collaboration with Queen's, agreed nearly a decade earlier, had not produced the anticipated rush of students, and there was some evidence of dissatisfaction with its operation in practice. The MTIB's desire to allow evening students to progress to degrees brought the matter to a head. The Queen's Senate dragged its feet on the matter, and its procrastination drove Forth to propose that the Institute be given a new 'constituent' status, which would permit its evening students to sit university examinations.[26] The Senate's rejection of that proposal, and its apparent reluctance to progress the matter further, caused

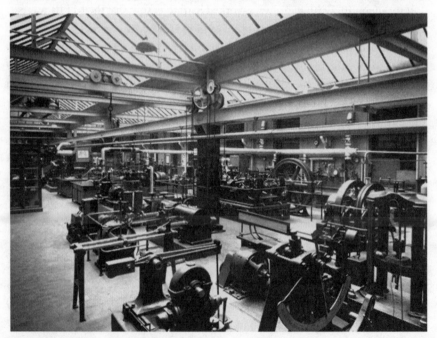

By the early 1920s, the Mechanical Engineering Laboratory was nearing perfection. (Belfast Metropolitan College Archive.)

great frustration in the ranks of the LTIC – so much so that in March 1919 a member proposed that the agreement with Queen's be terminated forthwith. The meeting, however, decided to adjourn the discussion until another day.

All was not lost: other opportunities for degree studies had presented themselves. A reorganised University of London allowed external students to sit for its degrees, and Forth and his colleagues were not going to allow such an opportunity slip by. Within a few months, the Institute's laboratories and workshops had been recognised by the University of London, and Forth was able to announce in 1918:

Arrangements have been made with the University of London for holding at the Municipal Technical Institute the matriculation examinations of the University in January and June each year, and the intermediate examinations in science and in engineering in both practical and theoretical subjects, whilst the question of holding the final examinations for the BSc degrees in Science and Engineering are under consideration.[27]

This was the first time that such a concession had been permitted outside of London.[28] Institute students were now able to get University of London degrees without leaving Belfast.

But recognition of evening classes by Queen's continued to be a central

BELFAST AND DISTRICT CHAMBER OF TRADE TECHNICAL CLASSES.

WITH the idea of encouraging and developing greater efficiency in business the BELFAST and DISTRICT CHAMBER of TRADE have arranged a COURSE of WINTER CLASSES in the TECHNICAL INSTITUTE, to commence this month, and a large sum has been subscribed for Scholarships and Prizes. Certificates will be issued at the close of the Season to those who pass the standard examination, and Business Houses will give preference to holders of these certificates when applications are made for vacancies.

STUDY OF TEXTILES—LINEN, COTTON, WOOL, &c.
1st Prize, £10; 2nd Prize, £5; 3rd Prize, £3.

COMMERCIAL ENGLISH AND ARITHMETIC.
1st Prize, £5; 2nd Prize, £3; 3rd Prize, £2.

SALESMANSHIP AND BUSINESS METHODS.
1st Prize, £5; 2nd Prize, £3; 3rd Prize, £2.

FRENCH AND SPANISH.
1st Prize, £3; 2nd Prize, £2.

WINDOW DRESSING, COLOUR SCHEMES.
1st Prize, £5; 2nd Prize, £3; 3rd Prize, £2.

BLOUSE AND DRESS CUTTING.
1st Prize, £3; 2nd Prize, £2; 3rd Prize, £2.

DRAWING AND LETTERING (with Special Reference to Window Ticket Writing).
1st Prize, £3; 2nd Prize, £2.

SPECIAL TRAVELLING SCHOLARSHIP.

ENGLISH AND FRENCH AND COLOUR CONTRASTS.

ONE WEEK IN LONDON, ALL EXPENSES PAID.

It has also been arranged to add another Travelling Scholarship—one week in Paris, all expenses paid—at the termination of the war.

Assistants engaged in either retail or wholesale drapery trades are entitled to attend these Classes, and should enrol at the Technical Institute before 12th September.

An advertisement for the Institute's commercial classes, *The Northern Whig*, 4 September 1918.

concern. Queen's was not entirely opposed to such a development, indeed, the Faculty of Commerce had first promoted the idea around the turn of the century when Professor H.O. Meredith, the Dean, had become convinced that the Faculty's viability depended on such a development.[29] However, part-time studies, and their close cousins – external degrees – were almost universally condemned by academic opinion at the time, so the Senate opposed their introduction in 1912. The Faculty of Commerce did not let the matter drop, however, and, in 1915, new regulations were introduced that allowed students to obtain a B.Com.Sc. by attending evening classes at the MTIB for two years, followed by three years at the University. That scheme provided the template for the scheme of collaboration that was ultimately adopted.

The new arrangements with the University of London gave the Institute confidence to put greater pressure on Queen's for revisions to the agreed scheme of collaboration. In April 1920, the Corporation authorised Principal Stanley 'to prepare proposals and submit same to the committee for better co-ordination between the Queen's University and the Municipal Technical Institute'. The Corporation's persistence, Stanley's wisdom and tact, and the Senate's realisation that something had to be done, brought early results with a new scheme of co-ordination in place in October 1920.

The scheme established a new Faculty of Applied Science and Technology, whose membership included the Vice-Chancellor and the University's Professors of Physics, Mathematics, Civil Engineering, and Chemistry. And the Institute was well represented by the Principal, along with the several extra-mural professors and lecturers in Mechanical Engineering, Electrical Engineering, Naval Architecture, Applied Chemistry, Design, and Mathematics. The subjects of the Faculty would include all the aforementioned disciplines, but the regulations also permitted the inclusion of certain subjects in the Faculties of Art and Commerce.

The introduction of regulations for evening students was a matter of celebration for the Institute. From 1921 onwards, its evening courses could qualify students for the award of Queen's degrees or diplomas in mechanical engineering, electrical engineering, naval architecture, architecture, and applied chemistry. In addition to aspirant scientists and technologists,[30] young people 'engaged in the business houses of Belfast' could use the MTIB's evening classes as stepping stones to a Queen's degree in commerce – BComSc. But evening students, whether in science or in commerce, had to meet several strict conditions: they had to study for at least five years, during which period they had to show evidence of concurrent employment in an appropriate industry, and their

The Institute's Weaving Shed in the early 1920s. (*Belfast Metropolitan College Archive.*)

fees would not be less than those of full-time students.

In addition to undergraduate degrees, the agreement with Queen's allowed the MTIB to prepare students for higher awards of the University – MSc and DSc. This encouraged the growth of research in the Institute. The establishment of the Textiles Testing House had been a step in that direction, but more needed to be done. The professors at the Institute were all capable of research, but some preferred to concentrate on mastering existing technologies, rather than developing new ones. The former focused on teaching, and displayed their expertise in the relevant technologies in various textbooks. Professor Fred Bradbury, for example, was a prolific author who, by 1914, had already established a reputation in textiles through five popular books including *Carpet Manufacture* (1905), and *Worsted Preparing and Spinning* (1914). Similarly, Stanley's textbook on *Wireless Telegraphy* (1917) remains a classic in the field. Of those more interested in research, many, such as Smith, Wren and Lloyd-Dodd, were able to display credentials such as the DSc degree. Smith's research made good use of the splendidly equipped mechanical engineering laboratory (e.g. his 1915 paper on 'Stress Strain Loops for Steel in the Cyclic State'). Professor Wren soon established a credible research programme in chemistry, as seen in his 1915 paper 'Configuration of the Stereoisomeric Diphenylsuccinic Acids'. The ability to conduct research was not the prerogative of the professoriate; W.J. Crawford, a teacher in mechanical engineering, was awarded a DSc by Glasgow University in 1911 for research into the elastic strength of flat plates.

The MTIB needed appropriate resources if it were to develop a credible research programme. In 1917, John Earls, then Acting Vice-Principal, wrote to the DATI seeking financial support for research at the Institute.[31] A positive response was received within a few weeks, and in September Forth applied for support for two research students – one in mechanical engineering, one in electrical engineering. There were other sources of funds for research: in 1919 the Scientific and Industrial Research Department, Westminster, provided a grant of £150 to support a research student in the Chemistry Department.[32] These developments laid the foundation of what was to become a substantial research activity in the Institute.

The Loss of the Founding Fathers

Technical education in Belfast suffered a great loss when Sir James Henderson, Chairman of the Library and Technical Instruction Committee, died suddenly on 1 May 1914. Services of remembrance were held in the City Hall and in the Municipal Technical Institute, where his portrait hangs to this day. Sir James was a man of great distinction. A lawyer by profession, his many positions of responsibility included first Lord Mayor of Belfast, first High Sheriff of the City and County of Belfast, Editor of the *Newry Telegraph*, and Managing Proprietor of *The Belfast Newsletter* and *Belfast Weekly News*. He was knighted in January 1899. He was a pioneering advocate of technical instruction, serving on the Board of Managers of the Belfast Government School of Art, and offering personal support to the Belfast Technical School. Sir James chaired the LTIC since its foundation in 1901 – indeed, he had presided at a meeting of the Committee on the day before his death. His portrait, which hangs in the Central Hall of the Institute, was unveiled in December 1914. Sir James was succeeded in the Chair by Alderman S.T. Mercier.

The Grim Reaper revisited the Institute in 1919. The combined tasks of Principal of the MTIB and Director of Technical Instruction in Belfast must have placed an extremely heavy burden on Francis Forth's shoulders. His responsibilities in the army would have added to that burden. There can be no doubt

W.G. MacKenzie's
portrait of Sir James
Henderson. (Belfast
Metropolitan College.)

Principal Francis
Charles Forth (*c.*1909).
(Belfast Metropolitan
College Archive.)

that these collective stresses and strains were the source of the failing health that began to show its effects in 1918. It was obvious to all that the Principal's health was on the wane. In August of that year he reluctantly advised the LTIC that, as the result of a medical examination he had recently undergone, he was compelled to go into a nursing home that evening for surgical treatmen.[33] But even his critical state of health could not deflect him from his responsibilities. He attended a meeting of the LTIC in December 1918, and early in 1919 he addressed a conference on education in his usual engaging manner. But the press reported that 'his physical powers were undermined by disease'.[34] The medical services of the day were not able to cope with his condition, and it was clear that the end was not far off. Forth wrote to the LTIC in February:

> It has been a great privilege and a great honour to me to have been associ-
> ated so long [over eighteen years] with the development of the Technical
> Instruction Scheme of Belfast. The Municipal Technical Institute, Belfast, has
> a great future before it, and in sending the Committee this farewell I earnestly
> trust that all the developments that are pending may be fully realised, and that
> the Committee's work may attain that high pinnacle to which it is so justly
> entitled.[35]

Francis Forth died on 28 February 1919 at the relatively young age of fifty-seven. The press described his passing as a grave blow to Irish technical education and to the city of Belfast. One report included the following, 'Mr Forth was a man of big ideas, sound judgement and quick apprehension, and in regard to education his optimism and enthusiasm were unbounded. His genial personality and sterling character endeared him to all who came in contact with him.'[36] He was buried in Knockbreda churchyard where his headstone can still be seen today.

This set of obituaries would not be complete without a brief reference to the death of William Gray, at the age of eighty-six, on 6 February 1917. Earlier chapters described Gray's breadth of vision concerning technical education, and his role in the development of the School of Art and the Free Library. His passing was noted in the minutes of the LTIC, but, surprisingly, his death attracted little comment in the press.

Housekeeping Matters

Ensuring that the necessary resources were in place was a primary responsibility of the LTIC. Income was attracted from the DATI, the Corporation, examining bodies like the City and Guilds, student fees, and a variety of miscellaneous sources. Most of the income found its way into the pockets of staff, both permanent and occasional, and the remainder was devoted to the general upkeep of the building, and to paying off outstanding debts. The annual statement for the year ending 31 March 1913 is given below.[37] Modern equivalences are given in brackets[38], but note that the value of the pound plummeted during the war years:

EXPENDITURE
Salaries and Wages, Permanent Staff: £12,814
Salaries, Occasional Staff: £2,857
Coal, Gas, Water, Electricity: £967
Printing, Stationery, Advertising: £1,043
Apparatus and Equipment: £3,243
Rents, Interest, and Sinking Fund: £6,190
Miscellaneous: £3,636
TOTAL EXPENDITURE £30,750 (approximately £2.2m today)

INCOME
Grants: £20,683
Fees: £2,704
Miscellaneous: £912
TOTAL INCOME £24,299 (approximately £1.7m today)

The statement shows a shortfall of £6,451. However, there is no reference to the penny-in-the-pound contribution from the rates – a sum that had risen from £5,409 in 1906/07 to £6,136 in 1912/13. So, overall, it seems that the Institute had overspent by £315 in 1912/13. Salaries were the dominant item of expenditure. The salaries of senior staff (April 1915) are listed overleaf:

F.C. Forth - £1,000 (around £70,000 today)

Professor Hall - £320

Professor Earls - £315

Miss Myerscough (Head of Women's Work) - £180

Professor Smith - £525

A.J. McCracken (Headmaster, TPS) - £265

Professor Stanley - £425

H.H. Dunlop (Registrar) - £300

Professor Bradbury -£425

R.A. Dawson (Headmaster, School of Art) - £425

Professor Wren - £400

J. Johnston (Engineer) - £220

Grants were dominated by a recurrent endowment of around £11,000 from the DATI, complemented by Science and Art grants from the same Department. In 1916/17, for example, the Institute attracted £8,608 from the latter source – £6,067 for classes in Science, and £2,541 for classes in Art.[39] Income from student fees was smaller, but significant nevertheless. Proportional to the number of students in attendance, and to the level of study pursued, fee income varied from year to year. The figure below shows that student numbers reached a first peak of 7,000 at the onset of the Great

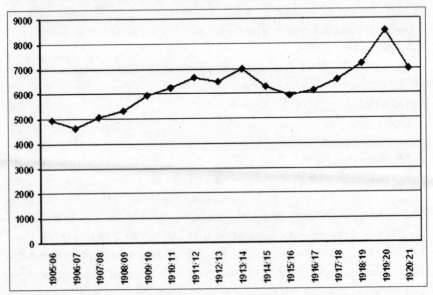

Numbers of students attending the Municipal Technical Institute, 1905-1921.

War in 1914. Thereafter they fell as some students enlisted, and some, who would otherwise have attended classes, were required to devote their days and nights to the manufacture of munitions. Numbers did not exceed the 7,000 mark again until the end of the war.

As numbers picked up towards the end of the war, the LTIC was chastised by the DATI in October 1917 for allowing enrolments to certain classes to exceed those permitted by regulations. The Department warned that it would not pay the grant for the excess numbers. This incensed Forth who immediately demanded that early consideration be given to the question of additional accommodation. Other factors affected attendance. The influenza epidemic of 1918 – the 'Great Flu' – affected both students and staff; the Trade Preparatory School was particularly hard hit, and had to be closed for a period in November 1918.

The euphoria of peacetime, combined with an increasing respect for technology, brought a resurgence in demand for classes. Enrolments rose to an all-time high of 8,500 in 1919, but the growth in numbers was soon strangled by a worsening of The Troubles: the impacts of local politics had replaced those of international politics. The severity of the violence on the streets led the authorities to introduce a curfew which, by its nature, was bound to have a negative impact on evening classes, especially on those students who had some distance to travel. The MTIB tried to ameliorate those difficulties by adjusting its timetable. Classes scheduled to commence at 7.30 or 8p.m. were moved forward to 7.15p.m., those due to start at 8.30 or 9p.m. were moved forward to 8p.m., and all classes were to close at 8.45p.m. However, student numbers had fallen by 20 per cent by the end of the 1920/21 year.

The Institute's staffing complement grew, but slowly. In 1921 there were 65 permanent staff (teaching and administration), and 166 occasional teachers.[40] This is to be compared with the situation eight years earlier when the respective numbers were 59 and 157.[41] Several senior appointments were made, including some new posts and some replacements. Professor Hall, Head of Commerce, resigned in 1915 and was replaced by Professor H.T. Lloyd-Dodd; I. Beaumont ARCA, an expert in Industrial Design, succeeded R.A. Dawson as Headmaster of the School of Art when the latter retired in 1919; T.R. Hampshire, from the Northern Polytechnic, London, was appointed Head of the Building Trades Department in October 1919, and Professor T.P. Matthewman, from Margate, became Head Of Physics and Electrical Engineering when Professor Stanley moved into the Principal's office in 1919.

As described earlier, many staff had joined the fighting forces. Most were granted some financial recognition by the LTIC. The Corporation minutes of

8 October 1914 refer to teachers joining the colours and include a decision to pay, depending on circumstances, half or full salaries to dependants. For example, when Thomas Wright, gymnastics instructor, enlisted in the 30th Brigade at the Curragh, his family was paid full salary. (Wright was later raised to the rank of Captain.) In Forth's case, his captain's salary of some £250 was topped up to the £1,000 he had been earning in the Institute at the time.[42] But others were not treated so generously; J. Brown, one of the Institute's workmen, requested half pay but was refused.[43]

Those who chose to remain at home during the war benefited from war bonuses which were intended to offset war-induced rises in the cost of living. These were substantial, with the value of sterling falling by 59 per cent between 1913 and 1920.[44] After intense negotiations with the trades unions, the Corporation agreed to pay bonuses to its weekly-paid employees – starting at one shilling per week for those earning less than £1 per week.[45] Salaried staff seemed to fare better. In September 1919, the advertisement for the Head of the Building Trades Department quoted a salary of £300, with war bonus of £120 per annum.

The appointment of Francis Forth's successor was a major event on the staffing front. After consulting with the DATI, the LTIC decided on a starting salary of £800, rising by £50 increments to £1,000. The minutes of the LTIC's meeting were received by the Council at its meeting on 11 April 1919, but advertisements for the post had already been placed in the press.[46] The number of applicants is unknown, but the DATI – who had the final say – decided on a shortlist of four, which included local men Earls and Stanley. However, the procedures from then on were, to put it mildly, decidedly *ad hoc*. The Committee, without interview, and apparently with Earls present, decided to recommend him for the post.

The recommendation was turned down by both Council and Department. The post had to be re-advertised at a salary of £1,000, and English and Scottish newspapers and some professional journals had to be involved this time round. In a fit of pique the LTIC requested that 'the Department will be good enough to consult the law officers of the Crown and advise the Committee as to their powers in the matter.'[47] But the DATI offered no solace, arguing that it was the Committee's established practice to seek ratification of their procedures by the Council, and there were no grounds for departing from that practice in this particular case. The re-advertisement in August attracted twenty-six applications, from which the DATI shortlisted eight.[48] A further distillation reduced this to three – Thomas Crossland (Burnley), and Earls and Stanley from the

> 1. **That every person within the County of the City of Belfast shall remain indoors between the hours of 10.30 o'clock p.m. and 5 o'clock a.m., unless provided with a Permit in writing from the Competent Military Authority or some person duly authorised by him.**
>
> 2. **That all Places of Entertainment within the County of the City of Belfast shall be Closed at 9.30 o'clock p.m., and that the Tramway Service within the same area shall be suspended at 9.30 o'clock p.m.**

A curfew was advertised widely in the press in 1920.

MTIB. All three were interviewed by the LTIC along with G. Fletcher, the DATI Assistant Secretary, and Dr Garrett, an Inspector. Members voted as follows: Crossland, seven; Earls, fifteen, and Stanley thirteen. However, when the matter was considered by the Council on the afternoon of the same day, the vote was as follows: Stanley, thirty-nine; Earls, twenty-one, and Crossland, one. So Major Rupert Stanley was appointed Principal of the Municipal Technical Institute and Director of Technical Instruction to the County Borough of Belfast. Professor Earls received some recognition of his valuable services to the Institute; he was appointed Vice-Principal at a salary of £650, and received a retrospective honorarium of £500 for having carried out many of the duties of Principal over a period of four years.

The new Principal soon had to cope with a new system of governance. A new Belfast Corporation was elected in 1920 and, with new brooms sweeping, the LTIC was disbanded and replaced by two committees – a Technical Instruction Committee (TIC), and a Library and Museums Committee.

Promotion

The MTIB's reputation was growing locally and internationally. Dr J.W. Robertson, Chairman of a Canadian Royal Commission on Industrial Training and Technical Education, paid a visit in late 1911. He was favourably impressed, and in 1914, a letter from the Industrial Art School in London, Ontario quoted him as follows, '[in] the matter of arrangement the Belfast Municipal Technical Institute surpasses any institute he has seen while abroad … it is an excellent example of organisation, plans and equipment to meet the industrial needs of the city'.[49]

Others took heed of Robertson's comments. Those responsible for a new Technical School in Minneapolis wrote seeking details of the Belfast scheme, and there was a regular stream of visitors from Great Britain, Canada, the United States, India, South Africa, and Australia.[50]

This growing reputation ensured that the MTIB was a regular stopping-off point for distinguished visitors. When the Lord Lieutenant Lord Wimborne visited Belfast in May 1915, he did a quick tour of the laboratories and, on reaching the Central Hall was 'loudly cheered by the boys of the Trade Preparatory School, while Professor Smith played the National Anthem on the piano.'[51]

Sir Edward Carson was another notable visitor. In February 1918, accompanied by Sir James Craig (later to be Northern Ireland's first Prime Minister), he inspected the Institute's Bakery Department where the equipment was being used to provide bread and cakes, free of charge, for the UVF Hospital.[52] During a visit to a classroom Carson wrote the equation $2+2=5$ on the blackboard, and put his signature beneath. Cut from the blackboard and framed, that particular piece of political creativity provided a conversation piece in the Principal's office for many years.

The day-to-day business of the Institute also helped to boost its reputation. Annual prospectuses were informative and attractive publications, and regular exhibitions in the Central Hall attracted large numbers of visitors.

Northern Ireland on the Horizon

The Troubles continued to have a stultifying and erosive effect on life in Belfast. The third Home Rule Bill passed twice through the House of Commons in 1912, but was defeated in the Lords on both occasions. However, a third successful passage through the Commons in 1914 ratified the Bill, since legislation did not allow the Lords to block it for a third time. The intervention of war in 1914 persuaded the Government to postpone the Bill's implementation until hostilities had ceased. In the meantime, however, the Easter Rising of 1916, the establishment of the Irish Volunteers, the oratory of Edward Carson, and the organisation of Protestant paramilitary forces in the north had together produced an inflammatory and well-nigh unmanageable situation. Street riots, killings, and curfews were the order of the day.

The Government of Ireland Act 1920 was intended to resolve the conflict. Two parliaments would be established – one for Southern Ireland, one for Northern Ireland – and both with the power to unite if they so wished. But the paper plan did not work out in practice. Whilst the Northern Ireland Parliament was opened by King George V on 22 June 1921, the first meeting of the Southern Ireland Parliament only attracted an attendance of 4 members out of 128. Another period of intense political manoeuvring and bloody conflict had to pass before the Anglo-Irish Treaty of 1921/22 established a new Irish Free State.

All of this was to bring substantial changes to education in the new Northern Ireland. A Ministry of Education was set up on 7 June 1921, and the Minister, Lord Londonderry, was soon consulting widely on the shape of the new province's education system. He appointed a committee in September 1921 to examine the whole spectrum of educational provision. The supporters of technical education wanted to be sure that their views would be heard. Stanley had already proposed changes that would bring the new MTIB more into line with practice in Great Britain; in April 1921 he persuaded the new Technical Instruction Committee to change the name of the Institute to the Municipal College of Technology, Belfast – after the pattern of other great colleges like Glasgow, Manchester and Bradford. The committee also agreed to rename the Trade Preparatory School the Junior Technical School. Name changes were important, but the TIC's desire for more sweeping change was reflected in the minutes of the meeting on 22 September 1921:

> A discussion arose as to the possible changes in the administration of technical education under the Government of Ireland Act (1920) and it was resolved: That the Chairman, Vice-chairman, Councillors McCartney, Twaddell, and Mr A. Taylor, with the Principal, be appointed to wait upon the Minister of Education of Northern Ireland to place before him the future requirements for technical education.

The views of the Principal – and Director of Technical Instruction to the County Borough of Belfast – probably shaped the views of the deputation:

> Our educational scheme should be such that all natural talent and genius, born into every rank of our community, can be discovered and properly developed for the advantage of our industries; that every child has an equal opportu-

An exhibition of Women's Work in the Central Hall (*c.*1920). (Belfast Metropolitan College Archive.)

nity of passing from the Primary School to the University, and that we shall not overlook young Kelvins, Bessemers, or Stephensons, whose genius may enrich the community by thousands of pounds and increase the opportunities for employment in our province. In such a scheme the Belfast Municipal College of Technology should take an important place; it should provide for Belfast and Ulster the same advantages as the Royal College of Science in Dublin provides for the rest of Ireland. At the same time its direct usefulness to the Belfast community which founded it must not be impaired; through its Junior Technical School, its evening courses, and a proper selection of capable apprentices for day time instruction, it should continue to raise the standard of workmanship in our local industries, and provide a supply of selected and well-trained recruits to fill the managerial and other responsible positions.[53]

Epilogue

The 120 years from the formation of the Union of Great Britain and Ireland in 1801, until its dissolution in 1921 saw enormous changes in Belfast and in Ireland as a whole. The growth of Belfast was phenomenal – from 30,000 citizens to 430,000 over the period. In the process, the small town at the mouth of the Farset developed from a modest mercantile community into a large, bustling industrial city. This impressive growth was largely driven by scientific and technological advances that spawned new industries and made old ones more efficient. Cotton, linen, shipbuilding and engineering led the way, supported by a plethora of service industries. Belfast was a leading industrial centre by the middle of the nineteenth century. By 1921 its wealth and potential productive output assured the economic viability of the new Northern Ireland.

As Belfast's size increased in the early decades of the nineteenth century, the need for an adequate education system for its growing population grew in step. But it was essential that any such system would adequately address the needs of the growing industrial base, and should provide sufficient numbers of people educated and trained to deal with the full range of industrial tasks. It was clear that all levels of education – primary, secondary and higher – would have to be involved. Much work was required at all three levels. At the most elementary level, a disorganised array of primary schools began to show some semblance of purpose following the introduction of National Schools in 1831. However, with the exception of a handful of Model Schools, the early primary school curriculum paid little attention to science and technology. A revised curriculum brought some improvements in this respect in the closing years of the nineteenth century.

Secondary, or intermediate education as it was known in Ireland, was in private and ecclesiastical hands, often supported by ancient endowments, throughout most of the nineteenth century. It was not until 1878 that the State decided to intervene and use its Intermediate Board to bring some order and focus to the sector's activities. Belfast's philanthropists had exercised enterprise as early as 1785 with the opening of the Belfast Academy, and later, in 1810 with the opening of the Belfast Academical Institution. Both organisations devoted meaningful portions of their curricula to science, and that pattern was followed as other schools were launched, such as the Ladies' Collegiate School (1859) and the Methodist College (1868). On the whole, however, Irish intermediate schools, including those in Belfast, tended to favour an academic and classical curriculum and, like the primary schools, science and technology had to play second fiddle in the curriculum right up to the end of the nineteenth century.

Higher education, which would be expected to provide an appropriate education for the future leaders of industry, was in an embryonic state in Ireland in the first half of the nineteenth century. Trinity College reigned supreme in Dublin from 1592, and Belfast's two ancient schools – the Academical Institution and the Academy – had in their different ways attempted to introduce higher education, albeit largely directed towards the needs of aspirant Presbyterian clergy. The former school established considerable credibility in the higher field and had six professors in post in the early decades of the century. However, higher education closely related to science and technology did not materialise until the formation of the Queen's Colleges in 1849. These three colleges, including Queen's, Belfast, worked to a common curriculum that included a Diploma in Civil Engineering, and a BA degree programme which included a good deal of science. Queen's Belfast achieved university status in 1908, and by 1921 was making a substantial contribution to higher technical education (although, often in collaboration with the Municipal Technical Institute).

On the whole, however, these conventional sources were tardy in providing an appropriate education for those individuals who wished to do their jobs better, and for the small but growing number of industrialists who recognised the need to improve business effectiveness through new technology. A specific technical education was required. The Mechanics' Institute was the earliest co-ordinated attempt to provide such an education in Belfast. Launched in 1825, the intention was to teach elementary science to practising artisans. However, the artisans soon tired of attending evening and weekend lectures that were often more concerned with morals than technical efficiency, and the Institute petered out within a couple of decades.

Subsequent developments in Belfast were influenced by the burgeoning technical education movement in Great Britain. The Government's growing awareness of foreign competition motivated the establishment of Schools of Design which were intended to improve the design, and hence the attractiveness and success of manufactured products. The Belfast Government School of Design, opened in 1849, had some early successes in this field, but it failed financially and was forced to close in 1858.

Financial viability was a major concern of the early pioneers of technical education. The Government's *laissez-faire* policy resulted in a technical education system that was dependant on self-help with occasional and modest encouragement from the Government. This approach was reinforced by the Victorian attitudes promulgated in books like Samuel Smiles's *Self Help*, which recorded and espoused the successes of self-made men like the great railway engineer Robert Stephenson.

Despite financial vulnerability, technical education continued to be driven forward by local demand, and by the Government's growing fear that foreign competition was getting out of hand. The great industrial exhibitions in London's Crystal Palace in 1851 and in Paris in 1867 confirmed those fears. By 1867, for example, it was clear that the British lead in dyeing, lace-making and engineering had gone.

Technical education was born of a fear of Continental competition, but with matters largely left to self-help, prophets, entrepreneurs and philanthropists were needed to devise, support and promote an appropriate system. In England men like T.H. Huxley, Lyon Playfair, Bernhard Samuelson, and Philip Magnus donned that mantle; in Ireland, Robert Kane, and T.P. Gill were two of the most active champions for the cause; and in Belfast, William Gray, Robert Barklie and James Henderson were amongst the town's many early proponents of technical education.

Local voluntary effort led to the establishment of four technical education institutions in Belfast in the second half of the nineteenth century – the Working Men's Institute (1866), the Belfast Government School of Art (1870), the Belfast Technical School (1884), and the School of Applied Science and Engineering (1886). These bodies had varying fortunes, but all made useful contributions to the enlightenment of the local populace and to local industrial effectiveness. The *Belfast Evening Telegraph* was able to report on 28 September 1886 that, 'There has been a great work silently and steadily accomplished in Belfast without the general public at our very doors knowing, except by means of annual reports, the immense amount of technical education being accomplished.'

All four schools suffered continuing financial difficulties, forcing them to operate on a hand-to-mouth basis for most of the time. Substantial donations were attracted from local philanthropists and businesses in the formative years, but these tapered off in later years. Industrialists were reluctant to throw their full weight behind these developments, fearing loss of trade secrets, and not convinced that a workforce knowledgeable in scientific matters would make any significant improvement to their company's productivity. On the whole, the industries of Belfast offered little support, either in cash or kind, to the technical education movement.

The Government offered some modest financial support, but most of it came through a system of 'payment on results' which turned out to have many drawbacks. The largesse of South Kensington's Department of Science and Art allowed Belfast schools to earn grants by entering their students for the Department's Science and Art examinations. But those examinations largely ignored the technological dimension of technical education; indeed, the technical education of the 1860s and 1870s was in reality a scientific education, and much of the so-called technical education was in practice of little relevance to the nation's needs of the times. Matters improved in 1880 when the City and Guilds of London Institute inaugurated its technically-orientated examinations, which also offered 'payments on results'. In Belfast, the Working Men's Institute and the Belfast Technical School fared reasonably well in these examinations.

The Government finally got the message that technical education needed and deserved substantial resources. To that end the Technical Instruction Act of 1889 empowered local authorities to raise a penny in the pound from the rates towards technical education. Unfortunately the administrative structures were not in place to deliver all of those benefits in Ireland. Nevertheless, the local champions continued to press the Belfast Corporation for a share of the rates. While it is unwise to judge past ages on standards only applicable to our own, the Council's total response of a mere £7,400 over the ten years (1891-1901) seems parsimonious and short-sighted in the extreme.

Fortunately for Irish technical education, the cavalry came storming over the hill in 1900 when, as a result of Horace Plunkett's valiant efforts, the Agriculture and Technical Instruction (Ireland) Act established a Department of Agriculture and Technical Instruction. The new Department brought immediate benefit to technical education. Substantial sums were promised to the Belfast Corporation, but on condition that a co-ordinated system of technical education would be devised, and that the Council would make a meaningful contribution to the costs of operation. After much work, most of it carried out by Principal Francis Charles Forth, a new scheme of technical education, subsuming the existing providers, got underway in 1902. A spanking new Municipal Technical Institute was opened in 1907.

The new Technical Institute made a mark on the city. A great success by any standards, it grew in size and status year on year, and its portfolio soon extended to include higher technical education in collaboration with the Queen's University of Belfast. When the new State of Northern Ireland was established, the Municipal Technical Institute helped to ensure its viability at a time when local and international conditions were not entirely propitious.

A closing note on the evolution of the Institute is appropriate. The Belfast College of Technology, as the Institute became known in 1922, was the nucleus of greater things to come. In the 1960s its higher-level engineering work was moved to the Ashby Institute as part of a collaborative arrangement with Queen's University. There, operating under a Joint Authority of University and Corporation, the scheme soon found itself suffering from stubbornness and lack of effective co-operation at the top. The resultant operational failure effectively left the door open for an alternative rationalisation of Belfast's higher technical education. It was no surprise, therefore, when the College of Technology's higher-level work was moved to Jordanstown in 1971 as part of a new Ulster College, which in turn became the Ulster Polytechnic, and again in turn part of the University of Ulster in 1984.

The College of Technology experienced further disruption in 1991 when it merged with the College of Business Studies and the Rupert Stanley College to form the Belfast Institute of Further and Higher Education. Further change followed in 2007, when the Belfast Institute and the Castlereagh College of Further Education were brought together in the Belfast Metropolitan College.

Endnotes

AR: Annual Report of the Belfast Government School of Art (location BCL)
BCL: Belfast Central Library
BNL: *Belfast News Letter*
BT: *Belfast Telegraph*
LHL: Linen Hall Library
LTIC: Minutes of Library and Technical Instruction Committee (location PRONI)
NW: *Northern Whig*
PRONI: Public Record Office Northern Ireland
TSC: Minutes of Technical School Committee (location PRONI)

Chapter 1: Belfast: Shaped by Science and Technology

1 Green, E.R.R., *Early Industrial Belfast. In Belfast; Origins and Growth of an Industrial City*. Editors: Beckett, J.C., Glasscock, R.E. (London: British Broadcasting Corporation, 1967).
2 Neeson, H., *The Origin and Development of Technical Education between 1850 and 1920, with Particular Reference to the Industrial Area of Belfast and its Surrounding* (DPhil Thesis, Coleraine, University of Ulster 1984).
3 *ibid*.
4 Coe, W.E., *The Engineering Industry in the North of Ireland* (Newton Abbott: David and Charles, 1969).
5 Green.
6 Robb, J.H., *The Book of the Royal Belfast Academical Institution*. (Belfast: Stevenson and Orr, 1913).
7 Coe.
8 McCracken, J.L., *Early Victorian Belfast. In Belfast; Origins and Growth of an Industrial City*, Editors: Beckett, J.C., Glasscock, R.E. (London: British Broadcasting Corporation, 1967).

9 Jones, E., *Late Victorian Belfast; 1850-1900. In Belfast; Origins and Growth of an Industrial City*, Editors Beckett, J.C., Glasscock, R.E. (London: British Broadcasting Corporation, 1967).

10 Anon., *Industries of the North One Hundred Years Ago* (Belfast: Friar's Bush Press, 1986).

11 Black, W., *Industrial Change in the Twentieth Century. In Belfast; Origins and Growth of an Industrial City*, Editors: Beckett, J.C., Glasscock, R.E. (London: British Broadcasting Corporation, 1967).

12 Coe.

13 Johnston, J., *Victorian Belfast* (Belfast: The Ulster Historical Foundation, 1993).

14 *ibid.*

15 Lynch, J.P., *An Unlikely Success Story* (Belfast: The Belfast Society and the Ulster Historical Foundation, 2001).

16 *ibid.*

17 Coe.

18 *ibid.*

19 *ibid.*

20 Kane, R., *Industrial Resources of Ireland* (Dublin: Hodges and Smith, 1844).

21 Young, A., *A Tour in Ireland* (London: Cassell and Company, 1897).

22 Kelham, B., McMillan, D.D.G., *Experimental Science in Ireland and the Scientific Societies. In Prometheus's Fire*, Editor: McMillan, N. (Carlow: Tyndall Publications, 2000).

23 Robb.

24 Killen, J., *A History of the Linen Hall Library; 1788-1988* (Belfast: The Linen Hall Library, 1990).

25 *ibid.*

26 Gray, W., 'Science and Art in Belfast' (Belfast: *The Northern Whig*, 1904).

27 Deane, A., *The Belfast Natural History and Philosophical Society; Centenary Volume 1821-1921* (Belfast, 1924).

28 *ibid.*

29 *ibid.*

30 Anon, *Prospectus. Belfast Library of Useful Knowledge,* number 1, 1831 (location, LHL).

31 Anon, *Belfast People's Magazine.* Number 5; Volume 1, May, 1847 (location, LHL).

32 Kane, R.

33 Cardwell, D.S.L., *The Organisation of Science in England* (London: Heinemann, 1972).

34 Anon, *Ireland Industrial and Agricultural* (Dublin: Browne and Nolan, 1902).

35 *ibid.*

36 Anon, *Apprentice Indentures* (location, PRONI, ref. D/3540/1).

37 Anon, *Commissioners of National Education in Ireland Twenty-Ninth Report.*

38 BNL 20/5/1857.

39 Barnes, J., *Irish Industrial Schools; 1868-1908* (Dublin: Irish Academic Press, 1989).

40 *ibid.*

41 *ibid.*

42 Kane, R.

Chapter 2: Technical Education Finds a place in the Curriculum

1 Anon, *Report of Commissioners of Irish Education Inquiry* (Dublin, 1825).

2 Hyland, A., Milne, K., *Irish Educational Documents* (Dublin: Church of Ireland College of

Education, 1987).

3 Coolahan, J., *Irish Education: Its History and Structure* (Dublin:Institute of Public Administration, 1981).

4 *ibid.*

5 Durcan, T.J., *History of Irish Education from* 1800 (Dublin: Dragon Books, 1972).

6 NW 28/4/1857.

7 Hyland & Milne.

8 Craig, A.R., McNeilly, N., *Belfast Model Schools 1857-1957* (Belfast: Northern Publishing Office, 1958).

9 BNL 20/5/1857.

10 Anon, *Commissioners of National Education in Ireland Twenty-Ninth Report.*

11 Anon, *Report of Commission of Inquiry into Primary Education (Ireland), 1868-1870* (Dublin,1870).

12 *ibid.*

13 Durcan.

14 Coolahan.

15 Hyland & Milne.

16 Durcan.

17 Stewart, A.T.Q., *Belfast Royal Academy; The First Century, 1785-1885* (Belfast, 1985).

18 Anon, *Statement of the Constitution of the Belfast Academy* (Belfast, 1829); (location LHL).

19 Moody, T.W., Beckett, J.C., *Queen's Belfast 1845-1949; the History of a University* (London: Faber and Faber, 1959).

20 Hyland & Milne.

21 *ibid.*

22 *ibid.*

23 BNL 14/1/1859.

24 Coolahan.

25 Coyne, W.P., *Science Teaching and Technical Instruction in Ireland Industrial and Agricultural* (Dublin, Department of Agriculture and Technical Instruction,1902).

26 McLorie, A.D., *Voluntary Bodies and the Development of Technical Education in Belfast During the Nineteenth Century* (Unpublished MA Thesis, Jordanstown, University of Ulster, 1987).

27 Jordan, A., *Margaret Byers; Pioneer of Women's Education and Founder of Victoria College Belfast* (Belfast: Institute of Irish Studies, Queen's University Belfast, 1989).

28 Robb.

29 NW 7/7/1886.

30 Coolahan.

31 Henderson, J.W., *Methodist College Belfast 1868-1938; Survey and Retrospect* (Belfast, 1939).

32 NW 14/9/1910.

33 NW 2/9/1890.

34 *Dublin Evening Mail.* 13/9/1892.

35 Stewart.

36 *ibid.*

37 BNL 6/5/1825.

38 Robb.

39 *ibid.*

40 Hyland & Milne.

41 *ibid.*

42 Moody & Beckett.

43 Robb.

44 Moody & Beckett.

45 *Report of the President of Queen's College Belfast for the Session Ending June 1864.* (Dublin: 1864)

46 Robb.

47 Coolahan.

48 NW 10/12/1909.

Chapter 3: Adult Education and the Belfast Mechanics' Institute

1 Muir, J., *John Anderson; Pioneer of Technical Education* (Glasgow: John Smith, 1950).

2 Smith, A., *An Introductory Lecture on the Past and Present Study of Science, as Regards the Working Classes. In Science and the Rise of Technology since 1800* (Milton Keynes: Open University Press, 1972).

3 *ibid.*

4 Millis, C.T., *Technical Education* (London: Edward Arnold, 1925).

5 Armytage, W.H.S., *Four Hundred Years of English Education* (London: Edward Arnold, 1970).

6 Tylecote, M., *The Manchester Mechanics' Institute, 1824-50. In Artisan to Graduate* (Manchester: Manchester University Press, 1974).

7 Abbott, A., *Education for Industry and Commerce in England* (Oxford: Oxford University Press, 1933).

8 Neeson.

9 Duffy, S., 'Treasures Open to the Wise; The Mechanics' Institutes of North-East Ulster.' In *Prometheus's Fire*; Editor: McMillan, N (Carlow: Tyndall Publications, 2000).

10 NW 6/1/1825.

11 NW 24/3/1825.

12 BT 4/3/1925.

13 NW 6/1/1825.

14 BNL 6/5/1825.

15 Anon, *Problems of a Growing City; 1780-1870* (Belfast: Office of the Economic and Social History Society of Ireland, 1973).

16 *Rules proposed for the Belfast Mechanics' Institute with Lists of the Donors and Members* (Belfast, 1825); (location BCL).

17 Neeson.

18 BT 4/3/1925.

19 Anon, *Belfast Peoples' Magazine*; number 2, Volume 1, February 1847, (location LHL).

20 McCormac, H., *On the Best Means of Improving the Moral and Physical Condition of the Working Class* (London: Longman, 1830), (location LHL).

21 NW 24/8/1826.

22 NW 26/11/1827.

23 McCormac.

24 Anon, *Problems of a Growing City; 1780-1870.*

25 BNL 13/5/1831.

26 Neeson.

27 Anon, *Belfast Peoples' Magazine*; number 2, Volume 1, February 1847.

28 NW 30/11/1838.

29 NW 6/12/1838.

30 Hudson, J.W., *The History of Adult Education* (London: Woburn Press, 1969).

31 Anon, *Problems of a Growing City; 1780-1870*.

Chapter 4: Teaching Art and Design in Belfast.

1 NW 28/11/1848.

2 Black, E., *Art in Belfast 1760-1888; Art Lovers or Philistines?* (Dublin: Irish Academic Press, 2006).

3 Bell, Q., *The Schools of Design* (London: Routledge and Kegan Paul, 1963).

4 *The Times.* 9/5/1845.

5 Cole, H., *Fifty Years of Public Work accounted for in his Deeds, Speeches, and Writings* (London: 1884).

6 *ibid.*

7 Black, E.

8 *ibid.*

9 Cole.

10 Anon, *Belfast Peoples' Magazine*, No 6, Vol.1, 5 June 1847 (Belfast, 1847); (location LHL).

11 NW 18/1/1849.

12 NW 31/5/1849.

13 Black, E.

14 NW 4/12/1849.

15 NW 8/3/1851.

16 Wilk, C., *Grand Design; a History of the Victoria and Albert Museum* (London, Victoria and Albert Museum, 2007).

17 NW 26/1/1850.

18 NW 30/3/1852.

19 NW 11/4/1850.

20 Black, E.

21 NW 20/3/1851.

22 NW 30/3/1852.

23 *Annual Report Belfast Government School of Design; 1852/53* (location BCL).

24 *Annual Report Belfast Government School of Design; 1853/54* (location BCL).

25 *ibid.*

26 NW 30/3/1852.

27 NW 8/3/1851.

28 NW 30/3/1852.

29 *Annual Report Belfast Government School of Design; 1853/54.*

30 NW 30/3/1852.

31 NW 8/3/1851.

32 *Annual Report Belfast Government School of Design; 1852/53.*

33 Cole.

34 Black, E.

35 BNL 20/12/1854.

36 Black, E.
37 BNL 13/11/1855.
38 Robb.
39 NW 29/12/1855.

Chapter 5: The Belfast Working Men's Institute and Temperance Hall

1 *Annual Report of the Working Men's Institute and Temperance Hall; 1871-1872* (Belfast, 1872), (location LHL).
2 *ibid.*
3 Gray, W.
4 *ibid.*
5 *Annual Report of the Working Men's Institute and Temperance Hall; 1871-1872.*
6 *ibid.*
7 *ibid.*
8 *Annual Report of the Working Men's Institute and Temperance Hall; 1871-1872.*
9 Black, E.
10 *ibid.*
11 *Annual Report of the Working Men's Institute and Temperance Hall; 1871-1872.*
12 Gray, W.
13 BNL 24/5/1876.
14 *ibid.*
15 *ibid.*
16 *ibid.*
17 *ibid.*
18 Anon, *Official Catalogue; Industrial Exhibition and Bazaar* (Belfast: Hugh Adair, 1876), (location LHL).
19 *ibid.*
20 *Annual Report of the Belfast Working Men's Institute and Temperance Hall; 1872-73,* (location BCL).
21 Anon, *Official Catalogue; Industrial Exhibition and Bazaar.*
22 *ibid.*
23 *Annual Report of the Belfast Working Men's Institute and Temperance Hall; 1878-79,* (location BCL).
24 McLorie.
25 *Annual Report of the Working Men's Institute and Temperance Hall; 1882-1883,* (location BCL).
26 Gray W.
27 *Annual Report of the Working Men's Institute and Temperance Hall; 1882-1883.*
28 *ibid.*
29 Gray, W.
30 NW 31/1/1887.
31 *Annual Report of the Working Men's Institute and Temperance Hall; 1879-1880,* (location BCL).
32 BT 28/9/1885.
33 *Reports of the Royal Commission on Technical Instruction* (London, 1884).

34 *ibid.*
35 *ibid.*
36 *ibid.*
37 Robb.
38 Walker, B.M., Dixon, H., *In Belfast Town* 1864–1880 (Belfast: Friar's Bush Press, 1984).
39 BNL 12/4/1895.

Chapter 6: A New Belfast School of Art

1 NW 21/4/1868.
2 Gray, W.
3 McLorie.
4 BNL 17/10/1870.
5 NW 23/9/1870.
6 NW 17/10/1870.
7 Programme of Examinations, 1900. Belfast Government School of Art (location BCL).
8 McLorie.
9 Gray, W.
10 4th AR 1874–1875.
11 12th AR 1882–1883.
12 15th AR 1885–1886.
13 25th AR 1895–1896.
14 4th AR 1874–1875.
15 7th AR 1877–1878.
16 8th AR 1878–1879.
17 12th AR 1882–1883.
18 BNL 10/10/1882.
19 12th AR 1882–1883.
20 3rd AR 1873–1874.
21 4th AR 1874–1875.
22 8th AR 1878–1879.
23 7th AR 1877–1878.
24 Black, E.
25 *ibid.*
26 10th AR 1880–1881.
27 19th AR 1889–1890.
28 22nd AR 1892–1893.
29 6th AR 1876–1877.
30 Programme of Examinations, 1900. Belfast Government School of Art.
31 McLorie.
32 28th AR 1898–1899.
33 24th AR 1894–1895.
34 28th AR 1898–1899.
35 1st AR 1871–1872.
36 Gray, W.
37 26th AR 1896–1897.
38 *ibid.*

Chapter 7: The Belfast Technical School

1 *Reports of the Royal Commission on Technical Instruction* (London, 1884).
2 NW 16/12/1882.
3 *Reports of the Royal Commission on Technical Instruction* (London, 1884).
4 *ibid.*
5 NW 12/8/1881.
6 McLorie.
7 NW 16/12/1882.
8 Gray, W.
9 *Reports of the Royal Commission on Technical Instruction* (London, 1884).
10 Gray, W.
11 *ibid.*
12 NW 8/2/1884.
13 *ibid.*
14 *ibid.*
15 *ibid.*
16 *ibid.*
17 McLorie.
18 NW 29/1/1885.
19 NW 19/6/1884.
20 BNL 26/9/1885.
21 *ibid.*
22 *ibid.*
23 NW 26/1/1886.
24 NW 29/1/1885.
25 NW 26/1/1886.
26 Gray, W.
27 NW 30/11/1888.
28 *ibid.*
29 McLorie.
30 *The Belfast Technical School Eleventh Annual Report, 1893-1894,* (location Belfast Metropolitan College Archive).
31 NW 15/11/1900.
32 NW 26/1/1886.
33 NW 30/11/1888.
34 *Belfast Evening Telegraph,* 12/9/1884.
35 NW 30/11/1888.
36 *The Belfast Technical School Eleventh Annual Report, 1893-1894.*
37 NW 15/11/1892.
38 NW 11/12/1886.
39 McLorie.
40 NW 6/12/1898.
41 NW 15/11/1892.

42 NW 30/11/1888.

43 NW 3/11/1892.

44 *The Belfast Technical School Eleventh Annual Report, 1893-1894.*

45 Anon, *The Industries of Ireland; Belfast and the Towns of the North* (London, Historical Publishing Company, 1891; reprinted Belfast, Friars Bush Press, 1986).

46 McLorie.

47 *The Belfast Technical School Eleventh Annual Report, 1893-1894.*

48 NW 6/12/1898.

49 *ibid.*

50 NW 15/11/1900.

Chapter 8: Brighter Prospects for Technical Education.

1 Earl of Belfast, *The Establishment of an Athenaeum in Belfast* (Belfast, 1852), (location LHL).

2 NW 24/4/1852.

3 BNL 26/9/1885.

4 BNL 5/1/1871.

5 BNL 1/1/1880.

6 Gray, W.

7 NW 21/4/1887.

8 Gray, W.

9 Cardwell.

10 Magnus, P., *Educational Aims and Efforts; 1880-1910* (London: Longmans, 1910).

11 *Reports of the Royal Commission on Technical Instruction* (London, 1884).

12 Cardwell.

13 *ibid.*

14 Argles, M., *South Kensington to Robbins* (London: Longmans, 1964).

15 *ibid.*

16 MacCartain, S., 'Technical Education in Ireland 1870 -1899'; in *Prometheus's Fire*; Editor McMillan, N (Carlow: Tyndall Publications, 2000).

17 *ibid.*

18 *ibid.*

19 Gray, W.

20 NW 18/11/1890.

21 Gray, W.

22 NW 31/3/1894.

23 *Reports of the Royal Commission on Technical Instruction* (London, 1884).

24 NW 20/1/1898.

25 Officer, 2007.

26 Gray, W.

27 Anon, *Ireland Industrial and Agricultural.*

28 Officer, 2007.

29 Anon, *Ireland Industrial and Agricultural.*

30 NW 20/1/1900.

31 Officer, 2007.

32 Neeson.

33 NW 12/6/1900.

Chapter 9: Planning a New System

1 NW 20/1/1898.

2 Gray, W.

3 *ibid.*

4 *ibid.*

5 *ibid.*

6 NW 15/1/1900.

7 TSC 29/1/1900.

8 Gray, W.

9 LTIC 4/10/1900.

10 LTIC 3/1/1901.

11 TSC 31/8/1899.

12 TSC 16/11/1899.

13 *ibid.*

14 TSC 21/11/1899.

15 *ibid.*

16 BNL 6/12/1899.

17 TSC 21/11/1899.

18 TSC 19/12/1899.

19 TSC 12/2/1900.

20 Gray, W.

21 Blair, R., *Survey of Belfast Schools, 1900* (Belfast, PRONI; ref. ED4/40).

22 *ibid.*

23 LTIC 23/11/1900.

24 *ibid.*

25 Officer, 2007.

26 LTIC 28/3/1901.

27 NW 15/8/1900.

28 BNL 15/8/1900.

29 Officer, 2007.

30 LTIC 16/8/1900.

31 Bell, H.V., McCloy, D., *Francis Charles Forth; Pioneer of Technical Education. In Great Ulster Engineers*; Editors Crossland, B., and Moore, J (Belfast, 2008).

32 *ibid.*

33 LTIC 28/3/1901; also see PRONI ref. LA/7/7AF/1/1.

34 *ibid.*

35 Gray, W.

36 LTIC 27/6/1901.

37 LTIC 26/8/1901.

38 Forth, F.C., *Technical Instruction in the City of Belfast* (Dublin: Department of Agriculture and Technical Instruction Journal, Number 3, Volume 7, 1907).

39 NW 1/6/1901.

40 NW 27/9/1901.
41 NW 26/9/1901.
42 LTIC 20/6/1901.

Chapter 10: A Dream Realised: the Municipal Technical Institute

1 Forth, F.C., *Technical Instruction in the City of Belfast*.
2 TSC 20/3/1900.
3 TSC 2/4/1900.
4 Brett, C.E.B., *Buildings of Belfast* 1700-1914 (London: Weidenfeld and Nicolson, 1969).
5 TSC 4/5/1900; also see PRONI ref. LA/7/7AF/1/1.
6 BNL 25/11/1902.
7 LTIC 21/8/1900, also PRONI ref. LA/7/7HD/2.
8 LTIC 25/1/1901.
9 NW 14/12/1900.
10 Gray, W.
11 BNL 25/11/1902.
12 LTIC 7/2/1901.
13 LTIC 28/1/1904.
14 NW 27/4/1901.
15 NW 5/8/1903.
16 LTIC 3/9/1903.
17 LTIC 15/8/1904.
18 Forth, F.C., *Technical Instruction in the City of Belfast*.
19 *ibid.*
20 NW 6/9/1901.
21 NW 15/12/1903.
22 NW 2/10/1907.
23 NW 8/1/1905.
24 NW 14/9/1903.
25 Forth, F.C., *Souvenir of the Opening of the Municipal Technical Institute* (Belfast: Municipal Technical Institute Belfast, October 1907).
26 *Prospectus of the Municipal Technical Institute Belfast 1909-1910* (location PRONI).
27 *ibid.*
28 Forth, F.C., *Technical Instruction in the City of Belfast* .
29 Forth, F.C., Letter to Students; Time Table of Classes (Belfast, Municipal Technical Institute Belfast, September 1909); see PRONI ref. LA/7/7HB.
30 *ibid.*
31 Forth, F.C., Letter to Students; Time Table of Classes.
32 *ibid.*
33 NW 5/8/1903.
34 NW 10/8/1903.
35 LTIC 20/4/1904.
36 NW 13/12/1905.
37 Forth, F.C., *Technical Instruction in the City of Belfast*.
38 *Irish News*. 16/10/1903.

39 NW 28/11/1906.

40 NW 22/11/1907.

41 NW 9/11/1906.

42 Forth, F.C., *Souvenir of the Opening of the Municipal Technical Institute*.

43 NW 9/11/1906.

44 NW 8/1/1905.

45 Forth, F.C., *The Belfast Municipal Technical Institute; its Aims and Aspirations* (Belfast: Belfast Natural History and Philosophical Society, December 1901); (location BCL).

46 NW 15/12/1903.

47 Forth, F.C., *The Belfast Municipal Technical Institute; its Aims and Aspirations*.

48 NW 13/12/1905.

49 *ibid*.

50 Bell, H.V., *Diligence and Skill; 100 Years of Education at Belfast Institute* (Belfast: the Belfast Institute of Further and Higher Education, 2007).

51 Forth, F.C., *The Belfast Municipal Technical Institute; its Aims and Aspirations*.

52 NW 13/12/1902.

53 LTIC 10/10/1901.

54 LTIC 2/5/1901.

55 NW 28/11/1906.

56 NW 22/11/1907.

57 *ibid*.

58 NW 5/11/1906.

59 NW 8/1/1905.

Chapter 11: Technical Education Recognised

1 LTIC 24/2/1901.

2 NW 31/10/1907.

3 Forth, F.C., *Souvenir of the Opening of the Municipal Technical Institute*.

4 NW 2/11/1907.

5 Forth, F.C., *Technical Instruction in the City of Belfast*.

6 Anon, *Irish Builder*, page 778 (Dublin, 1907).

7 NW 31/10/1907.

8 Pevsner, *Cities of London and Westminster. Vol. 1* (London, 1957).

9 Hayward, R., *Belfast Through the Ages* (Belfast, 1952).

10 Brett.

11 *ibid*.

12 NW 21/9/1910.

13 Belfast Metropolitan College Archive.

14 Crawford, W.J., 'Description of the New Mechanical Engineering Laboratory' (London: Engineering, December 8, 1911).

15 LTIC 10/7/1912.

16 NW 4/9/1918.

17 Neeson.

18 Anon, Timetable of Classes 1909-1910, (location PRONI; ref. LA/7/7HB/2).

19 Belfast Metropolitan College Archive.

20 LTIC 22/2/1912.

21 LTIC 17/12/1914.

22 NW 5/6/1909.

23 LTIC 4/3/1915; also see PRONI ref. LA/7/7HD/9.

24 *ibid.*

25 LTIC 28/5/1913.

26 Anon, Timetable of Classes 1909-1910.

27 NW 21/9/1910.

28 NW 29/9/1910.

29 LTIC 7/10/1910.

30 NW 21/9/1910.

31 NW 4/5/1910.

32 *ibid.*

33 Brett.

34 LTIC 1/6/1910.

35 NW 7/12/1910.

36 Perry, J., *Technical Institute Problems* (London, Nature, 28 December 1911).

37 Forth, F.C., *Technical Instruction in the City of Belfast.*

38 Moody & Beckett.

39 BNL 25/11/1902.

40 LTIC 16/1/1903.

41 NW 11/2/1903.

42 NW 2/9/1903.

43 Moody & Beckett.

44 LTIC 9/6/1910.

45 LTIC 7/7/1910.

46 NW 12/10/1910.

Chapter 12: War, Politics and the End of an Era

1 LTIC 19/11/1914.

2 LTIC 3/6/1915.

3 LTIC 14/6/1917.

4 LTIC 10/1/1918.

5 Bell, H.V., Diligence and Skill.

6 BNL 2/5/1914.

7 LTIC 27/8/1914.

8 Stanley, R., *History of the Scheme; Municipal College of Technology, Belfast* (Belfast: Municipal College of Technology, 1921).

9 LTIC 19/11/1914.

10 Neeson.

11 LTIC 22/6/1916.

12 TIC 17/6/1920.

13 TIC 10/3/1921.

14 LTIC 21/1/1914.

15 BNL 3/9/1919.

16 Stanley.
17 TIC 23/3/1921.
18 LTIC 4/3 1915.
19 NW 4/9/1918.
20 Stanley.
21 BNL 3/9/1919.
22 TIC 16/6/1921.
23 LTIC 1/3/1916.
24 LTIC 17/12/1914.
25 *ibid.*
26 LTIC 2/5/1918.
27 LTIC 4/9/1918.
28 Neeson.
29 Moody & Beckett.
30 BNL 4/9/1920.
31 LTIC 25/1/1917.
32 LTIC 18/9/1919.
33 LTIC 5/9/1918.
34 BNL 16/1/1919.
35 LTIC 1/3/1919.
36 BNL 3/3/1919.
37 LTIC 5/6/1913.
38 Officer, 2007.
39 LTIC 18/4/1918.
40 Stanley.
41 LTIC 4/3/1915.
42 LTIC 1/1/1917.
43 LTIC 3/12/1914.
44 Officer, 2007.
45 Belfast City Council Minutes. 3/5/1915, (location PRONI).
46 NW 9/4/1919.
47 LTIC 23/5/1919.
48 LTIC 25/9/1919.
49 Belfast City Council Minutes.
50 Neeson.
51 NW 21/5/1915.
52 Bell, H.V., Diligence and Skill.
53 Stanley, R.

Index